# RELIGION AND POPULAR CULTURE

# RELIGION AND POPULAR CULTURE

## STUDIES ON THE INTERACTION OF WORLDVIEWS

EDITED BY
DANIEL A. STOUT
JUDITH M. BUDDENBAUM

IOWA STATE UNIVERSITY PRESS/
AMES

DANIEL A. STOUT is an associate professor and associate chair in the Department of Communications at Brigham Young University. He coedited *Religion and Mass Media: Audiences and Adaptations* (Sage) with Judith M. Buddenbaum and has written articles for the *Journal of Mass Media Ethics, Information and Behavior, Newspaper Research Journal, Public Relations Review,* and *Southern Speech Communication Journal.* He received his MA from the University of Georgia and his PhD from Rutgers.

JUDITH M. BUDDENBAUM is a professor in the Department of Journalism and Technical Communication at Colorado State University. A former religion reporter, she is the author of *Reporting News about Religion: An Introduction for Journalists* (Iowa State University Press) and of numerous scholarly research articles and book chapters on various aspects of religion and the media. She earned an MA in journalism and a PhD in mass communication from Indiana University, Bloomington.

Iowa State University Press
2121 South State Avenue, Ames, Iowa 50014

Orders:    1-800-862-6657
Office:    1-515-292-0140
Fax:       1-515-292-3348
Web site:  www.isupress.com

♾ Printed on acid-free paper in the United States of America

First edition, 2001

Library of Congress Cataloging-in-Publication Data
Religion and popular culture : studies on the interaction of worldviews / edited by Daniel A. Stout, Judith M. Buddenbaum.
    p. cm.
  Includes bibliographical references and index.
  ISBN 0-8138-2276-9 (alk. paper)
    1. Popular culture—Religious aspects. 2. Popular culture—United States. 3. Religion and culture—United States. 4. United States—Religion—1960- I. Stout, Daniel A. II. Buddenbaum, Judith Mitchell.

  BL65.C8 R445 2000
  291.1'7—dc21                                                    00-061372

The last digit is the print number: 9 8 7 6 5 4 3 2 1

# Contents

## Part III
Empirical Studies, Essays, and Case Studies

*Dedicated to Kayna Stout and Warren Buddenbaum*

# RELIGION AND POPULAR CULTURE

CHAPTER 1

# Beyond Culture Wars: An Introduction to the Study of Religion and Popular Culture

## DANIEL A. STOUT

ew topics in media criticism are as divisive and controversial as the relationship between religion and popular culture. Despite decades of mass communication research, great confusion still exists about how members of religious groups use media within contexts of institutional expectations of belief and behavior. Recent historical investigations, for example, reveal that religious participation in popular culture is more complex and difficult to assess than previously thought. A case in point is seventeenth-century Puritan America, a time associated with religious ambivalence regarding the role of art in the church. Robert Hughes' (1997) provocative discussion of the Old Ship Puritan Meeting House illustrates how public displays of art and images were avoided, while less obvious forms of popular communication were simultaneously embraced. For example, the building lacks decoration of any sort and is highlighted by the same simplicity that characterizes a hull of a ship. "They were people of the Word, not the Image," he argues, and truth "lived in the Word, but the Image could deceive" (p. 25). Therefore, the tourist finds few paintings

on the walls and none of the sculptures that adorn Catholic and Angli-
can churches. Such icons were seen as detractors and unnecessary sub-
stitutes for God. Hughes, however, dismisses the notion that Puritans
were "narrowly art-hating and repressively pleasure-denying" (p. 29).
On the contrary, portrait paintings were common and reinforced values
of reverence and commitment through a consistent tone and style.
While religious and landscape paintings were rejected as "graven images," Puritan writing, furniture, silverware, and even decorative grave-
stones reveal "sparks of culture amid the wilderness" (p. 30).

Hughes' discussion of Puritan art teases out the main question addressed by this book: How do members of religious groups make decisions about the use of media of popular culture? And, related to this,
is the equally compelling issue of whether our explanations of these
choices have been accurate. In the same way that we harbor a *Scarlet
Letter* mythology about the narrowness of Puritan art, do we make similar false assumptions about the ways Baptists, Mormons, Muslims,
Buddhists, and other groups use media of popular culture today?

Recent events suggest that these questions have sociological relevance. The worldwide condemnation of Salman Rushdie's novel *The
Satanic Verses* by Islamic leaders demonstrates concern about the
power of mass media. Upset by what is perceived to be a growing number of unsavory films and television programs, the Southern Baptist
Convention declared an official boycott of Disney entertainment products (see Chapter 11). According to various news reports, these and
other incidents are evidence of a growing "culture war" between religious institutions and the entertainment industry. This book seeks a
deeper understanding of the relationship between religion and popular
culture. It examines the role religion plays in framing the public discourse about popular culture and presents a number of theoretical investigations of the topic.

For centuries, religious groups have had an impact on the production, content, and use of the media of popular culture. The printing
press is one important example given its historical role in the Reformation and Renaissance (Eisenstein, 1979). The popularization of
Bible reading was an initial step toward widespread literacy and the
eventual marketing of literary texts (see Schement and Stephenson,
1996). Historically, religious music was also enjoyed by large audiences, as illustrated by Johann Sebastian Bach's performance of
"church music" in large concert halls in the 1700s (Boorstin, 1992).
While popular culture is often considered a postindustrial phenome-

non, religious involvement in the popular arts occurs well before the printing press. Museum artifacts provide evidence of religious influence on the creation of architecture, sculpture, pottery, and painting in a number of ancient civilizations (Schroeder, 1980). Yet, despite religion's salient role in communication history, it is often missing from much of the research on media and society.

## Questioning the "Culture Wars" Paradigm: The Search for New Theoretical Frameworks

Popular culture refers to the art, entertainment, and cultural objects "which have proved most successful in garnering a significant audience" (Rockett, 1993, p. 150). It refers to the beliefs and practices of "many people" (Gans, 1974, p. vii). Genres of popular culture range widely from TV soap operas to country western music; in print media it might include romance novels and comic books. The term *culture war* was popularized in the 1980s and 1990s by writers seeking a descriptive label for what they perceived to be religious reaction to popular forms of communication. When competing moral beliefs conflict in public discourse, a culture war emerges (Hunter, 1991). Medved's (1992) book, *Hollywood vs. America,* and Carter's (1993) *The Culture of Disbelief* draw a line in the sand between the culture of mass media and mainstream culture. Culture wars have also been examined in the field of education (Yamane, 1996; Sargeant and West, 1996; Waterman and Kagel, 1998). *In Dumbing Down: Essays on the Strip-Mining of American Culture,* Washburn and Thornton (1996) lament that American education "has somehow begun sliding down a long, steep chute into nullity" (p. 13). According to Bloom (1994), a culture war is being fought over the classical canon of Western literature, which must be protected from postmodern scholars who want to study TV sitcoms, soap operas, popular films, romance novels, and other genres of popular culture.

The question is, how accurately does the culture wars framework describe the complex relationship between religious institutions and the larger popular culture? Can such a relationship be framed in terms of cultural conflict in the ongoing social situations of everyday life? Culture wars researchers identify values that citizens do not agree on; they raise awareness about the sometimes dangerous tensions between groups and subcultures. They have not, however, offered conceptually and theoretically rich explanations of how members of religious sects use media of popular culture.

The concern with the culture wars idea is dualism, which has created several obstacles in the study of religion and media (see Hoover and Venturelli, 1996). When a researcher approaches the study of religion and popular culture using this framework, the analysis is reduced to descriptions of opposing sides. According to the orthodox view, consumers of popular culture are in danger of losing their faith in God, while the progressive vision holds that they are impervious to influence. This book takes the position that while social conflicts do occur between religious institutions and popular culture, an exclusive focus on these conflicts rarely brings "these choices together in faithful and creative ways" (Wuthnow, 1989, p. 186). While philosophers, sociologists, and theologians rarely agree on a precise definition of dualism, it is used here to describe the rhetoric of social critics and researchers who reduce the question of religion and popular culture to contrasting positions that can never be synthesized or viewed simultaneously. In his popular book, for example, film critic Michael Medved (1992) uses dualistic terminology in criticizing contemporary movies and TV programs:

> The distortions and insults about organized religion will continue unabated as long as our popular culture continues its overall campaign against judgment and values. A war against standards leads logically and inevitably to hostility to religion because it is religious faith that provides the ultimate basis for all standards. (p. 89)

Although she disagrees sharply with Medved, popular author Sarah Ban Breathnach also speaks in a dualistic style in assessing the value of television:

> Television is a spiritual gift. Anytime you can communicate to millions of people it's a spiritual gift. TV is getting better; the creative decisionmakers . . . realize that people want authentic stories. (Rudolph, 1997, p. 37)

To Medved, the relationship between religion and popular culture comes down to the depiction of values, which he concludes are loosening moral standards. For Breathnach, on the other hand, these values are getting better, and the medium's ability to spread them throughout the world makes TV a spiritual medium. The question of media and popular culture is boiled down to dualistic categories that limit the range of questions that can be asked. While this type of rhetorical dualism is useful in some situations, its conceptual flatness inhibits a deeper more thorough study of popular culture. Lengermann and Niebrugge-Brantley (1990) comment on this:

> By "dualistic rhetoric," we mean that Westerners think in terms of distinctive, relatively impermeable, and contrasting categories and that they see, cognitively organize their relationships to, and often experience the world in terms of such categories. But sometimes experiences of the world do not slip easily into preexisting dualistic categories. (p. 332)

This book examines some of these "experiences of the world," which are not accounted for by the contrasting categories of culture wars dualism. From the culture wars perspective, research questions rarely probe beyond the comparison of values. While such a comparison is essential, it is not complete without addressing additional social and cultural arguments for the study of religion and popular culture.

## Resisting the Rhetoric of Dualism: Three Arguments for the Study of Religion and Popular Culture

A number of issues surrounding the study of popular culture are covered up by the dualism of culture wars rhetoric. First, researchers concentrating on the "effects" of media on religious audiences tend to overlook the fact that religious institutions also create and participate in popular culture. Second, studies of religion and the media often omit the concept of cultural context. That is, how members of religious groups experience popular culture cannot be fully understood outside the families, groups, and subcultures that help shape the experiences of everyday life. Lastly, the study of religion and popular culture contributes to *media literacy*. Both logical and inevitable, religious criticism of popular culture is an essential part of life in many faith communities. Regardless of the particular church or sect, however, the quality of this critique can be enhanced through deeper, more informed analysis. I now elaborate on these three arguments.

## Argument One: Religious Groups Create as Well as Criticize Popular Culture

Religious groups are often at odds with popular culture, but they also help create and sustain it. For centuries, denominational structures have promoted those popular arts that help them reach their spiritual, social, and sometimes financial goals. When Benedictine monks mass marketed a CD of musical prayers in 1994 called *Chant,* it sold over six million copies and was played on major radio stations throughout the world (Schement and Stephenson, 1996; Thigpen, 1995). This illustrates one of the weaknesses of the culture wars hypothesis. It is insufficient to examine religious groups only as critcs; they must also be studied as creators of and participants in popular culture. In some ways, *religion is popular culture* and can never be completely detached from it.

An historical examination indicates that while religious leaders often feared the secularizing powers of new forms of communication (Spigel, 1992; Pool, 1983), religion turns out to be a consistent element in popular culture throughout much of history. The diffusion of the printing press in seventeenth-century Europe, for example, did not obscure the fact that the more common forms of popular culture included household shrines of religious relics and statues (Orr, 1980), pious images, religious art, family devotionals, manuals of prayers, popular religious literature, hagiographic documents (Boglioni, 1980), and apocryphal writings (Benko, 1980). Religious involvement in popular culture is not easily reduced to points of conflict over particular technologies or texts; it must be studied in ways that take into account a wide variety of media and genres.

Religious groups are increasingly involved in the popular arts. While politicians speak of cultural "warfare," TV programs, film, popular books, and other forms of entertainment are helping to achieve religious goals and solicit donations. The industries of televangelism, religious publishing, and gospel music are flourishing (see Chapters 15 and 16). In addition, religion is blending with secular art forms to create interesting hybrids. Pat Robertson's *700 Club* TV program borrows sets and formats from traditional news programs to create a religious news and talk show that includes prayer and sermons. Contemporary Christian Music (CCM) is also a synthesis of the sacred and the secular; it combines spiritual messages with secular soft rock music. "Gospel rap" is also a music genre that combines religious and secular art forms (Gooch, 1996). In addition, studies by Zaleski (1997) and Cobb (1998) indicate that religion is emerging rapidly on the Internet, creating new types of interactive religious experiences. When these media are taken into account, the culture wars metaphor unravels as a theoretical construct; it fails to account for the dialectical nature of popular culture where religion is both friend and foe.

## Argument Two: Religion and Popular Culture Are Best Understood within Social Contexts

The culture wars metaphor implies that there is unity in the fight against mass media. Homogeneity rarely exists within and across religious groups, however. Various denominations may share particular beliefs but are usually distinctive in terms of specific norms, lifestyles, and values. Major religious traditions (e.g., Islam, Christianity, Judaism, Buddism, etc.) in the United States often vary in their teachings about the role of education, art, and entertainment. For example, leaders of the Southern Baptist Convention led a boycott of Disney entertainment products because of perceived offenses to religious values. However, such direct admonitions are not likely to be found in Reformed and Conservative Judaism, which are different types of knowledge cultures.

Within religious groups themselves, there are also different contexts that create variations in the ways popular culture is defined and used. Age, gender, income, social networks, and particular geographic regions help create these contexts of divergence. Such differences may go undetected by culture wars assumptions that claim unity of voice in protesting media texts. One example is "Generation X" (made up of adults, 18–24 years of age), which appears to be outwardly irreverent yet religious in nontraditional ways. While rock music, music video, and Internet web sites have drawn criticism from some religious leaders, there is growing evidence that these entertainment genres are also channels of religious expression. Beaudoin (1998) makes this argument in a recent book on the topic:

> It may seem odd to examine popular culture to learn about religion, but for Xers, popular culture is a major meaning-making system. Thus, religious statements about the generation must take popular culture into account. . . . We express our religious interests, dreams, fears, hopes, and desires through popular culture. (p. xiv)

Social context, as it pertains to the study of religion and popular culture, recognizes that the role of media cannot be fully understood outside the cultural dynamics of society (see Hoover and Lundby, 1977). Whether it be families, informal social groups, or larger subcultures, more can be learned about how these collectivities shape perceptions of art and entertainment. Research on this topic must not only expand knowledge about religious experience in general but also deepen understanding of the sociology of knowledge and how such processes proceed in environments of cultural conflict.

One area that has inspired this book is the sociology of knowledge, particularly the contributions of Peter Berger. He encouraged researchers to understand the differences between institutional religion and the ways the sacred is defined at the level of personal experience. Rather than focus on religious doctrine exclusively, Berger's focus is the "plausibility structure," or personal network of family, friends, and coworkers that negotiates the border between religious expectations and the values of the larger society (Berger, 1967, p. 134). This volume applies this perspective in emphasizing *the audience as the primary unit of analysis* in the study of religion and popular culture.

## Argument Three: The Study of Religion and Popular Culture Promotes Media Literacy

The final reason for studying this topic is the quality of past critiques. Many assumptions about the impact of popular culture are based on conjecture and hearsay. The substantive and theoretical issues defining the relationship between religion and popular culture have not yet been adequately identified. It is possible that the culture wars metaphor has framed the debate about popular entertainment in terms that are so general as to favor the sensational over media literacy. According to the *Media Literacy Resource Guide* (1992), *media literacy* is the ability to "respond thoughtfully to the media we consume" (p. 12). To Kubey (1991), it means having sufficient skills to "appreciate, interpret, and analyze the media" (p. 1). Regardless of whether one would call oneself religious or not, the following five components of media literacy outlined by Silverblatt (1995) are highly sought after:

1. An awareness of the impact of the media on the individual and society.
2. An understanding of the process of mass communication.

3. The development of strategies with which to analyze and discuss media messages.
4. An awareness of media content as a "text" that provides insight into our contemporary culture and ourselves.
5. The cultivation of an enhanced enjoyment, understanding, and appreciation of media content (pp. 2–3).

While it is recognized that some denominations reject the use of various mass media outright, within the world's major religious traditions, millions watch TV programs, view films, listen to popular music, and surf the Internet. This fact has spawned a number of public debates both within and without religious communities that require critical media skills. African-American religious leaders do not always agree about the acceptability of rap music (Gooch, 1996), and historically, Christian Fundamentalists have had sharp disagreements about the appropriate use of radio in religious life (Bendroth, 1996). The popular press reports conflicting views among religious leaders about television's spiritual influence (Rudolph, 1997), and the controversial film *The Last Temptation of Christ,* although assailed by many conservative churches, drew contrasting reactions by religious audience members (Lindlof, 1996). This book does not attempt to resolve these debates, but it does identify the relevant theories, contexts, and audience descriptions that inform them and provide depth. This information does not necessarily provide specific answers but helps guard against a discourse on religion and popular culture that is overly casual and anecdotal.

The absence of theoretical exploration of these issues can have unfortunate consequences. One illustration often cited by historians is that of Anthony Comstock and the New York Society for the Suppression of Vice (NYSSV) in the late nineteenth century. Armed with support of the New York Police Department as well as the Young Men's Christian Association, Comstock embarked on a benevolent effort to restore religious values to a city rife with pornography, prostitution, and unwholesome entertainment. As a number of historians attest, however, his efforts were later considered extreme and inconsistent with majority religious views about art and popular culture. His group arrested individuals for possessing contraceptives and photo reproductions of classical French paintings; Comstock pressured one of Walt Whitman's publishers not to print his classic book of poetry *Leaves of Grass,* forcing Whitman to find another publisher in Philadelphia

(Beisel, 1997). Beginning in the 1870s, Comstock's group engaged in censorship that included "books, plays, and pictures which were pornographic only by the widest stretch of the imagination" according to historians Brown and Leech (1927, p. 267). Comstock's actions included the arrest of a young woman distributing pamphlets for the Art Student's League containing reproductions of nude drawings (Trumbull, 1913). Despite early support from local religious leaders, Comstock's extremism ultimately spawned the term "Comstockery," which became synonymous with prudery for many years (Beisel, 1997).

The point of this brief case study is not to reject Comstock's initial assumptions about unwholesome entertainment and its threat to families but to illustrate the inexpedient results of public discussion lacking the basic components of media literacy (i.e., attention to audience and aesthetics as well as message). Speaking about television, Browning, et al. (1997) stress media literacy in their book *From Culture Wars to Common Ground: Religion and the American Family Debate:*

> The emphasis here should be on providing criticism and well-grounded evaluations. . . . Nor should criticism be voiced in ways that obscure the good that educational television can do and the positive images that some programs and movies convey. . . . Rather than portraying the media as uniquely and single-mindedly seditious . . . it is better to follow . . . dialectical analysis. (p. 333)

It is hoped that the scholarly studies in this book will help achieve these "well-grounded evaluations" of the religion and popular culture paradox. They represent a first step toward "critical awareness," which, according to Silverblatt (1995), means becoming well informed about media-related issues and developing a set of terms or tools for more in-depth analysis.

## Scope and Organization of the Book

Based on these issues, *Religion and Popular Culture* is divided into three parts: theoretical, institutional, and empirical perspectives. Part I theorizes about the relationship between religion and popular culture. While much has been speculated, articles in this section go deeper than the often superficial "culture wars" analysis found in consumer magazines and TV talk shows. Authors explore religiosity as a phenomenon that works to simultaneously embrace and reject cultural forms. Each chapter draws on particular sociological and critical theories in identifying issues and operational definitions necessary to a substantive and credible analysis of religion and popular culture.

Part II provides an overview of institutional perspectives on religion and popular culture. It describes media teachings of several world religions (i.e., Judaism, Christianity, Islam, and Eastern religious philosophy) as well as how religious leaders take particular stands on issues related to popular culture. These chapters give appropriate attention to divergent strains within each particular tradition.

Lastly, Part III contains empirical studies of particular religious audiences as well as essays on related topics.

# References

Beaudoin, T. (1998). *Virtual faith: The irreverent spiritual quest of Generation X.* San Francisco: Jossey-Bass.

Beisel, N. (1997). *Imperiled innocents: Anthony Comstock and family reproduction in Victorian America.* Princeton, NJ: Princeton University Press.

Bendroth, M. (1996). Fundamentalism and the media, 1930–1990. In D.A. Stout and J.M. Buddenbaum (Eds.). *Religion and mass media: Audiences and adaptations.* Thousand Oaks, CA: Sage. 74–84.

Benko, S. (1980). Popular literature in early Christianity: The apocryphal New Testament. In Fred E.H. Schroeder (Ed.). *5000 years of popular culture: Popular culture before printing.* Bowling Green, OH: Bowling Green University Popular Press. 173–190.

Berger, P. (1967). *The sacred canopy: Elements of a sociological theory of religion.* Garden City, NY: Anchor Books.

Bloom, H. (1994). *The western canon: The books and school of the ages.* New York: Riverhead Books.

Boglioni, P. (1980). Some methodological reflections on the study of medieval popular religion. In Fred E.H. Schroeder (Ed.). *5000 years of popular culture: Popular culture before printing.* Bowling Green, OH: Bowling Green University Popular Press. 191–200.

Boorstin, D. (1992). *The creators: A history of heroes of the imagination.* New York: Vintage Books.

Brown, H. and Leech, M. (1927). *Anthony Comstock: Roundsman for the Lord.* New York: Albert and Charles Boni.

Browning, D.S., Miller-McLemore, B.J., Couture, P.D., Brynoff Lyon, K., and Franklin, R.M. (1997). *From culture wars to common ground: Religion and the American family debate*. Louisville, KY: Westminister John Knox Press.

Carter, S.L. (1993). *The culture of disbelief: How law and politics trivialize religious devotion*. New York: Basic Books.

Cobb, J.F. (1998). *Cybergrace: The search for God in the digital world*. New York: Crown Publishers.

Eisenstein, E.L. (1979). *The printing press as an agent of change: Communications and cultural transformations in early modern Europe*. Cambridge, UK: Cambridge University Press.

Gans, H.J. (1974) *Popular culture and high culture: An analysis and evaluation of taste*. New York: Basic Books.

Gooch, C.R. (1996). Rappin' for the Lord: The uses of gospel rap and contemporary music in black religious communities. In D.A. Stout and J.M. Buddenbaum (Eds.). *Religion and mass media: Audiences and adaptations*. Thousand Oaks, CA: Sage. 228–242.

Hoover, S.M. and Lundby K., eds. (1997). *Rethinking media, religion, and culture*. Thousand Oaks, CA: Sage.

Hoover, S.M. and Venturelli, S. (1996). The category of the religious: The blindspot of contemporary media theory? *Critical Studies in Mass Communication*. 13(3): 251–265.

Hughes, R. (1997). *American visions: The epic history of art in America*. New York: Alfred A. Knopf.

Hunter, J.D. (1991). *Culture wars: The struggle to define America*. New York: BasicBooks.

Kubey, R. (1991, March 6). The case for media education. *Education Week X(24)*, 1.

Lengermann, P.M. and Niebrugge-Brantley, J. (1990). Feminist sociological theory: The near-future prospects. In G. Ritzer (Ed.). *Frontiers of social theory: The new synthesis*. New York: Columbia University Press. 316–344.

Lindlof, T.R. (1996). The passionate audience: Community inscriptions of "The Last Temptation of Christ." In D.A. Stout and J.M. Buddenbaum (Eds.). *Religion and mass media: Audiences and adaptations*. Thousand Oaks, CA: Sage. 148–168.

*Media Literacy Resource Guide*. (1992). Toronto: The Ontario Department of Education.

Medved, M. (1992). *Hollywood vs. America: Popular culture and the war on traditional values*. New York: HarperCollins.

Orr, D.G. (1980). Roman domestic religion: The archaeology of Roman popular art. In Fred E.H. Schroeder (Ed.). *5000 years of popular culture: Popular culture before printing*. Bowling Green, OH: Bowling Green University Popular Press. 155–172.

Pool, I. de Sola. (1983). *Technologies of freedom*. Cambridge, MA: Harvard University Press.

Rockett, W. (1993) Crossing wire borders: Concepts of popular culture in film and television studies. In R.B. Browne and R.J. Ambrosetti (Eds.). *Continuities in popular culture: The present in the past and the past in the present and future.* Bowling Green, OH: Bowing Green State University Popular Press. 143–159.

Rudolph, I. (1997, March 29). You gotta have faith: Ten prominent spiritual thinkers reflect on TV's treatment of God and religion. *TV Guide,* 36–38.

Sargeant, K.H. and West, E.L. (1996). Teachers and preachers: The battle over public school reform in Gaston County, North Carolina. In J.L. Nolan, Jr. (Ed.). *The American culture wars: Current contests and future prospects* (pp. 89–113). Charlottesville: University of Virginia Press.

Schement, J.R. and Stephenson, H.C. (1996). Religion and the information society. In D.A. Stout and J.M. Buddenbaum (Eds.). *Religion and mass media: Audiences and adaptations.* Thousand Oaks, CA: Sage. 261–289.

Schroeder, F. (1980). *5000 years of popular culture: Popular culture before printing.* Bowling Green, OH: Bowling Green University Press.

Silverblatt, A. (1995). *Media literacy: Keys to interpreting media messages.* Westport, CT: Praeger.

Spigel, L. (1992). *Make room for TV: Television and the family ideal in post-war America.* Chicago: University of Chicago Press.

Thigpen, D.E. (1995, May 22). Leaving little to chants. *Time 45(21),* 72.

Trumbull, C.G. (1913). *Anthony Comstock, fighter.* New York: Fleming H. Revell Company.

Washburn, K. and Thornton, J., Eds. (1996). *Dumbing down: Essays on the strip-mining of American culture.* New York: W.W. Norton.

Waterman, B. and Kagel, B. (1998). *The Lord's university: Freedom and authority at BYU.* Salt Lake City, UT: Signature Books.

Wuthnow, R. (1989). *The struggle for America's soul: Evangelicals, liberals, and secularism.* Grand Rapids, MI: Eerdmans.

Yamane, D. (1996). The battle of the books at Berkeley: In search of the culture wars in debates over multiculturalism. In J.L. Nolan, Jr. (Ed.). *The American culture wars: Current contests and future prospects.* Charlottesville: University of Virginia Press. 3–34.

Zaleski, J. (1997). *The soul of cyberspace: How new technology is changing our spiritual lives.* San Francisco: Harper Edge.

# PART I

## Theoretical Perspectives on Religion and Popular Culture

CHAPTER 2

# The Media, Religion, and Public Opinion: Toward a Unified Theory of Cultural Influence

JUDITH M. BUDDENBAUM

*[The American pioneer] is, in short, a highly civilised being, who consents, for a time, to inhabit the backwoods, and who penetrates into the wilds of the New World with the Bible, an axe, and a file of newspapers.*

Alexis de Tocqueville

ollowing his 1831 visit to America, Alexis de Tocqueville (1841/1889) noted approvingly ways in which both the press and religion served democratic ideals. But where Tocqueville's analysis suggests the importance and value of both press and of religion, today people are more likely to see one or the other (and sometimes both) as a powerful but pernicious influence.

Where one group sees the media as contributing to and perhaps causing harm, another sees them as promoting or re-enforcing conventional values—or, at the very least, supporting the status quo (Buddenbaum, 1998). Conversely, and perhaps simultaneously, one group sees religion, or at least true religion, as the source of all that is good within a culture while another fears it is, or can be, a repressive and dangerous force. For some, the media are the primary concern. For others, the concern is religion and its effects.

Out of those contending sides, culture wars are born and fought. In choosing sides, people give voice to their hopes and fears about how things are, how they will be, and how they should or might be. In battle, each arms itself with favorite statistics culled from the research literature. However, what is missing from the literature is work contributing to an understanding of reciprocal, joint, and independent individual and societal effects of the media and of religion (Buddenbaum and Stout, 1996). Therefore, this chapter brings together evidence from communication research and from the sociology of religion to show how an expanded theory of agenda setting could account for the shaping of popular culture through the effects of both mass media and religion on public opinion.

## Mass Media Agenda Setting

As early as 1831, Tocqueville noted the core principle of agenda setting when he wrote:

> [N]othing but a newspaper can drop the same thought into a thousand minds. . . . The effect of a newspaper is not only to suggest the same purpose to a great number of persons, but also to furnish means for executing in common the designs which they may have singly conceived. (1841/ 1889, Vol. 2, p. 102)

However, agenda setting, as a way of investigating and understanding media effects, became the dominant framework only after McCombs and Shaw (1972; Shaw and McCombs, 1977) documented significant, positive correlations between the issues emphasized by the news media and the issues people in Chapel Hill, North Carolina, regarded as most important in the 1968 presidential election.

In the 15 years following publication of that first study, more than 100 articles in the research literature examined the agenda-setting effect (Rogers and Dearing, 1988). While much of the work has been done in connection with elections, the very similar "cultivation" studies of television violence produced similar findings (Signorielli and Morgan, 1990). Indeed, even a single television program can enhance the salience of its subject (Ball-Rokeach, Rokeach, and Grube, 1984; Miller and Quarles, 1984). Although early correlational studies produced rather weak evidence of effects, more recent work by Iyengar and his colleagues (1987; Iyengar and Kinder, 1987; Iyengar, Peters and Kinder, 1982) clearly shows that the direction of the media coverage and the ways issues are framed affect people's understanding of who or what is responsible for problems and for their solution. Their work also provides evidence of a priming effect. That is, prior coverage of candidates or issues influences the language people use in describing candidates; it also affects the criteria they use for interpreting and evaluating people, events, behaviors, and issues the media subsequently bring to public attention.

However, even influencing the criteria people use in reaching their conclusions does not guarantee that people will reach the same conclusions. Every study turns up evidence of people who nominate issues as important to themselves, to others, or to society that are not on the media agenda; others replace media evaluations with their own judgments (Weaver et al., 1981, Chap. 9). To some extent seeming anomalies can be explained by demographics (Mullins, 1977; Weaver et al., 1981, Chap. 3), motivations for media use (Weaver, 1977; Graber, 1988, Chap. 6), judgments about media credibility (Rogers and Dearing, 1988, p. 569), and by social context (Csikszentmihalyi, 1991; Moscovici, 1991). Although susceptibility to agenda setting varies from person to person, relatively few studies have tapped into the abundant literature linking media effects to individual differences (Wanta, 1997). However, more recent work has linked agenda setting to at least 10 other theoretical perspectives (Beniger and Jones, 1990). Of those, the most fruitful for teasing out individual differences may be cognitive processing, especially when it is linked to the uses and gratifications approach.

## Mass Media and Cognitive Processing

Whereas agenda setting is usually approached as a societal-level phenomenon, cognitive processing is internal to the individual (Wanta, 1997, p. 1). In cognitive processing, the focus is on the decisions individuals make about media use, their reasons for those decisions and on the ways they understand, interpret, and ultimately use the information to which they are exposed. Thus, linking cognitive processing to agenda setting moderates the agenda-setting concern for "what the media do to people" by recovering the idea of an "active audience" inherent in the uses and gratifications approach (McCombs and Weaver, 1985). In its qualitative form, research on cognitive processing combines cognitive theories (Lau and Sears, 1986; Markus and Zajonc, 1985; Graber, 1988, Chap. 2) with the tenets of symbolic interactionism (Blumer, 1969) to explore how meanings of messages are negotiated in a particular social context. To do that, researchers most often examine written self-reports or transcripts of in-depth interviews and small group discussions for clues to the ways people select, understand, transform, and use information.

Graber notes that quantitative agenda-setting research, like most other quantitative approaches to the study of political communication, focuses on the "what" and "why" questions (1988, p. 2). In contrast, qualitative research is better suited to exploring questions of "how" people use the media and make up their minds. That is, the work tries to explain effects by examining the decisions people make about media use.

Both Graber's work and similar studies by Gamson (1992) and by Neuman, Just, and Crigler (1992) portray an audience more active than that implied by traditional agenda-setting research. These studies indicate that people cope with the constant flow of news by attending primarily to the stories they find interesting and useful for their purposes. For the most part, they find those stories in the most readily available sources. That usually means people get their information from the mass media. Then they fit whatever information they happen to come across and that strikes their fancy into a few readily available frameworks.

Many of those frames come from the mass media; others are derived from American culture. In some contexts and on some issues, cultural frameworks are also the media frames. Through coverage that is deferential to the country's political structure, its values, and its elected and appointed officials, the media transmit "the same basic values as well as some specific schemata about the political process" that are, in turn, adopted by most Americans. Graber calls these frameworks "the cultural norm cocoon" (1988, pp. 210–212). Gamson (1992, Chap. 8) refers to them as "cultural resonances," and they are, of course, part of the "common knowledge" that gives rise to the title of the book by Neuman, Just, and Crigler (1992).

From their rather casual surveillance of the media, people learn to recognize the media agenda and get enough information to justify their opinions, but agenda-setting effects on issue salience or positions tend to be context- and issue-specific. In the intervals between episodes of intense media coverage, direct effects on salience and on evaluations are mitigated by past personal experiences and by information from alternative sources.

As Lane (1972, p. 310) points out, people develop a "strategy of news intake." In part, that strategy depends on a person's need for information from which to learn about the world, form opinions, and make decisions. Those with a stronger need for this kind of information will make more use of information sources, including the mass media, than will those with lower information needs. More importantly, as Weaver (1977) has demonstrated, those with a greater "need for orientation" are the ones most susceptible to agenda-setting effects.

## Religion and Cognitive Processing

While the need for orientation is usually linked to the declining role of political parties as information sources, it could as plausibly be argued that those with a high need for orientation are not getting their cues from other organizations such as churches. In his work linking terminal and instrumental values to choice of a medium, Nimmo (1990) found that ranking "salvation" as a low priority was linked to choosing NBC, CBS, and *Time* magazine. This suggests that people for whom a religious value such as salvation is salient may not feel they need mass media because they are getting information from other sources.

Wanta (1997) makes a plausible case that highly educated people are more susceptible to agenda setting because they possess the kind of cognitive skills needed to link issues in the ways suggested by the studies exploring the role of framing and priming. He also argues quite plausibly that differences in susceptibility between liberals and conservatives may be related to the nature of the issues examined and the ways they were framed, as well as to people's levels of education and tolerance. But there is also reason to believe religion may be involved.

Attention to alternative sources, such as information from clergy or religious leaders, may affect both the credibility some people attach to particular mass media and their use of it. Cues from those sources may also make schema other than those provided by the mass media more available for use in processing information and reaching conclusions.

Here, the differences in the way conservatives and liberals process information and the conclusions they reach (Wanta, 1997, pp. 33–34) may be related to the accessibility of other schema, at least some of which may come from religious sources (Buoma and Clyne, 1995; Lupfer, Brock, and DePaola, 1992; Lupfer et al., 1994; Shah, Domke, and Wackman, 1997).

While evidence of religious influence from those quantitative studies is circumstantial at best, the qualitative research employing discourse analysis turns up evidence that people do use religious schema in thinking about political issues, forming their opinions, and making political decisions.

Graber (1988, pp. 41–43), for example, appears to have uncovered some evidence of religious influence on schema formation, but stronger evidence of that comes from Neuman, Just, and Crigler (1992, pp. 72–75), who found that 15 percent of their subjects used a morality framework in discussing issues even though mass media used it in only 4 percent of their stories. The examples they quote come from discourse about AIDS and drug use, but the authors say moral language occurred in discussions of all issues. Similarly, Gamson found that "outbursts of moral indignation" occurred in all groups (1992, pp. 57–58).

Although Gamson does not offer religion as an explanation, those outbursts may have their roots in the religious beliefs of his subjects. So too, may apparently secular frameworks such as Neuman, Just, and Crigler's "us-them" and "human impact-empathy" frames (1992, pp. 62, 69), Gamson's "we-they" and "humankind-individualist" ones (1992, pp. 84–87), and Graber's "Horatio Alger–give unto the poor" cultural norm (1988, pp. 212, 237). Indeed, "give unto the poor" suggests a biblical command.

But none of those studies was designed to examine religious influences. For that, one must look to researchers from sociology, psychology, and political science who have examined the links between religion and public opinion more carefully.

## Religious Agenda Setting

Those who study the effects of religion on public opinion work on the assumption that people's beliefs, attitudes, opinions, and behaviors should be consistent with official church teachings. Because those teachings differ from religion to religion and even from congregation to congregation, the emphasis, then, is on establishing correlations between particular kinds of religions and both issue salience and issue positions.

Although a few researchers report little evidence that messages attributed to church leaders have any effect on people's political opinions (McKeown and Carlson, 1987), others find that people do learn from the religious messages they receive (Gaddy and Pritchard, 1986; Pargament and Silverman, 1982). In general, religious conservatives take conservative political positions; religious liberals hold more liberal ones. For conservative Protestants, personal morality issues such as abortion tend to be most salient; more liberal Protestants generally attach more importance to justice issues. Catholics, African-American Protestants, and members of non-Christian religions tend to be swing voters, siding with conservative Protestants on issues of sexual morality and with liberal Protestants on civil rights and economic issues (Fowler, Hertzke, and Olson, 1999).

However, as Lopatto (1985, p. 44) points out, patterns of issue salience and issue positions within traditions can be "quirky," especially among religious moderates. But some of that "quirkiness" can be attributed to the fact that researchers rarely examine the messages people actually receive from their churches or from particular religious media. Instead, the evidence rests on survey findings of similarities between the positions of clergy and laity within a religious tradition and differences among traditions.

Because there may be differences among congregations within the same religious tradition as well as contradictory messages within the same congregation, detecting religio-political message effects from survey data is very difficult. Using survey data usually requires treating as equivalent all members of the same or similar denominations even though they attend different churches and are exposed to different messages.

However, a few studies have found important differences at the congregational level that may be related to the information available in them. In his study of 13 congregations, for example, Jelen (1991, 1993) found differences among congregations on a host of political issues that he attributed to religious beliefs and teaching styles. According to his analysis, the belief within conservative Protestantism in an inerrant Bible coupled with a rhetorical style that links a specific Bible verse to each statement gives a normative dimension to clergy pronouncements that is much more conducive to political mobilization than the liberal Protestant emphasis on individual autonomy and reason (see also Lehman, 1997; Nelson and Baxter, 1981). Thus, clergy-lay opinions are much more similar within conservative Protestantism than they are in liberal Protestantism. Within Catholicism, pronouncements tied to both the Bible and authoritative papal statements are most effective on issues such as abortion that also enjoy certain cultural resonances.

Jelen's findings are consistent with cognitive processing research showing that religious broadcasting has a priming effect (Hollander, 1998) that makes religious conservatives more likely than other Christians to make religious attributions in their political discourse (Lupfer, Brock, and DePaola, 1992; Lupfer et al., 1994; Watson, Morris, and Hood, 1990). However, Jelen discusses clergy opinions in one book (1993) and lay opinions in another (1991) so that direct evidence of agenda setting and mobilization rests primarily on differences in opinions across traditions and similarities between clergy and lay opinions within a religious tradition.

While Johnson (1966, 1967) argues that clergy pick up cues from congregation members and from the community and tailor their messages accordingly, work by Welch et al. (1993) indicates that church members' attitudes can be affected by the cues they believe they are receiving from their pastors. Although Welch et al. did not examine actual messages, their work suggests that religious communication can have its own agenda-setting effect. In the study most closely approximating those in the agenda-setting literature, Wald (1992) used public opinion polls to document changes in attitudes toward the Vietnam War in the wake of the Catholic bishops' peace pastoral that were consistent with the bishops' message. But whether the brief but short-lived reaction against military spending resulted from the pastoral or from media coverage of the pastoral and of the war itself is unclear (see also Tamney, Burton, and Johnson, 1988).

Similarly, Fetzer (1992) found an effect of pastoral persuasion on lay attitudes toward the Gulf War that remained even with sophisticated statistical analysis to control for other possibilities. However, that analysis combined churches into "peace" and "other" categories. Therefore, evidence of persuasion again rested on measurements of clergy and lay attitudes to war, not on the messages actually presented by clergy to lay members.

However, research combining a survey of the general population with ethnographic observation in six congregations and in-depth interviews with leaders and average members of those congregations in the context of the 1992 presidential election indicates that messages congregation members receive from their clergy leaders have an effect on their use of mass media and on their political opinions.

During the 1992 presidential election campaign, religious communication apparently kept abortion on the public agenda even though mass media attention was minimal. For a small number of subjects, all members of fundamentalist churches that encouraged their members to see a threat to their freedom, constitutional issues ranging from prayer in public schools to support for gun ownership were the most important issues even though those concerns were not part of media discourse about the presidential election (Buddenbaum, 1992).

However, religious message effects may be mediated by demographic characteristics of the hearers (Maguire, 1980; Pargament and DeRosa, 1985; Pargament and Silverman, 1982; Rigney and Hoffman, 1993; Schmalzbauer, 1993), motives for church membership and degree of involvement (Buddenbaum, 1996a; Eckberg and Blocker, 1989; Newman and Wright, 1980; Lenski, 1963; Allport, 1954/1979), prior beliefs (Buddenbaum, 1996b; Pargament and Silverman, 1982; Ragsdale and Durham, 1986), or effect of the pastor and the pastor's rhetorical style (Avery and Gobbel, 1980; Pargament and Silverman, 1982; Price, Terry, and Johnston, 1980).

## Cross Pressures

Real people do not live alone in a world in which the mass media are their only source of information, nor do even the most devout adherents to a religion spend all their time in church. People are subject to a host of influences that can exert cross pressures tearing them in opposite directions. For the mass media, competition for audiences is a fact of life. Churches, too, compete for members, then go to great length to keep them.

Although researchers working in the agenda-setting tradition frequently note that the medium they are studying is not the only one available to people or the only one they might use, most research on the effect of alternate sources of information has centered on the role of interpersonal communication.

In general the effect of cross pressures from conversation with other people depends on the frequency and intensity of interpersonal communication, the participant's role in the communication, perceptions of the credibility of other people versus that of the mass medium in question, and whether or not information from interpersonal sources is consistent or inconsistent with the media messages. However, in the most complete model of interpersonal effects, Wanta (1997) did not take into account the credibility of interpersonal sources or the content of conversations. Therefore, the most one can conclude from the available literature is that talking to others may sometimes enhance agenda setting (McLeod, Becker, and Byrnes, 1974), inhibit the effect (Atwater, Salwen, and Anderson, 1985; Erbring, Goldenberg, and Miller, 1980), or have no effect (Lasorsa and Wanta, 1990).

Attempts to examine the agenda-setting effect of different mass media are similarly inconclusive. Differences are undoubtedly related to the information content and presentation style employed by each medium. They may also stem from the kinds of people who use each medium, how much credibility they attach to the media or a particular medium, as well as to differences in how people process information they must read versus information communicated to them via the spoken word and/or pictures.

Although studies of the effect of cross pressures set up by using truly competing information sources are rare, the available evidence suggests that specialized sources, as exemplified by messages from clergy leaders and from religious media, affect agenda setting by the mass media at the preprocessing stage and again by providing additional resources for evaluating information and forming opinions.

In general, conservative Christians may be less susceptible to agenda setting by the mass media, both because of the teachings of their church and because of the rhetorical styles employed by their clergy leaders. Those factors do make them more inclined than others to employ religious schema in interpreting information and forming opinions. However, susceptibility to mass media agenda setting increases with increasing exposure to mass media. Therefore, religious leaders often caution against relying on mass media as a source of information. Such concern is generally strongest among conservative Protestant clergy and less pronounced among liberal Protestants and Jews (Buddenbaum, 1997; Johnson and Tamney, 1986).

Following cues from their religious leaders, members' evaluations of the mass media and their use of them generally conform to church teachings (Stout and Buddenbaum, 1996). Conservative Protestants

who are tightly tied to their religious tradition are most inclined to
avoid the dangers of cross pressures from mass media by limiting their
exposure (Buddenbaum, 1996a; McFarland, 1996; Hamilton and Rubin, 1992), even to the point of engaging in boycotts of media content
about which they have no real knowledge (Lindlof, 1996; Swatos,
1988; Tamney and Johnson, 1997).

Exposure to mass media or to other outside information sources can
increase the salience of issues that are not a part of a church's religio-
political agenda, although use of those sources does not always lead to
taking issue positions contrary to those of the church and of other
church members. Susceptibility to mass media rather than religious
communication influence occurs primarily among those whose religious beliefs are at odds with official church teachings and who have
weak ties to the religious community. It also occurs in cases where
people receive unclear or mixed messages from religious sources.

Use of mass media can, in fact, decrease the influence of religious
leaders and their messages. In the aftermath of the PTL scandal, support for televangelists among all viewers of the "700 Club" generally
decreased in the wake of heavy mass media coverage, especially
among those most heavily exposed to secular, mass media. The decrease was greatest for reactionary viewers who generally disagreed
with the televangelists but watched them for surveillance purposes; it
was smallest for fundamentalists who had traditionally supported televangelists and for ritualized viewers who watched religious television
for devotional reasons (Abelman, 1990, 1991; Hougland, Billings, and
Wood, 1990).

While Abelman's findings also illustrate the influence of initial beliefs and the perceived credibility of competing information, his conclusion that exposure to mass media coverage of the scandal contributed to the decline in perceived credibility of televangelists is
consistent with Zaller's work on the influence of contradictory messages (1991).

Although mass media messages can create cross pressures for people who attend to both mass media and religious sources of information, some of the most severe cross pressures from mixed messages can
be internal to the religious community. There are so many strains
within Christianity that religious reasoning can justify both liberal and
conservative positions. These conflicting strains coexist within the
same denomination (Donohue, 1993; Dudley and Hernandez, 1992;
Mock, 1992; Welch and Leege, 1991; Wald et al., 1990) and even

within the same congregation (Becker et al., 1993) largely because of the mobility of church members (Babchuk and Whitt, 1990; Hadaway and Marler, 1993).

However, cross pressures within a religious group also result from awareness of and attention to multiple religious sources with conflicting messages. Welch and Leege (1991; see also Dudley and Hernandez, 1992; Welch, Johnson, and Pilgrim, 1990) found that evangelically oriented Catholics took their political cues both from the Catholic Church and from the New Christian Right. On issues such as abortion, where the messages from both groups were clear and concordant, the evangelically oriented Catholics held relatively strong positions in the direction of the concordant position; where the positions of the two groups were equally clear but divergent, issue positions taken by the Catholics with dual reference groups followed Catholic teaching. However, where the positions were divergent but of unequal clarity, the evangelically oriented Catholics tended to follow the clearer message.

## Conclusion

From the available information, it seems obvious that both mass media and religion shape public opinion. Agenda-setting research clearly indicates that people learn from the mass media which issues are publicly recognized as most important. From mass media, people also get much of the information they use to evaluate issues and candidates and the language to describe them. But mass media influence less often extends to issue positions.

At the same time, other research documents consistent links between membership in particular kinds of churches and particular opinions. That link between religious affiliation and opinion is almost certainly the result of communication through religious channels. The effect of that communication on the salience church members attach to issues and on their opinions about those issues is similar to the mass media agenda-setting effect.

In both cases, the issues emphasized and the issue positions of the communicator generally match the salience attached to those issues and the positions on them taken by the audience. The available evidence also suggests that the mass media and religion sometimes work together to enhance issue salience and to promote particular issue positions and at other times work at cross purposes in ways that limit each other's effects. However, the relative influence of mass media and of religion, as well as the conditions under which each exerts influence and the processes by which they operate, are virtually unexplored territory.

The fact that, in each line of investigation, correlations are sometimes weak and findings are occasionally contradictory is, in part, due to the assumptions that both inform a theoretical perspective and flow from it. Agenda-setting research sees public opinion primarily as the aggregate of opinions formed as people attend to information from the mass media. Students of religion take more seriously the influence of group norms and group dynamics. But because these two lines of research have developed separately, neither has taken advantage of insights from the other.

In agenda-setting research, including measures of religion that are sensitive to the beliefs that shape people's worldviews and their attitudes toward and use of the media could help identify those who consider media issues salient and those who do not. Including religion as an independent variable or as a confound could also provide greater insight into the relationships between susceptibility to agenda setting and people's level of education, their degree of conservatism/liberalism and tolerance, perceptions of media credibility, and motives for media use. At the same time, those who study religion could take a cue from the agenda-setting literature. Many of the weak correlations and sometimes contradictory findings about the relationship between religion and issue salience may stem from the general tendency to treat as equivalent people who are exposed to very different religio-political messages through their churches, through religious media, and through the mass media. Attention to message content and framing could help explain the overall strength of observed relationships as well as identify the requirements for effectively transmitting a religious worldview.

Because neither mass media use nor church attendance occur in a vacuum, both lines of research could benefit from including measures that would tap use of multiple information sources. From the available literature it is clear that, as Tocqueville observed more than a century ago, both religion and the mass media help shape the mores of a people. But what is not clear is their relative strength. To determine the individual and collective influence of religion and of mass media, as well as the conditions under which each exerts its power to influence a culture through the public opinion process, will require including in the same study equivalent attention to mass media and religious communication as competing information sources.

# References

Abelman, R. (1990). Pat Robertson's fall from grace: Viewer processing of PTL scandal information. In S. Kraus, (Ed.). *Mass communication and political information processing* (pp. 113–130). Hillsdale, NJ: Lawrence Erlbaum Associates.

Abelman, R. (1991). Influence of news coverage of the "scandal" on PTL viewers. *Journalism Quarterly 68,* 101–110.

Allport, G.W. (1979). *The nature of prejudice* (25th annu. ed.). Reading, MA: Addison-Wesley. (Original work published 1954.)

Atwater, T., Salwen, M.B., and Anderson, R.B. (1985). Interpersonal discussion as a potential barrier to agenda-setting. *Newspaper Research Journal, 6,* 37–43.

Avery, W.O., and Gobbel, A.R. (1980). The word of God and the words of the preacher. *Review of Religious Research, 22,* 41–53.

Babchuk, N., and Whitt, H.P. (1990). R-order and religious switching. *Journal for the Scientific Study of Religion, 29,* 246–254.

Ball-Rokeach, S., Rokeach, M., and Grube, J.W. (1984). *The great American values test: Influencing behavior and belief through television.* New York: The Free Press.

Becker, P.E., Ellingson, S.J., Flory, R.W., Griswold, W., Kniss, F., and Nelson, T. (1993). Straining at the tie that binds: Congregational conflict in the 1980s. *Review of Religious Research, 34,* 193–209.

Beniger, J.R., and Jones, G. (1990). Changing technologies, mass media, and control of the pictures in people's heads: A preliminary look at U.S. presidential campaign slogans, 1800–1984. In S. Kraus (Ed.). *Mass communication and political information processing.* Hillsdale, NJ: Lawrence Erlbaum Associates.

Blumer, H. (1969). *Symbolic interactionism: Perspective and method.* Englewood Cliffs, NJ: Prentice-Hall.

Buddenbaum, J.M. (1992, November). If Jesus could vote: Religious beliefs about political behavior. Paper presented at the meeting of the Religious Research Association, Washington, D.C.

Buddenbaum, J.M. (1996a). The role of religion in newspaper trust, subscribing and use for political information. In D.A. Stout and J.M. Buddenbaum, (Eds.), *Religion and mass media: Audiences and adaptations* (pp. 123–234). Thousand Oaks, CA: Sage.

Buddenbaum, J.M. (1996b). Use of mass media for political information in a Middletown Quaker meeting. In D.A. Stout and J.M. Buddenbaum,

(Eds.), *Religion and mass media: Audiences and adaptations* (pp. 197–210). Thousand Oaks, CA: Sage.

Buddenbaum, J.M. (1997). Reflections on culture wars: Churches, communication content, and consequences. In M. Suman (Ed.). *Religion and prime-time television* (pp. 47–68). Westport, CT: Praeger.

Buddenbaum, J.M. (1998). Media influence on traditional values. In W.D. Sloan and E.E. Hoff (Eds.). *Contemporary media issues* (pp. 24–38). Tuscaloosa, AL: Vision Press.

Buddenbaum, J.M., and Stout, D.A. (1996). Religion and mass media use: A review of the mass communication and sociology literature. In D.A. Stout and J.M. Buddenbaum (Eds.). *Religion and mass media: Audiences and adaptations* (pp. 12–34). Thousand Oaks, CA: Sage.

Buoma, G.D., and Clyne, M. (1995). Articulating religious meaning in conversation: Variations in linguistic style of subdenominational religious groups. *Review of Religious Research, 37,* 132–146.

Csikszentmihalyi, M. (1991). Reflections on the "spiral of silence." In J. A. Anderson (Vol. Ed.). *Communication yearbook, 14* (pp. 288–297). Newbury Park, CA: Sage.

Donohue, M.J. (1993). Prevalence and correlates of New Age beliefs in six Protestant denominations. *Journal for the Scientific Study of Religion, 32,* 177–184.

Dudley, R.L., and Hernandez, E.I. (1992). *Citizens of two worlds: Religion and politics among American Seventh-Day Adventists.* Berrien Springs, MI: Andrews University Press.

Eckberg, D.L., and Blocker, T.J. (1989). Varieties of religious involvement and environmental concern. *Journal for the Scientific Study of Religion, 28,* 509–517.

Erbring, L., Goldenberg, E.N., and Miller, A.H. (1980). Front-page news and real-world cues: A look at agenda-setting by the media. *American Journal of Political Science, 24,* 16–49.

Fetzer, J. (1992, November). The role of the local pastor in shaping evangelicals' attitudes on the morality of war. Paper presented at the meeting of the Society for the Scientific Study of Religion, Washington, D.C.

Fowler, R.B., Herzke, A.D. and Olson, L.R. (1999). *Religion and politics in America: Faith, culture, and strategic choices.* Boulder, CO: Westview Press.

Gaddy, G.D., and Pritchard, D. (1986). Is religious knowledge gained from broadcasts? *Journalism Quarterly, 63,* 40–844.

Gamson, W.A. (1992). *Talking politics.* New York: Cambridge University Press.

Graber, D.A. (1988). *Processing the news: How people tame the information tide* (2nd ed.). New York: Longman.

Hadaway, C.K., and Marler, P.L. (1993). All in the family: Religious mobility in America. *Review of Religious Research, 35,* 97–116.

Hamilton, N.F., and Rubin, A.M. (1992). The influence of religiosity on television viewing. *Journalism Quarterly, 69,* 667–678.

Hollander, B.A. (1998). The priming of religion in political attitudes: The role
of religious programming. *The Journal of Communication and Religion, 21,* 67–83.

Hougland, J.G., Jr., Billings, D.B., and Wood, J.R. (1990). The instability of
support for television evangelists: Public reactions during a period of
embarrassment. *Review of Religious Research, 32,* 56–64.

Iyengar, S. (1987). *Is anyone responsible? How television frames political issues.* Chicago: University of Chicago Press.

Iyengar, S., and Kinder, D.R. (1987). *News that matters: Television and American opinion.* Chicago: University of Chicago Press.

Iyengar, S., Peters, M.D., and Kinder, D.R. (1982). Experimental demonstra-
tions of the "not-so-minimal" consequences of television news programs. *American Political Science Review, 76,* 848–858.

Jelen, T.G. (1991). *The political mobilization of religious beliefs.* New York:
Praeger.

Jelen, T.G. (1993). *The political world of the clergy.* Westport, CT: Praeger.

Johnson, B. (1966). Theology and party preference among Protestant clergy-
man. *American Sociological Review, 31,* 200–208.

Johnson, B. (1967). Theology and the position of pastors on public issues.
*American Sociological Review, 32,* 433–442.

Johnson, S.D., and Tamney, J.B. (1986). The clergy and public issues in Middletown. In S.D. Johnson and J.B. Tamney (Eds.). *The political role of
religion in the United States* (pp. 45–70). Boulder, CO: Westview Press.

Lane, R.E. (1972). *Political life.* New York: The Free Press.

Lasorsa, D.L., and Wanta, W. (1990). Effects of personal, interpersonal and
media experiences on issue salience. *Journalism Quarterly, 67,* 804–813.

Lau, R.R., and Sears, D.O. (Eds.) (1986). *Political cognition: The 19th annual
Carnegie Symposium on cognition.* Hillsdale, NJ; Lawrence Erlbaum
Associates.

Lehman, E.C., Jr. (1997). Correlates of lay perceptions of clergy ministry
style. *Review of Religious Research, 38,* 211–230.

Lenski, G. (1963). *The religious factor: a sociologist's inquiry.* Garden City,
NY: Anchor Books.

Lindlof, T.R. (1996). The passionate audience: Community inscriptions of
The Last Temptation of Christ. In D.A. Stout and J.M. Buddenbaum
(Eds.). *Religion and mass media: Audiences and adaptations* (pp.
148–166). Thousand Oaks, CA: Sage.

Lopatto, P. (1985). *Religion and the presidential election.* New York: Praeger.

Lupfer, M.B., Brock, K.F., and DePaola, S.J. (1992). The use of secular and
religious attributions to explain everyday behavior. *Journal for the Scientific Study of Religion, 31,* 486–503.

Lupfer, M.B., DePaola, S.J., Brock, K.F., and Clement, L. (1994). Making secular and religious attributions: The availability hypothesis revisited. *Journal for the Scientific Study of Religion, 33,* 162–171.

Maguire, J.T. (1980). A scale on preaching style: Hortatory vs. interactive preaching. *Review of Religious Research, 22,* 60–65.

Markus, H., and Zajonc, R.B. (1985). The cognitive perspective in social psychology. In G. Lindzey and E. Aronson (Eds.). *Handbook of social psychology, Vol. 1,* (3rd ed., pp. 137–230). New York: Random House.

McCombs, M.E., and Shaw, D.L. (1972). The agenda-setting function of mass media. *Public Opinion Quarterly, 36,* 176–187.

McCombs, M.E., and Weaver, D.H. (1985). Toward a merger of gratifications and agenda-setting research. In K.E. Rosengren, L.A. Wenner, and P. Palmgreen (Eds.). *Media gratifications research* (pp. 95–108). Beverly Hills, CA: Sage.

McFarland, S.G. (1996). Keeping the faith: The role of selective exposure and avoidance in maintaining religious beliefs. In D.A. Stout and J.M. Buddenbaum (Eds.). *Religion and mass media: Audiences and adaptations* (pp. 173–182). Thousand Oaks, CA: Sage.

McKeown, B., and Carlson, J.M. (1987). An experimental study of the influence of religious elites on public opinion. *Political Communication and Persuasion, 4,* 93–102.

McLeod, J.M., Becker, L.B., and Byrnes, J.E. (1974). Another look at the agenda-setting function of the press. *Communication Research, 1,* 131–166.

Miller, M.M., and Quarles, J.P. (1984, August). Dramatic television and agenda-setting: The case of "The Day After." Paper presented at the meeting of the Association for Education in Journalism and Mass Communication, Gainesville, FL.

Mock, A.K. (1992). Congregation religious styles and orientations to society: Exploring our linear assumptions. *Review of Religious Research, 34,* 20–33.

Moscovici, S. (1991). Silent majorities and loud minorities. In J.A. Anderson (Vol. Ed.). *Communication yearbook, 14* (pp. 298–308). Newbury Park, CA: Sage.

Mullins, L.E. (1977). Agenda-setting and the young voter. In D.L. Shaw and M.E. McCombs (Eds.). *The emergence of American political issues* (pp. 133–148). St. Paul, MN: West.

Nelson, H.M., and Baxter, S. (1981). Ministers speak on Watergate: Effects of clergy role during political crisis. *Review of Religious Research, 23,* 150–166.

Neuman, W.R., Just, M.R., and Crigler, A.N. (1992). *Common knowledge: News and the construction of political meaning.* Chicago: University of Chicago Press.

Newman, W.M., and Wright, S.A. (1980). The effects of sermons among lay Catholics: An exploratory study. *Review of Religious Research, 24,* 54–59.

Nimmo, D. (1990). Principles of information selection in information processing: A preliminary political analysis. In S. Kraus (Ed.). *Mass communication and political information processing* (pp. 3–18). Hillsdale, NJ: Lawrence Erlbaum Associates.

Pargament, K.I., and DeRosa, D.V. (1985). What was that sermon about? Predicting memory for religious messages from cognitive theory. *Journal for the Scientific Study of Religion, 24,* 119–236.

Pargament, K.I., and Silverman, W.H. (1982). Exploring some correlates of sermon impact on Catholic parishioners. *Review of Religious Research, 24,* 33–39.

Price, D.L., Terry, W.R., and Johnston, B.C. (1980). The measurement of the effect of preaching and preaching plus small group dialogue in one Baptist church. *Journal for the Scientific Study of Religion, 19,* 186–197.

Ragsdale, J.D., and Durham, K.R. (1986). Audience response to religious fear appeals. *Review of Religious Research, 28,* 40–50.

Rigney, D., and Hoffman, T.J. (1993). Is American Catholicism anti-intellectual? *Journal for the Scientific Study of Religion, 32,* 211–222.

Rogers, E.M., and Dearing, J.W. (1988). Agenda-setting research: Where has it been, where is it going? In J. A. Anderson (Vol. Ed.). *Communication yearbook, 11* (pp. 555–594). Newbury Park, CA: Sage.

Schmalzbauer, J. (1993). Evangelicals in the new class: Class versus subcultural predictors of ideology. *Journal for the Scientific Study of Religion, 32,* 330–343.

Shaw, D.L., and McCombs, M.E. (Eds.) (1977). *The Emergence of American political issues: The agenda-setting function of the press.* St. Paul, MN: West.

Shah, D.V., Domke, D., and Wackman, D.B. (1997). Values and the vote: Linking issue interpretations to the process of candidate choice. *Journalism Quarterly, 74,* 357–387.

Signorielli, N., and Morgan, M. (Eds.) (1990). *Cultivation analysis: New directions in media effects research.* Newbury Park, CA: Sage.

Stout, D.A., and Buddenbaum, J.M. (Eds.) (1996). *Religion and mass media: Audiences and adaptations.* Thousand Oaks, CA: Sage.

Swatos, W.H., Jr. (1988). Picketing Satan enfleshed at 7-Eleven: A research note. *Review of Religious Research, 30,* 176–185.

Tamney, J.B., and Johnson, S.D. (1997). Christianity and public book banning. *Review of Religious Research, 38,* 263–271.

Tamney, J.B., Burton, R., and Johnson, S.D. (1988). Christianity, social class and the Catholic bishops' economic policy. *Sociological Analysis, 49,* S78–S96.

Tocqueville, A. de (1889). *Democracy in America.* (Vols. 1, 2). (H. Reeve, Trans.). London: Longmans, Green and Co. (Original works published 1835, 1841.)

Wald, K.D. (1992). Religious elites and public opinion: The impact of the bishops' peace pastoral. *The Review of Politics, 54,* 112–143.

Wald, K.D., Owen, D.E., and Hill, S.S., Jr. (1990). Political cohesion in churches. *Journal of Politics, 52,* 197–215.

Wanta, W. (1997). *The public and the national agenda: How people learn about important issues.* Mahwah, NJ: Lawrence Erlbaum.

Watson, P.J., Morris, R.J., and Hood, R.W. (1990). Attributional complexity, religious orientation, and indiscriminate pro-religiousness. *Review of Religious Research, 32,* 110–121.

Weaver, D.H. (1977). Political issues and voter need for orientation. In D.L. Shaw and M.E. McCombs (Eds.). *The emergence of American political issues* (pp. 107–120). St. Paul, MN: West.

Weaver, D.H., Graber, D.A., McCombs, M.E., and Eyal, C.H. (1981). *Media agenda-setting in a presidential election: Issues, images, interests.* New York: Praeger.

Welch, M.R., and Leege, D.C. (1991). Dual reference groups and political orientations: An examination of evangelically oriented Catholics. *American Journal of Political Science, 35,* 28–56.

Welch, M.R., Johnson, C.L., and Pilgrim, D. (1990). Tuning in the spirit: Exposure to types of religious TV programming among American Catholic parishioners. *Journal for the Scientific Study of Religion, 29,* 185–197.

Welch, M.R., Leege, D.C., Wald, K.D., and Kellstedt, L.A. (1993). Are the sheep hearing the shepherds? Cue perception, congregational responses, and political communication processes. In D.C. Leege and L.A. Kellstedt (Eds.). *Rediscovering the religious factor in American politics* (pp. 235–254). Armonk, NY: M.E. Sharpe.

Zaller, J. (1991). Information, values, and opinion. *American Political Science Review, 85,* 1215–1237.

CHAPTER 3

# Touched by Angels and Demons: Religion's Love-Hate Relationship with Popular Culture

## QUENTIN J. SCHULTZE

I
n this chapter I address the relationship between American religion and popular culture, especially popular television. Religion
and popular culture have long shared a love-hate relationship, alternately courting and criticizing each other.

First, I propose that religious groups often see religious popular culture as a means of converting people to their beliefs. Protestants, in
particular, have viewed media technologies as a way to evangelize the
world. Today, Evangelicals, the conservative Protestants, champion
evangelistic popular culture.

Second, I propose that mainstream (or "secular") popular culture
pushes American religion simultaneously in opposite directions. On
the one hand, it *unifies* religious movements that organize in response
to common cultural enemies perceived in popular culture. Religious
groups establish antimedia movements, for example, to express shared

The author thanks research assistant Sara Toering for her excellent help in preparing
this manuscript.

moral concerns publicly and to try to reform the media. As they battle against mainstream popular culture, however, these unified religious movements "restructure" American religion into ideologically polarized, cross-denominational categories (Wuthnow, 1988).

On the other hand, mainstream popular culture *dilutes* the authority of established religious traditions. Commercial popular culture, in particular, constantly creates a lowest-common-denominator religiosity that implicitly challenges the particular beliefs of virtually all religious groups. Like the popular television program *Touched by an Angel,* popular culture expresses an amorphous faith that flattens religious traditions.

## Protestant Evangelization through Religious Popular Culture

Miller (1965) reveals how Protestants associated missionary activity with technology during the nineteenth century. By 1848 the American "mind had become so adjusted to the technological revolution" that "public orators identified missions with the industrial 'scene of astonishing activity'" (p. 52). Protestants saw mass communication technologies as God-given means for popular evangelism. In other words, American Protestants were "technologically minded" (Schultze, 1991, p. 179), quickly seizing popular media as a means to spread the Gospel.

Historically speaking, Protestants championed religious popular culture, or what McDannell (1995) calls "material Christianity." Hatch (1989) shows how preaching, music, and printing generated a multimedia explosion of Protestant evangelization in early America. Protestants established Bible and tract societies, which revolutionized mass printing and distribution during the 1830s (Nord, 1984). In the 1920s and 1930s, Protestants were strongly committed to the evangelistic power of religious radio (Schultze, 1990; Voskuil, 1990).

In the twentieth century, broadcasting offered religious underdogs, especially Evangelicals, a means to create publicly their own popular culture. If mainline Protestants controlled elite culture, Evangelicals believed that they could use popular culture to connect directly with the common people. Religious radio in Chicago was thoroughly dominated in the 1930s and 1940s by Evangelical groups, such as Holiness and Pentecostal churches (Betts, 1932; FCCCA, 1938; Parker and

Eastman, 1942). The Jehovah's Witnesses, Christian Scientists, and many smaller groups also used early radio (Schultze, 1988). Local mainline pastors publicly criticized early Evangelical radio programs, recognizing that Evangelicals could now directly evangelize members of mainline churches (Berkman, 1988). Evangelicals adopted broadcasting not only as a means of building their own organizations but also as a way of competing with their mainline rivals (Carpenter, 1984, 1997; Schultze, 1988).

## Popular Culture's Unifying Impact

Secular popular culture is a very important socio-religious force that unifies conservative religious people against a common enemy. Conservatives often use popular culture not just to evangelize but also to gain a public voice in "culture wars"—public disagreements over whose values and beliefs should guide the nation (Hunter, 1991). Evangelicals created the Moral Majority, for instance, to gain political power on moral issues. Today's Evangelical movement to redeem popular culture and reform the media is a "confluence of religious convictions and conservative political ideology" (Romanowski, 1996, p. 54).

Popular culture's unifying impact is evident in the new, specialized religious movements that form in response to the perceived evils of mainstream popular culture. As believers respond to what they do not like in mainstream popular culture, they *reorganize* American religious life into new, relatively temporary moral crusades and political movements. These movements create their own popular culture that links existing believers to a shared socio-political agenda.

Religious television, for instance, battles the evils of Hollywood, such as gay and lesbian television characters, liberal news reporting, excessive profanity in movies, and violent children's commercials, comic books, and video games. These types of moral concerns unify viewers of religious television. The vast majority of televangelists do not merely evangelize. They build quasi-religious, cross-denominational organizations that coalesce supporters around particular moral and political causes.

Consumers support religious popular culture partly by identifying with a movement's politically charged symbols. They participate in what Boorstin (1973) calls "consumption communities"— cross-geographical communities of individuals who do not know each other personally but who identify with a common product brand. In a sense, they "consume" the moral causes by identifying with the mass-mediated religious "community" and contributing financially to the movement. In fact, many of the contributors to religious television are not viewers (Hoover, 1988, p. 80); they participate *symbolically* in the ministry by reading ministry newsletters, following the ministry's efforts in the news, and eventually making contributions. In this way, religious popular culture symbolically unifies consumers who are concerned about the evil effects of mainstream popular culture.

The Reverend Jerry Falwell's religious television broadcast, *The Old-Time Gospel Hour,* is an excellent example. The program enabled him to create the Moral Majority, which offered members the opportunity to participate in a moral crusade with clear political purposes, including the presidential election of Ronald Reagan and American support for the nation of Israel (Simon, 1984). Other moral-political agendas included overturning *Roe vs. Wade* in order to criminalize abortion, returning prayer to the public schools, and supporting "pro-family" legislation (Fitzgerald, 1981). In addition, Falwell's television ministry appealed to viewers for contributions that would alleviate hunger and suffering in Africa, support missionaries who were spreading the Gospel, and educate committed young Christians at Falwell's Liberty University (Falwell, 1987). Using his broadcast program, Falwell unified hundreds of thousands of moral conservatives around these issues.

The unifying role of religious popular culture in American Christianity presents two potential problems. First, religious popular culture can polarize groups within society by antagonizing people who do not share the same beliefs. Religious popular culture often politicizes religion for the purposes of quickly mobilizing audiences and raising funds. It sometimes even demonizes others for the benefit of its own religious cause.

Second, religious popular culture can weaken established religious traditions. Religious television, for instance, one day addresses the portrayal of family values on the *Murphy Brown* television series. The next day it leads a battle cry against the portrayal of a lesbian in the show *Ellen.* Each new moral campaign whips religious consumers from one current agenda to another. But the religious rhetoric usually fails to show how the moral agendas relate to any particular religious tradition. Why should a Roman Catholic or a Jew, for instance, take a specific stand on either of these television programs?

## Popular Culture Dilutes Religious Traditions

Religious popular culture's power to foster new religious movements pales in contrast to mainstream popular culture's massive ability to dilute religious traditions. Most popular culture homogenizes and deflates traditional religious beliefs. Mainstream television, in particular, challenges the authority of religions to define reality (Goethals, 1990). The real television preachers in America are not the televangelists, but the writers and producers of prime-time fare. Secular network programs reach about two-thirds of the population every evening, compared with religious television's audiences in the hundreds of thousands or occasional millions (Hoover, 1987).

Secular popular culture breeds secularism in society by replacing distinct religious worldviews with quasi-religious entertainment. Through a kind of Gresham's Law, secular popular culture replaces overtly religious popular culture.

Religious broadcaster Pat Robertson discovered this when he built a major cable-TV network out of his Evangelical *700 Club* broadcast. Once an avid televangelist with a small audience of religious viewers, he eventually leveraged *The 700 Club* into the Christian Broadcasting Network, and then into the family-oriented and far more secular Family Channel. He finally sold the already secularized Family Channel to Rupert Murdoch's Fox Entertainment, which dubbed the network the "Fox Family" channel. Each step along the way, as audiences and revenues grew, the network's religious fare gave way to secular programming, such as old sitcoms and movies-of-the-week.

Prime-time television is amazingly secular. Skill and his colleagues (1994) found virtually no distinctly religious content on 100 episodes of series appearing on ABC, CBS, NBC, and Fox. Of the 1,462 speaking characters in the program sample, only 81 had an identifiable religious affiliation. Moreover, researchers found a total of only 115 "religious behaviors," most of which were something like a character uttering "Thank God!" after a close call. Skill concluded that there were no central characters who were significantly religious and no plots in which religion was central to the story. Moreover, when religion was apparent, it was often framed as a personal, private activity, not as a public or group activity. Ferré (1992) suggests, "The good news is that critics exaggerate television's hostility toward religion. The bad news is that television rarely takes religion seriously" (p. 14).

Successful television producer Luck (1999) says, for instance, that the program *Touched by an Angel* flattens and trivializes faith. "To watch one hour of that show is the equivalent of eating 4,000 spiritual Twinkies," he argues. Instead of providing only spiritual substance, the program merely makes "everyone's taste buds tingle." Finally, he says, the show may represent "nothing less than the birth of a new media religion."

Secular and traditional religious culture exist in tension. Religion and television for example, are "competition in cultural context" (Newman, 1996). Television stories generally assume that people are naturally good, whereas some religious groups believe that people are prone to evil. Television also stereotypes entire races or ethnic groups as evil. Most significant of all, television rarely assumes that God exists, let alone that immorality is a sin against God.

Jewish writer Lerner (1990) says that the show *thirtysomething* reflects "a world in which Judaism has been emptied of content and daily life has been emptied of political possibility" (p. 8). He suggests that it "apparently never occurred to the writers . . . that generations of martyrs died to keep Judaism alive precisely because there was . . . a message and a meaning." This television Jewishness "amounts to little more than criticism, a bat or bar mitzvah party after a child has memorized a Torah reading that she/he finds largely incomprehensible, some gifts for Chanukah, and a family meal at Passover" (p. 6). Lerner concludes, "We have yet to see a single portrayal on national television of a Jew who has some good reason other than family tradition for holding on to Judaism" (p. 6).

Even when popular culture recognizes ethnic and cultural identity, it tends to ignore religiosity. Critic Rosen (1989) explained how *thirtysomething* did this in an episode about the problems of an interfaith marriage. The main character, Michael, "toys with the idea of going to a synagogue and thereby reaffirming his identity as a Jew. He wanders by the place, but he can't bring himself to have a serious discussion with the young rabbi" (p. 32). As Rosen describes the episode, Michael never looks the rabbi in the eye and never seriously asks what it means to be a Jew. Instead, Michael "ends up confessing to his cousin Melissa a vague belief in God. . . . What Michael refuses, then, is any system of belief that would forbid or require certain conduct. It is Hanukkah he wants to observe, not Yom Kippur" (p.32).

Occasionally the tension between popular culture and religious faith seems to disappear when popular culture implicitly embraces the beliefs of a particular religion. Millions of religious people view *Touched by an Angel,* even though the show's religious worldview is probably more New Age than Christian, Jewish, or Muslim. Father Greeley (1988) argues that popular culture is "a theological place—the locale in which one may encounter God" (p. 9). Greeley even suggests that the *Cosby Show* provides "moral paradigms and displays warm and renewing love" (p. 125).

In other words, consumers often find religious meaning even in popular culture that might not have been produced for religious purposes. Theil (1983) concludes that the final episode of *M\*A\*S\*H,* like the Bible in Luke 13:1–5, asked why humans suffer. And he argues that the series was successful because it brought a "touch of humor and humility—and a lot of God-blessed humanity—to an otherwise unbearable situation" (p. 305). The show was, in his view, a "story of 'conversion' or 'regeneration'" (p. 305). At the program's best, "there was always the element of faith, of hope, and of love" (p. 306).

Nevertheless, there seems to be more tension than harmony between popular culture and religion. Goldsmith (1983) contends that commercial television has become the "common school of America" (pp. 421–422) as traditional schools have become more multicultural. In her view, a show like *Star Trek* is supremely American, preaching a naive faith in the values of freedom and progress. Sullivan (1983) agrees that "commercial television is a moral educator, the bard for the glorification of technology, science, expertise and the value of competition" (p. 12). Wall (1991) argues that religion on television always takes the form of "hypocritical piety" (p. 539) or meaningless ceremony.

Mainstream popular culture, then, elicits both criticism and praise from traditional faith communities. Sometimes the critics are prophets of doom, like Muggeridge (1977) and Ellul (1985), who warn the Christian community that television may be incompatible with the faith. More often, religious critics hope that the media could help traditions reestablish authentic communities of faith.

Roman Catholics are especially likely to look to the media for opportunities to reinvigorate traditional faith. Mann (1987), for example, believes that a revitalized Roman Catholicism will occur only when "individual Catholics and Catholic groups can be seen and heard telling their stories, sharing their experiences and discovering together what unites and what divides them. . . . The identity and uniqueness of Catholicism is at stake" (p. 372). Film producer Bullert (1987) agrees with Bellah (1985) that prime-time television reflects the radical individualism that makes religious community so difficult to achieve in America, but she looks to the electronic media for images that might inspire Catholics to construct cities based on the common good. In the PBS documentary *God and Money,* about U.S. Catholic bishops' pastoral letter on the economy, Bullert optimistically profiles three types of projects: the citizen's lobbying organization, the cooperative, and the community organization. In the midst of the popular culture wars, some religious people hope that media can revitalize traditional religions.

## Conclusion

Religious groups have always expressed a love-hate relationship with American popular culture. Protestants hoped that they could use mass media to evangelize the unsaved. But they found that popular culture also sparks culture wars.

As popular culture both unifies and dilutes religious culture in the United States, it reflects the tensions between *democracy* and *theocracy.* Democracy opens the nation to all religious and secular voices. But when religious groups criticize popular culture, they generally hope to conform public life to their own religious convictions. Taken to the extreme, they wish that their religious beliefs would set the agenda for the entire society—a kind of theocracy ruled by religious leaders from their own traditions.

The tension between religion and mainstream popular culture waxes and wanes in the United States. Indeed, the tension may flow from Americans' own unease about religion in public life as well as from the nation's growing religious diversity. Popular culture is one battleground *about* which and *through* which Americans debate their different religiously inspired moral visions for the future of the country. This may be why popular culture seems both highly religious and deeply secular; it all depends on who one asks! Popular culture touches the love-hate relationships that religious groups have with both the angels and demons of American culture.

## References

Bellah, R.N. (1985). The sociological implications of electronic media. In *The electronic media, popular culture and family values.* A proceedings report: United States Catholic Conference (pp. 13–21).

Berkman, D. (1988). Long before Falwell: Early radio and religion—as reported by the nation's periodical press. *Journal of Popular Culture,* 21(4), 296–297.

Betts, G.H. (1932). Radio's contribution to religion. In J.H. MacLatchy (Ed.), *Education on the air* (pp. 37–51). Columbus: Ohio State University Press.

Boorstin, D.J. (1973). *The Americans: The democratic experience.* New York: Random House.

Bullert, B.J. (1987). Television and the vision of the common good. In O.F. Williams and J.W. Houck (Eds.). *The common good and U.S. capitalism* (pp. 375–387). Lantham, MD: University Press of America.

Carpenter, J.A. (1984). From fundamentalism to the new evangelical coalition. In G.M. Marsden (Ed.), *Evangelicalism in modern America* (pp. 3–16). Grand Rapids, MI: Eerdmans.

Carpenter, J.A. (1997). *The reawakening of American fundamentalism.* New York: Oxford University Press.

Ellul, J. (1985). *The humiliation of the word.* Grand Rapids, MI: Eerdmans.

Falwell, J. (1987). *Strength for the journey.* New York: Simon and Schuster.

Federal Council of the Churches of Christ in America, Department of Research and Education. (1938). *Broadcasting and the public.* New York: Abingdon Press.

Ferré, J.P. (March 16, 1992). Prime-time piety? It hardly exists. *The Banner,* 127, 14–15.

Fitzgerald, F. (May 18, 1981). A reporter at large—a disciplined, charging army. *The New Yorker,* 57, 53–141.

Goethals, G.T. (1990). *The electronic golden calf: Images, religion, and the making of meaning.* Cambridge, MA: Cowley.

Goldsmith, M.H. (1983). Video values education: Star Trek as modern myth. *Religious Education,* 78, 421–422.

Greeley, A.M. (1988). *God in popular culture.* Chicago: Thomas More Press.

Hatch, N.O. (1989). *The democratization of American Christianity.* New Haven, CT: Yale University Press.

Hoover, S.M. (December, 1987). The religious television audience: A matter of significance or size? *Review of Religious Research,* 29(2), 135–156.

Hoover, S.M. (1988). *Mass media religion: The social sources of the electronic church.* Newbury Park, CA: Sage.

Hunter, J.D. (1991). *Culture wars: The struggle to define America.* New York: Basic Books.

Lerner, M. (November/December, 1990). "thirtysomething" and Judaism. *Tikkun,* 5, 6–8.

Luck, C. (1999). Touched by a fallen angel. *The Tongue.* Available: *http://www.thetongue.com/columnist/luck/archive/luckb.html.*

Mann, P. (1987). Media and the common good: The search for justice. In O.F. Williams and J.W. Houck (Eds.), *The common good and U.S. capitalism* (pp. 364–374). Lantham, MD: University Press of America.

McDannell, C. (1995). *Material Christianity: Religion and popular culture in America.* New Haven, CT: Yale University Press.

Miller, P. (1965). *The life of the mind in America.* New York: Harcourt, Brace, and World.

Muggeridge, M. (1977). *Christ and the media.* Grand Rapids, MI: Eerdmans.

Newman, J. (1996). *Religion vs. television: Competitors in cultural context.* Westport, CT: Praeger.

Nord, D.P. (1984). The evangelical origins of mass media in America. *Journalism Monograph,* 88.

Parker, E.C., and Eastman, F. (January, 1942). Religion on the air in Chicago. *The Chicago Theological Seminary Register, 22,* 12–22.

Romanowski, W.D. (1996). *Pop culture wars: Religion and the role of entertainment in American life.* Downers Grove, IL: InterVarsity Press.

Rosen, J. (July/August, 1989) "thirtysomething." *Tikkun,* 4, 29–32.

Schultze, Q.J. (1988). Evangelical radio and the rise of the electronic church, 1921–1948. *Journal of Broadcasting and Electronic Media, 32,* 289–306.

Schultze, Q.J. (1990). Keeping the faith: American Evangelicals and the mass media. In Q.J. Schultze (Ed.), *American Evangelicals and the mass media: Perspectives on the relationship between American Evangelicals and the mass media* (pp. 23–46). Grand Rapids, MI: Zondervan/ Academie.

Schultze, Q.J. (1991). *Televangelism and American culture.* Grand Rapids, MI: Baker Book House.

Simon, M. (1984). *Jerry Falwell and the Jews.* Middle Village, NY: Jonathan David.

Skill, T., Robinson, J.D., Lyons, J.S., and Larson, D.B. (March, 1994). The portrayal of religion and spirituality on fictional network television. *Review of Religious Research, 35*(3), 251–276.

Sullivan, E.V. (1983). Commonsense and valuing. *Religious Education,* 78, 5–12.

Theil, S.L. (October, 1983). An epilogue for *M*A*S*H*: A prologue for human suffering. *Currents in Theology and Mission,* 10(5), 304–306.

Voskuil, D.N. (1990). The power of the air. In Q.J. Schultze (Ed.), *American Evangelicals and the mass media: Perspectives on the relationship between American Evangelicals and the mass media* (pp. 69–95). Grand Rapids, MI: Zondervan/Academie.

Wall, J.M. (May, 1991). A show in which prayer is all in the family. *Christian Century,* 108, 539–540.

Wuthnow, R. (1988). *The restructuring of American religion: Society and faith since World War II.* Princeton: Princeton University Press.

CHAPTER 4

# Religion, Media, and the Cultural Center of Gravity

## STEWART M. HOOVER

There has been great change in recent years in the way we think about relations between religion and the media. There was a time not too long ago when very little attention was given at all. To the extent anyone noticed, most were concerned with effects that religion and the media might be having on each other. Two phenomena were of primary concern: the way religion was constructed within "secular" media such as the news media and the effects of religious television on conventional religion.

But these were far from complete or satisfying approaches to what is a much more complex and involved question. These studies of religion and the media need to be complemented by other perspectives and approaches. In particular, they could benefit from attention to *culture*. Within communication studies in general, culture has come to be a more and more important issue. The set of theories that have come to be known collectively as *cultural studies* (Grossberg et al., 1992) have called attention to the need to understand that the media play a role beyond their *direct effects* on beliefs or behaviors. They also participate in the *construction of meaning* and the definition of the structured relationships within which individuals live their lives (Moores, 1993). These are substantially *cultural* tasks.

And, as the media are involved in such areas as the construction of

**49**

*meaning,* they might be said to have *religious* implications or conse-quences. But, to see things this way, we must abandon one of the as-sumptions that has supported much of the research that has gone on be-fore: the idea that the media and religion are separate and competing spheres and that, on some level, they inhabit the roles of "sacred" (re-ligion) and "profane" (the media) influences in contemporary life.

As attractive and broadly accepted as this notion is, I want to sug-gest that to think of things in this way—as if a clear demarcation ex-ists between the voluble and effervescent religion of the private sphere and the cool, rational, pragmatic religion of the public sphere—misses a vital point about contemporary religion and contemporary media.

That point is that the whole cultural center of gravity has now shifted. What was once easily understood as a line between private and public has been or is being erased as a result of forces at work in con-temporary religion and contemporary media. What has emerged in place of an old dualism between the private and the public, between the religious and the secular, and between the sacred and the profane is a less definite space where those distinctions exist in a state of fluidity and flux.

Several social trends are bringing this about. First, religious practice has undergone great change in the decades since the 1960s. Described by observers such as Robert Bellah (1985), Robert Wuthnow (1988), Catherine Albanese (1993), and Wade Clark Roof (1993), religion is coming to reside more and more in the hands of individuals and less and less in the hands of institutions, denominations, congregations, or para–church groups.

Sociologists call this the rise of *personal autonomy* in matters of faith. It is rooted in the twentieth-century revolution that has brought the *self* and the construction of the *self* and *personal identity* to the fore as the central logics of social practice (Giddens, 1991).

We are now much more self-conscious and calculating about identity—that is, about faith, belief, taste, and value—than was the case in the preindustrial past, and we feel a greater sense of ownership over both the quest and the outcome. Wade Clark Roof (1993) calls the religious valence of this identify-formation "seeker" or "quester" reli-giosity. It is not the totality of religious practice today, but it is the im-portant religious momentum at this point in history.

At the same time, the world of the media is changing, too. Fractur-ing, atomization, diversification, and restructuring are the facts of life there. More and more channels, more and more sources, and a greater range of goods and services are emerging. Look at television. The old general-interest networks are in decline. In their place we find an explosion in specialized channels and services.

And of special interest here is the fact that in this new media marketplace there is an increasing range of programs, products, and services that are either explicitly or implicitly religious. Recent television seasons, for instance, have seen unprecedented numbers of television series that directly involve religion, as well as religious themes showing up in many other series on a less regular basis. *Touched by an Angel,* one of the top-rated shows for several seasons, and *Nothing Sacred,* which failed in the ratings wars in 1998, are only two of dozens of examples in television alone. Similar trends can be found in film and in other media.

This means that we are, in fact, seeing the media marketplace function as a *marketplace*. The rise of autonomous religious seeking has led to a supply to meet that demand. It goes without saying that this is interesting and somewhat unprecedented. Heretofore, religion, either explicit or implicit, was much less a feature of media content than it has now become (Hoover, 1998).

While it is helpful to think of what has emerged as a marketplace, it is much more like a bazaar or a flea market than it is like Main Street or a department store. It is a marketplace made up of the plethora of television, radio, cable, and direct-broadcast channels; the World Wide Web; the publishing industry; the self-help industry; the recording industry; the film industry; and their allied fields. It is a marketplace within which people are increasingly seeking and finding religious insight and religious meaning. And it provides resources to fit all tastes. Everything from Christian kitsch to crystal healing to "the Goddess," to Joseph Campbell, to Deepak Chopra, to 12-step programs, to the PBS documentary *From Jesus to Christ,* to anything by Bill Moyers. It is all there.

What this means is that in contemporary life the ways of being religious have moved out of the protected sphere of religious institution and tradition and into the open ground of the symbolic marketplace. The rise of the autonomous self and the increasing diversity of the media marketplace are necessary but not sufficient explanations of this trend, however.

This marketplace approach to religion has deep roots in what Nathan Hatch (1989) calls the "democratization" of American religion. Briefly, Hatch argues that the religious ferment of the American

"Great Awakenings" had at its base an individualistic, anti-institutional spirit. That spirit connected the democratic ideals of the political sphere with a set of ideals in the religious sphere that valued individual conscience and choice over institutional loyalty. This spirit of religion, in fact, is what gave rise to nonconformist denominational movements such as Methodism, the Disciples of Christ, and Evangelicalism more generally.

It is important to remember that this democratic spirit within American religion has both *rejected* institutions and their prescribed doctrine and at the same time *embraced* certain modes of religious practice that are rooted in and confirm this rejection. Religious authority, for example, has traditionally been suspicious of visual imagery, both two- and three-dimensional. One only need think of the curious and contested place of Warner Sallman's "Head of Christ" in American piety to see this. Think about where Sallman's "Head" has been "permitted" in Protestant practice. In which churches does it hang in the chancel, in the basement, in the storeroom, or not at all?

But Sallman's "Head" also represents a kind of resistive practice among the laity (Morgan, 1996). Regardless of how the theological elites felt about it, it found an important, meaningful place in the hearts and homes of people. American religion has always had this tension or struggle within it. On the one hand, religious institutions and religious authorities, doing their job as guardians of the faith and of doctrine. On the other hand, a laity empowered by their social, cultural, and historical context to actually contest and resist those definitions.

The kind of contestation and struggle represented by popular appropriation and use of Sallman's "Head" in the past is today exploding as more and more images, artifacts, services, organizations, and locations have emerged to satisfy a popular religiosity that has overflowed its banks. And a wide range of things come into play. It is not just visual imagery such as Sallman's "Head." It is also objects, rituals, and experiences, both embodied and more cerebral.

Let's think for a moment about what people get from all this. Objects, for example, have traditionally been derogated within mainline Protestant culture. They are what Colleen McDannell (1995) calls "Material Christianity" or what others have called "Christian Kitsch." They are tacky, profane, material, and sullied by commerce. One can take an alternative view, however. In an address several years ago to a religion sociology conference, Barbara Wheeler (1995) of Auburn Seminary recounted her experience doing research in an Evangelical seminary. One part of her reflection focused on the role of objects within Evangelicalism. She said:

> Evangelicals turn out stuff: thousands of Christian recordings: even more books—a new Christian gothic novel, I was told by an avid reader of them, is published every week—along with almost every other kind of fiction, poetry, Bible translations and paraphrases, advice, celebrity biography, and countless devotional volumes; magazines pamphlets, newspapers, broadsides, leaflets; plaques, posters, greeting and note cards, bumper stickers, ceramics, jewelry. As various as they are, and as much as they have in common with the rest of American mass material culture, most evangelical artifacts are self-evidently evangelical. . . . Evangelicals have a vast and distinctive material culture. Almost anything that you can imagine they make, they probably do.

By contrast, she observed about mainline Protestantism:

> [M]ainline Protestantism does not have enough of a culture. By comparison with the prolix popular culture of the evangelicals, mainline protestantism's inventory of symbols, manners, iconic leaders, images of leadership, distinctive language, decorations, and sounds is very low indeed.
>
> Without these elements of culture, mainline Protestantism cannot create something a religious tradition must have to survive: a piety. By that term I mean to include much more than explicitly religious forms of activity. . . . I mean piety in the classic protestant sense: a whole way of life—shared practices, a catalog of virtues, models of Christian adequacy in the church and the world. Mainline Protestantism, I now think, is struggling because we have not established among us patterns of life, some of them religious in the conventional sense but many not so, that are fitted to our religious identity.
>
> In fact, mainline Protestants do not handle much of anything. I never would have realized this if I had not done research in such a different milieu. What I further gained from the evangelicals and now have to offer my own religious community is the realization that our lack of paraphernalia is a dangerous situation. We do not need the evangelicals' particular dry goods or pious practices, but we, like the evangelicals, are bodied beings, and a religious tradition that has little or nothing to look at, listen to, and touch cannot sustain us very long.

In his recent book on the visual piety of American religion, David Morgan (1997) makes a similar point. In a helpful amplification, he places the salience of such objects and images in a psychological context. Citing the work of Mihaly Czikszentmihalyi and Eugene Rocheberg-Halton (1981), Morgan posits that the value of objects, be they visual or tactile, lies in their ability to ground identity. They give us touchstones in our lives, linking us to our past, grounding us in the present, and giving a hint of our future expectations. This is important, says Csikszentmihalyi, because without such objects, we risk falling into a state of confusion and entropy.

We can extend this argument to the artifacts, objects, and programs of the media sphere. These ways of doing religion—popular, material, commodity based—represent more and more of what American religiosity *is* today. And, they are gradually moving the center of religious culture into the center of media culture.

Consider the progress of a large-scale study of religion and meaning-making in the media age (Hoover, 1999). The research centers on the marketplace of symbols, with researchers thinking of it as an inventory out of which people select and adopt symbols, values, and ideals that inform their identities, both religious and social. Researchers are conducting interviews and observations in a wide range of households, attempting to understand how, in the context of daily life, this symbolic inventory is accessed, related to, and used. In the end they want to be able to say something about how meanings are made in a time and context that are in many ways unprecedented, and which have been left unexamined by previous research.

This is very different from the approaches taken by most previous research on the media. Rather than taking the perspective of media producers or owners, and thus looking at media in terms of their effectiveness at conveying messages, this study radically stands with the receivers of those messages, looking back, with them, at the whole inventory that they have available and from which they choose.

What is the research finding? First of all, there is a good deal of confirmation for the conceptual approach laid out here. It turns out to be quite useful to conceive of things in this way. People very much encounter the media environment as a source of symbols and values—some of which they adopt, some of which they throw away, some of which they reinterpret and reconstruct for themselves. They do not, by and large, see the world as a dualistic struggle between the sacred spheres of the home, church, or tradition against a secular or profane sphere of the media. For them, in their practices of daily life, it is all part of a universe of symbols.

In fact, when they *do* seem to center their meaning-making around the symbolic resources of the public sphere, they use those resources according to one or more of three systems of logic we are calling "media discourses."

First, there are the discourses *in* the media. These are the symbols, ideas, impulses, values, and narratives that enliven media texts and artifacts. People, on some level, are attracted to, and derive meaning from, participating in these discourses. They like, and derive pleasure and meaning from, being conversant in *The X-Files,* or the *Simpsons, or Friends.*

Second, there are the discourses *about* the media. People find great value and meaning in being able to use the symbols, values, ideas, languages, and practices they encounter in the media sphere as resources for their daily social interactions. Conversations within and beyond the household are often based on shared knowledge and a sense of common feeling derived from media experience.

Third, there are the discourses of the media. Everyone we have interviewed has had a sense of how they *should* think and behave with regard to the media. People know they should watch more public television and less *Baywatch.* Parents know their children should watch less television and play fewer video and computer games. Children know they should not watch violence or sex. Everyone thinks of his or her media behaviors, on some level, as guilty pleasures. These conditioning ideas about media experience have long been thought of by social scientists as impediments to understanding what people really "do." They'll tell you what they know they should about their media behaviors, but you can never be certain what they are actually doing. This can be looked at differently, though. How do these "shoulds" relate to and contribute to the meanings people make from their media experiences.

What draws people to media symbols and artifacts in the first place? There seem to be three broad categories here. First, there is a category we might simply call "I like it." There is some indefinable attraction or motivation that draws people into images, artifacts, programs, and experiences in the media sphere. A wide range of psychological theories, from subliminal to Freudian to behaviorist, have been directed at explaining these tastes and desires, but to no avail. The fact that more new programs, films, books, and other media fail than succeed, suggests to me that on some level we will never know or be able to predict more than that some things are liked and some things rejected.

The second category of attraction and motivation is more familiar: that is one we might call "function" or "information." There are those times when a television program is only a television program. News viewers, for example, are probably partly drawn to news for "the news." They want some information, and that is where they go to get it. This is where we would also place the function of social connection mentioned earlier. People really do consume media messages in order to maintain contact, both within the household and beyond it.

The third category is the most interesting and in some ways most important. That is, that people seem to go to media for the kind of reason suggested by David Morgan (1997) and Mihaly Csikszentmihalyi and Eugene Rocheberg-Halton (1981). Media artifacts have an important function as objects that ground identity. They are touchstones through which people define themselves and their place in the social and cultural landscape. The media provide the symbolic resources through which these definitions take place. Their power is not a power *to convict* or *to manipulate* so much as it is a power to provide the means within culture *to define* and *to name*.

There are some things this research can say about the "effects" of media on religion, when seen in this way.

First, there is a "flattening" of symbols. The overall framework presented here would predict that religious symbols would be becoming submerged in the general universe of symbols of the media sphere. There is evidence of this in research interviews. Religious symbols, traditionally legitimated by religious doctrine, history, and practice, today struggle to find any particular or special place. The former situation in which symbols such as the cross could be held in a hierarchical relationship to other, more secular or cultural symbols, has broken down. Today, for instance, Madonna can take the crucifix off the wall and (to borrow a phrase) "get down" with it or place it on her body in juxtapositions that formerly would have been thought blasphemous, with the consequence that it becomes in part her property, her symbol.

The outlines of this flattening are best seen in relationship to practice. And there is a generational effect here (Clark, 1998). One of the ways that the traditional hierarchy of legitimacy was maintained was through institutional loyalty and participation. People who went to church heard the stories, celebrated the traditional symbols and values, and participated in their maintenance and reconstitution.

Sociologists tell us that a huge generational shift is coming when the children of the Baby Boom—who came late or never to conventional participation in formal religion—themselves come to the fore as young adults. They lack the cultural memory of religion that would support the traditional view of the cross, for example. Which symbols are in the canon and which are not, and the relationship between them, will be of little interest when these postboomers themselves become parents.

An early hint of this shift in understanding came several years ago on NBC's *Saturday Night Live.* The Irish pop singer Sinead O'Connor, who was a musical guest of the program, ended her last song by holding up a photograph of John Paul II, tearing it in half, and saying "fight the real enemy." This sent shock waves through a predominantly young audience that had for several years been consuming images of Madonna's cavorting with the crucifix with little reaction. In contrast, the reaction to O'Connor's act was huge—and telling. The cross, as an object of history and tradition, had lost much of its power to shock and convict. The Pope, by contrast, was someone known, in the here and now, and understood via his media presence to be a real human being.

A second area of effect has to do with the range of symbols that are present in the media inventory. One of the traditional areas of media effects was called "canalization" by early pioneers in the field. This has also been called the "agenda-setting" (McCombs and Shaw, 1972) function of the media. That is, that their effect is not so much in telling us "what to think" as "what to think about." The range of topics covered in news serves to direct public comment and public discourse within a narrower, defined range than the universe of possible topics. In the same way, we might say that if what I've written earlier is correct, that the symbolic marketplace of the media sphere is coming to be the place where religious meanings are made, then the raw material of those meanings will necessarily be a narrower set of resources than all possible ones.

Finally, it may follow from all of this that certain narratives, symbols, and stories come to be established at the expense of others. For example, it would make sense that dominant American cultural myths would also dominate in the narratives of prime-time television. The struggle between individualism and commitment, as described by Robert Bellah (1986), is a common theme in television narratives. Cultural critics call this process "naturalization" or the "making natural" of certain symbolic constructions and the denial of others.

So what are some of the implications of all this? First, the major message here for religious institutions is that to exist in today's public culture, it is necessary to exist in the media. To withdraw entirely in the face of an omnipresent media sphere is to choose marginalization and loss of voice.

Second, for those who would study these things, it is necessary to abandon efforts that set up dualisms between religion and media as separate spheres, authentic and sacred on the one hand and inauthentic and secular or even profane on the other. That is simply not the way people think about or use media today. The media are a *given,* a taken-for-granted environment of meaning and cultural commerce. They are not all-encompassing or all-pervasive. They are, however, a reality to be reckoned with.

Third, we need to understand, along with culturalist media theory more generally, that meaning happens not in the messages produced but in the *audiences* that receive them. As one important sociologist of religion has observed, it is important to realize that we must study religion as *achieved,* not as *ascribed* (Warner, 1993).

This analysis rests on the realization that contemporary religion and contemporary media are coming together and also on the realization that the way we study religion and media must also come together. The emergence of a new religious marketplace has arisen at the same time as the emergence of a new media marketplace. But in order to understand their relationship, it is necessary to adopt methods that are sufficiently historically and culturally rooted to give us an appropriate standpoint.

Looking at things this way, we can come to some understandings of how people's religious understandings support their practices as media consumers. We have long thought that religion would lead to certain kinds of media behaviors (though there is quite a bit of disagreement about exactly which directions this influence would flow). Highly religious people might be expected to have particularly powerful or compelling ways of integrating media into their lives. To use the language introduced earlier, they might be expected to have strong and determinative "discourses *of*" the media.

But, as was observed earlier, the way people talk about their use of media may have little to do with the way they actually behave. In fact, it may say more about what they would like to believe or to present about themselves than about what they actually *do*. Instead, we have to start thinking about their media diets on their own terms, without preconceptions as to the way religious belief might relate to media use. What we will then find is that these relationships are complex, subtle, and nuanced.

This means that the influence of religion on media or the influence of media on religion is best seen as something that is not direct or linear. Instead, we need to understand it as recursive, cyclical, and constructed. People don't simply "consume" media; they experience media images, symbols, and messages as part of an ongoing flow of experience in their daily lives. Specific programs and images have less prominence than we often think. They are consumed within the larger frameworks of motivation and meaning-making we discussed earlier. Media are more of a resource than an influence. As resources, they both *represent* religious meaning and, at the same time, *constitute* religious meaning for certain viewers at certain points in time.

The cultural view of media and religion thus opens up new and intriguing ways of looking at things. We no longer have to limit ourselves to the possibility that religion is influencing media behaviors or vice versa. Both are happening, and the evidence would suggest that in their interaction, new ways of understanding both media and religion in the lives of viewers and adherents emerge.

# References

Albanese, Catherine (1993). Fisher kings and public places: The old new age in the 1990s. *Annals of the American Academy* 527: 131–45.

Bellah, Robert, Madsden, R., Sullivan, W.M., Swidler, A., and Tipton, S.N. (1985). *Habits of the heart: Individualism and commitment in American life.* Berkeley: University of California Press.

Clark, Lynn Schofield (1998). "Identity, Discourse, and Media Audiences: A Critical Ethnography of the Role of Visual Media in Religious Identity-Construction among U.S. Adolescents, Ph.D. Dissertation, the University of Colorado.

Csikszentmihalyi, Mihaly, and Rocheberg-Halton, Eugene (1981). *The meaning of things: Domestic symbols and the self.* New York: Cambridge.

Giddens, Anthony (1991). *Modernity and self-identity.* Stanford: Stanford University Press.

Grossberg, L., Nelson, C., and Treicheler, P., Eds. (1992). *Cultural studies.* London: Routledge.

Hatch, Nathan (1989). *The democratization of American Christianity.* New Haven: Yale.

Hoover, Stewart (1998). *Religion in the news: Faith and journalism in American public discourse.* Newbury Park: Sage.

Hoover, Stewart (1999). Toward a fourth (and a fifth?) paradigm for the study of television and religion, paper delivered to the Conference on Religion and Television, University of Heidelberg, February.

McCombs, Maxwell, and Shaw, Donald (1972). The agenda-setting function of the mass media. *Public Opinion Quarterly* 36: 176–87.

McDannell, Colleen (1995). *Material Christianity: Religion and popular culture in America.* New Haven: Yale.

Moores, Shawn (1993). *Interpreting audiences.* London: Routledge.

Morgan, David (1996). "Introduction," in Morgan, D., Ed., *Icons of American Protestantism.* New Haven: Yale.

Morgan, David (1997). *Visual Piety.* Berkeley: University of California Press.

Roof, Wade Clark (1993). *A generation of seekers: The spiritual journeys of the baby boom generation.* San Francisco: Harper.

Warner, R. Stephen (1993). Work in progress toward a new paradigm in the study of American religion. *American Journal of Sociology* 5: 1044–93.

Wheeler, Barbara (1995). "We who were far off," Address to the Religious Research Association, St. Louis.

Wuthnow, Robert (1988). *The restructuring of American religion.* Princeton: Princeton University Press.

CHAPTER 5

# Religion and Popular Culture: Notes from the Technological School

## DANIEL A. STOUT

D
ebates about religion and popular culture are heating up. The subject surfaces frequently in such fields as art, communication, political science, and sociology. In fact, some scholars perceive the schism between the entertainment industry and religion to be so deep as to warrant the term, "culture wars" (Hunter, 1991; Browning et al., 1997). Concerned about violence, sexual imagery, and a lack of deferential treatment of religion, some media critics see mass media as oppositional to mainstream religious values (Medved, 1992; Dobson and Bauer, 1990; Carter, 1993). On the other hand, some denominations are using media of popular culture more than ever, creating religious talk shows (Moore, 1994), rock music (Rohter, 1999), Internet web sites (Ramo, 1996), and sophisticated advertising campaigns (Niebuhr, 1995). The relationship between religion and popular culture is indeed paradoxical; its complexity renders it difficult for sociologists of religion to assess. Few agree on the role mass media play in secularization, religious community, and formation of cultural values. Given this situation, the time may be right to evaluate current research and explore fresh ideas for theory-building in this emerging area of media studies.

Theorizing about religion and popular culture is difficult given the level of divergent research interests and lack of consistent conceptual frameworks (see Stout and Buddenbaum, 1996). For example, while some contend that news media trivialize religious devotion (Carter, 1993; Olasky, 1988), Silk (1995) argues that journalistic content is highly consistent with religious belief. Although Fore (1987) sees popular culture as essentially antithetical to religious values, Beaudoin (1998) insists that mass media are important sources of religious experience, especially for youth. Despite philosophical and methodological disagreement, however, one thing is certain: the study of religion and popular culture is in need of creative synthesis of theoretical concepts that cuts across interdisciplinary lines.

One such perspective might be *medium theory,*[1] sometimes referred to as the *technological school*[2] of mass communication. While researchers are bound up in a seemingly endless debate about the effects of specific messages, this school is more interested in the role of technology in creating and sustaining culture through time. Medium theory is the idea that each communication technology helps form a unique information environment or context that promotes particular lifestyles, cultural values, and patterns of behavior (see summary in Meyrowitz, 1994). When Mumford (1934, 1986) analyzed the cultural role of the mechanical clock, for example, he bypassed the actual message (i.e., time of day) in order to speculate about the device's encouragement of efficiency, industry, and task-orientation within the cultural context of "modern civilization." According to Mumford (1986), civilization "represents the convergence of numerous habits, ideas, and modes of living, as well as technical instruments" (p. 324). The salient result of the clock, then, is how it works alongside other cultural developments to discourage spontaneity and informality in American culture; its accuracy in communicating hours, minutes, and seconds has consequences far beyond the mechanical precision of gears and metal wheels. Phrases such as "time is money" and "as regular as clockwork" characterize the cultural environment of the "orderly punctual life" that the clock promotes indirectly and gradually (Mumford, 1986, p. 327).

Today, new questions about contemporary media are raised by both religious leaders and social scientists. What is the role of television in cultivating cultural values? Do movies have a secularizing influence? How does the Internet reshape social networks within religious communities? In medium theory, *social context* holds the key to such questions, and *information* is essential to understanding such contexts. As a leading theorist on the complexities of medium theory, Joshua Mey-rowitz (1990) explores the sociological connection between context and technology:

> One way to think of contexts, then, is as information systems, that is, as specific patterns of access/restriction to social information, of access/ restriction to the behavior of other people. The concept of information-systems suggests that physical settings and media settings are part of a con-tinuum rather than a dichotomy. Places and media both foster set patterns of interaction among people, while set patterns of social information flow. (p. 74)

This perspective could have implications for the study of religion and popular culture. The role of online computers, for example, may have as much to do with new settings of religious worship and relationships than with specific messages on the screen. These new exchanges of re-ligious information may not have existed had the technology not been invented. Similarly, television viewing is as much about the level and topics of conversation it fosters within a religious community as it is about the direct effect of specific programs (see Postman, 1985). To ignore the macrolevel question of how technology helps create infor-mation environments within evolving religious communities is theo-retically perilous; to do so would impede the analysis of religious groups from the sociological perspective of information flow and so-cial interaction.

## Theoretical Foundations of Medium Theory

If one accepts the basic assumptions of Berger (1967), Durkheim (1912), Park (1915), and Weber (1963), information exchange is essen-tial to understanding religious community. Nevertheless, medium theory has not been applied to the study of religion and popular culture within a consistent explanatory framework. This is partly due to a rejection of the approach on grounds of "technological determinism," or the idea that medium theory is a contextless, causal approach that is too simplistic and linear to adequately describe the complex processes of mass communi-cation. Lundby and Hoover (1997), for example, argue that this per-spective is "based in a more or less deterministic view of media" (p. 303). McQuail (1994), on the other hand, says that to "label this body of thinking 'determinist' does not do justice to the many differences and nuances" (p. 85). Likewise, Katz (1987) calls the technological school one of three emerging "paradigms" in the study of mass communication: "the technological paradigm challenges communications research to consider why we invest so much energy in exploring the influence of media on opinion and ideology and so little on social organization" (p. 34). Meyrowitz (1994) also deflects the determinism label by referring to "second generation" medium theory, which links information technology with sociological processes of everyday interaction.

A rich, interdisciplinary body of work provides the foundational literature for future research on medium theory (see Meyrowitz, 1985, 1994). Examples include studies of the transition from orality to literacy (Goody, 1987; Ong, 1982; Havelock, 1976; McLuhan, 1964), the shift from script to print (Eisentein, 1979), and technological aspects of the rise of political empires (Innis, 1950, 1951). In general, medium theory is that area of research that focuses on "the historical and cross-cultural study of the different cultural environments created by different media of communication" (Meyrowitz, 1985, p. 16).

## Medium Theory and Religious Community

A unifying concept is necessary before medium theory can be applied consistently to the study of religion and popular culture. *Community* is a phenomenon around which the sociological application of medium theory can be built. Regarding the relationship between community and media, Meyrowitz (1997) argues that "each evolution in communication forms has involved a shift in social boundaries and hence a shift in the relationship between self and others" (p. 62). Researchers are interested in such shifts within religious groups. Schement and Stephenson (1996), for example, suggest that information technologies may play a role in how members of religious groups think about community:

> The resurgence of enthusiasm for spirituality and religion may be traced in part to the decline of community brought about by the fragmenting tendencies of the information society. The more people take advantage of the increased interconnectedness made possible by information technologies, the more they depend on secondary relationships for their daily interactions, and the more they feel disconnected from their immediate surroundings. (p. 278)

According to Bellah et al. (1985), social relationships are synonymous with community: He defines a community as "a group of people who are socially interdependent, who participate together in discussion and decision making, and who share certain *practices* [which see] that both define the community and are nurtured by it" (p. 333). In discussing religious community, Berger (1967) makes the distinction between "ideological rhetorics" of institutions, and the "sphere of everyday social activity" occurring within "family and social relationships" (p. 133). Do media of popular culture help structure such relationships, and if so, what impact does this have on religious communities?

The most important question regarding religion and popular culture, then, turns out to be the role of technology in structuring a community's information sphere (e.g., social organization, networks, information flow, etc.). The purpose of this chapter, then, is to identify those components of community that cannot be adequately explained without some attention to communication technology. First, media and the formation of social *relationships* is discussed. Next, the concept of social *roles* is explored from a technological perspective. Lastly, information technology's role in the *rituals* of religious communities is addressed. The concepts of social relationship, role, and ritual provide a framework for a more focused application of medium theory to the study of religion and popular culture. In addition, the conceptual connection between these phenomena and social context shields against a research approach that is linear and deterministic.

## Communication Technology and Relationships

Winner (1986) contends that "a technical system that involves human beings as operating parts brings a reconstruction of social roles and relationships" (p. 11). His comment is an invitation to explore how "technical systems" created by media help structure the social relationships that define religious community. So far, researchers are divided about how, precisely, this takes place. Bellah et al. (1985), for example, chide television for not depicting an ideologically healthy view of relationships. The medium is simply too "abrupt and jumpy" to present relationships in ways that are instructive and insightful. "Except for the formula situation comedies (and even there, divorce is increasingly common), relationships are as brittle and shifting as the action of the camera. Most people turn out to be unreliable and double-dealing" (p. 281).

Bellah's concern rests in television's inadequacy as a model of healthy relationships. There is also, however, the matter of technology and the number and nature of relationships that people have. The Internet, in particular, has been the focus of speculation about the need for new relationships in a complex and hectic society. "Today's heightened consciousness of incompleteness may predispose us to join with others" through the Internet (Turkle, 1997, p. 261). According to Cobb (1998), computer technology is forming "our connections to one another" on levels that impact our "sense of psychological health" (p. 20).

The study of religious community is incomplete without attention to technology and the formation of personal relationships. Almost 200 million have access to the Internet worldwide, and 80 million in the United States (The Dawn, 1999, p. 40). Furthermore, e-mail is now the preferred activity on the Internet (Leonard, 1999, p. 59). Religiously speaking, 410,000 Web pages mention God, and 146,000 reference Jesus Christ (Ramo, 1996, p. 62). In response to this situation, Campbell (1999) discusses the multiplicity of information options that comprise religious life today with limitless access to newsgroups, chat groups, and Internet sites. The question is not whether these developments directly alter relationships within religious community but how technology creates social opportunities for those who do not find them in their neighborhood houses of worship. For a number of demographic segments and subcultures, this desire for new relationships is likely to grow. It is compelling, therefore, to think about these trends in light of both Roof's (1999) thesis that a "spiritual marketplace" is blurring the social boundaries of religious communities and recent data indicating that the Internet facilitates the expansion of community networks (Wellman and Gulia, 1999).

These developments coincide with a paradigmatic reconceptualization of community in sociology from a geographic construct to one based on social networks and interpersonal relationships. In the words of Fischer (1982), one cannot understand "residential communities" without examining "personal communities," and Wellman (1979; 1988) considers social networks to be the most defining aspect of community. Likewise, religious communities are as much about social interaction as they are about actual houses of worship (Cornwall and Thomas, 1990). Therefore, because communities tend to be "geographically dispersed," sociologists are increasingly interested in the question of whether information technologies create and sustain weak or strong ties within networks that form one's personal community (Wellman and Gulia, 1999).

Potential shifting in the nature, frequency, and quality of relationships may alter our thinking about how denominations accommodate each other in the future, as well as how they assimilate within the larger society. How media-facilitated relationships weigh in to ongoing processes of secularization is also a vital question.

## Communication Technology and Social Roles

In addition to relationships, religious communities are also comprised of a number of social roles (i.e., women, men, priest, parishioner, churchgoer, nonchurchgoer, etc.). It is interesting to consider how such roles are evolving in an age characterized by communication media and increasing emphasis on information retrieval and dissemination. While traditional local congregations are durable and contribute significantly to American life (Marty, 1994; Wind and Lewis, 1994), media are impacting the social roles that make such congregations central to religious life. According to Schement and Stephenson (1996), the roles of the "lay worker," and "religious worker," for example, are blurring as they perform similar tasks:

> Information workers possess verbal and literary skills once reserved for the clergy. Literacy skills necessary for personal interaction with religious texts are now the fundamental skills for all information work tasks. In addition, religious leaders have taken on roles comparable to those of idea experts in secular fields such as business, science, and technology. (p. 271)

Similarly, the role of churchgoer is being questioned as media create a number of religious experiences outside of, or in addition to, the neighborhood church (see Cobb, 1998; Zaleski, 1997). It was recently reported, for example, that one in every six teenagers (16 percent) said they expected to substitute the Internet for church-based religious worship in the next five years (The Cyberchurch, 1998, p. 1), thus calling into question conventional ideas about what it means to be a participating church member.

This situation demands a more theoretically grounded examination of media and religious roles, however. The work of Joshua Meyrowitz provides a general sociological foundation for the theoretical connection between technology and social role formation:

> [Social roles] are not only based on physiological and cognitive growth, but also on what might be called specific "patterns of access to social information." Every stage of socialization involves both exposure to, and restriction from, social information. (Meyrowitz, 1984, p. 26)

For Meyrowitz, each medium (e.g., television, Internet, magazines, etc.) is a social context that influences social roles in some way:

> Media-induced changes in social contexts, then, ought to have an impact beyond individual psychological experience. Changes in social-information systems also alter basic elements of the social structure and reshape broad categories of social statuses and roles. (Meyrowitz, 1990, p. 85)

Postman (1982), for example, discusses the blurring of adulthood and childhood in the television environment, as does Meyrowitz (1984, 1985). In addition, Meyrowitz (1985, 1994) explores technological implications for growing similarity between gender roles as well as the lowering of political figures to the level of the general populace. Here, I briefly mention a number of social roles in which this line of inquiry can be applied.

## Priest and Parishioner

One of the key questions regarding new media is how they help blur the lines between religious leaders and parishioners. In this regard, Zaleski (1997) observes: "Online, the words of the Dalai Lama look no different than those of an everyday Buddhist practitioner. How will this potential eroding of hierarchy change the way we worship?" (pp. 4–5). Electronic media erode religious hierarchies by providing public platforms and audience access to a number of lay members who may or may not be trained within traditional institutions. Through televangelism, publishing, and the Internet, one can acquire information accessible only to clergy in the past.

This situation is similar to the "leveling effect" of television, which Roof (1999) claims has diminished "old dichotomies like private/public and holy/unholy" (p. 68) and replaced them with a softer spiritual rhetoric that deemphasizes traditional religious structure and truth claims.

## Churchgoer and Nonchurchgoer

Religious experience outside the traditional congregation remains a compelling issue. While traditional congregations remain essential to spiritual experience, social and economic factors are creating religious interactions outside church buildings. "Generation X" is one example of this phenomenon. According to Beaudoin (1998), Generation X is that group of young adults who, as "latchkey children," grew up as frequent and independent consumers of popular culture. "For a generation of kids who had a fragmented or completely broken relationship to 'formal' or 'institutional' religion, pop culture filled the spiritual gaps" (p. 21). Beaudoin's point is that technology offers a religious experience to those "who have grown up with such a tense relationship to formal communities of faith and who are so well suited to nonfamilial, ad hoc communities" (p. 88). Again, a recent survey reported that one out of six teens (16 percent) plan to substitute the Internet for current church-based religious experience (The Cyberchurch, 1998, p. 1). About this situation, Campbell (1999) writes:

> The emergence of cyberchurches is exciting and a bit worrisome. Will we see an exiting of the faithful of the sanctuary in favour of fellowship in front of the computer screen? . . . [I]t is key to note that the cyberchurch challenges our traditional images of interacting within the Christian community. (Campbell, 1999, pp. 55, 56)

Parishioners are demanding religious information from other media as well. Prayer telephone lines, televised sermons, and radio call-in programs are popular options. In fact, 56 percent of U.S. TV viewers sampled feel that "not enough" attention is being paid to religion on prime-time television (Kaufman, 1997, p. 33).

## Gender Roles in the Church

One of the most vital issues is how information technology serves the interests of women in their religious worship and study. For example, Hall (1990) contends that religious information sources and opportunities are more difficult for women to obtain, and Schement and Stephenson (1996) argue that "voices in the information age remain marginalized by gender and ethnicity" (p. 265). Considerable disagreement exists about how new media contribute to the development of gender roles. One school of thought sees cyberspace as an equalizer of roles. According to Turkle (1997), social roles blur when people are not physically present; men can become women and vice versa through interactive technology. This is similar to the "cyborg" concept of how computers reduce gender "dualisms" present in face-to-face interaction (Haraway, 1991, p. 181). On the other hand, as church members seek religious information on the Internet, such interactions may not be preferable to all women. Some argue that artificial intelligence has not sufficiently promoted the plurality of views consistent with feminist theory (Adam, 1998), nor is the style of Internet communication that permits "flaming" (anonymous aggressive criticism) and male Internet dominance reflective of women's communication style (Adams, 1996; Balsamo, 1996). In terms of religious groups, it remains unclear how new media will structure information contexts for women. The use of information technology within particular religious subcultures is crucial to a future understanding of these questions.

## Communication Technology and Religious Rituals

The use of media in the performance of religious rituals is also important to this discussion. Ritual, according to Shils and Janowitz (1948), is one of the necessary conditions for community, and for Durkheim (1912), it is a key element of religion itself (also see Alexander, 1997; Carey, 1988; Goethals, 1997). Sermons, sacraments, healings, offerings, blessings, and prayer are common practices in many denominations, and in recent years have been mediated or disseminated to larger audiences through information technology. A compelling example is the CD *Chant,* a collection of musical prayers by Benedictine monks that sold six million copies in 1994 (Thigpen, 1995). The telephone prayer line of the Redemption Christian Center in Knoxville, Tennessee, also illustrates the idea of mediated ritual (Stout, 1998). Through a computer-based phone system, a number of prerecorded prayers can be accessed by callers. "Televangelism," or the use of television to teach biblical religion, has enabled the broad-cast of numerous religious rituals from healing to paying tithes (Schultze, 1991; Abelman and Neuendorf, 1985; Hoover, 1990).

One concern for the religion–popular culture researcher is the con-vergence of sacred rites and practices with commercially based enter-tainment media. Concerns result from technology's symbolic nature; television, for example, is a medium of leisure and entertainment. In-corporating religious ritual into entertainment formats has been con-troversial; it raises questions about the bias of technology in endorsing particular values. While Innis (1950, 1951) recognized the bias of par-ticular media toward various systems of government and economics, scholars are also addressing how information technology emphasizes certain values in religious settings. As Ellul (1964) states, technology is not neutral and has "unforeseeable" consequences that are difficult to ponder when first introduced.

According to Postman (1985), "Each medium, like language itself, makes possible a unique mode of discourse by providing a new orien-tation for thought, for expression, for sensibility" (p. 10). And, with tel-evision, "entertainment is the supra-ideology of all discourse" (p. 87). Religious television, therefore, has not escaped the lure to entertain.

On cable television's *700 Club,* for example, viewers may join in a prayer ritual, but only in the context of a program that looks very much like talk shows such as *Good Morning America* or *Dateline NBC.* Host Pat Robertson welcomes the audience and introduces a news reporter who reviews the day's top stories. Next, he previews a film short on teenagers and sexual abstinence. Later in the program he bows his head, asking the audience to join him in prayer. Intermittently through-out the show, he announces, "We'll be right back after these messages." The messages turn out to be in-house commercials for religious tapes and books.

In the case of television, not only is the sacred treated in an envi-ronment of entertainment but it is mixed with forms of commercialism as well. According to one view, television is symbolic of excessive ma-terialism that contradicts values of selflessness and prudence. On the other hand, the medium is an efficient way to do missionary work; some religious leaders applaud television's ability to proselyte to large groups that simply could not be reached face-to-face (Niebuhr, 1995).

The *Benny Hinn Ministry* is a program that introduces ritual in an environment that is both commercial and entertainment oriented. In ad-dition to showing dramatic healing rituals on stage, the show sold 50 million dollars worth of videotapes, religious publications, and gift items in one year (Impact, 1997). In one part of the program, individuals are shown lining up to go on stage. Reverend Hinn inquires about each person's illness or affliction, pronounces a blessing, and promises that he or she will be healed. This is followed by an advertisement asking audience members to send a "love gift" donation to assist the healing efforts of the ministry. At the end of the commercial, the announcer says, "Your miracle is on the way."

This example illustrates how medium theory has a dual application in the study of religion and popular culture. Commercial television is paradoxical in that it is alternately embraced and criticized by researchers operating within different theoretical domains. From the perspective of critical studies, televised ritual has much to do with hegemony and trivialization. The frequent and ubiquitous depiction of sacred ritual contributes to what Baudrillard (1983) terms an overproduction of signs leading to a destabilization of meaning. The problem has to do with how television fills cultural space previously reserved for entertainment, art, and educational fare. Of religious symbols, Postman (1992) argues that this destabilization "is a function not only of the frequency with which they are invoked but of the indiscriminate contexts in which they are used" (p. 167).

On the other hand, the theoretical line of medium theory can be taken in another direction to explore some of the more pragmatic questions of information dissemination. For religious leaders faced with perceived realities of competition, television is just one step in a social and economic process where denominations have made regular use of dominant communication forms. History bears out that when information technologies are invented, many religious groups tend to exploit them quickly. Ancient Sumerians used clay tablets, and Jews recorded their histories on papyrus. When Gutenberg invented movable type, it wasn't long before religious texts were printed. Paintings, stained glass, tapestries, and various forms of architecture all demonstrate a reliance on a wide range of media in communicating God's word.

## Summary and Conclusion

This chapter explores religion and popular culture from the perspective of technology rather than message; it summarizes work in the area of medium theory to show how media are impacting information environments within denominational structures. Using the sociological concept of community to summarize research in this area, the chapter looks at information technology within the specific contexts of social relationships, roles, and mediated ritual. While prior work in this area has had disparate application across a number of disciplines, this chapter synthesizes a number of medium-theoretical ideas into a coherent discussion of the religious community and how it is evolving. In the case of relationships, young adults seek new interactions through new media, and more specialized discussions across denominations are likely. Building on the work of Meyrowitz, technology and social roles are an important area of future study of religious community. Changing contexts of information acquisition suggest that the lines between priest and parishioner as well as churchgoer and nonchurchgoer may blur in coming years. Technological implications for gender roles in religious settings is more difficult to assess, with some arguing that interactive media marginalize women's roles, while others see opportunities for empowerment. Finally, the issue of mediated ritual, especially in television, has created fodder for both critical studies researchers, who see the medium in terms of trivialization of religious symbols, and pragmatists, who associate mediated ritual with the functional goal of information dissemination. In summary, the application of medium theory to community concepts of relationships, roles, and mediated ritual creates a coherent agenda for future research within this paradigm.

It isn't likely that medium theory will escape the determinism label that serves to discourage research in this area. However, by grounding medium theory in the sociology of communities, with particular attention to personal networks and social organization, this chapter strives for a softer determinism that recognizes patterns of social context and cultural change. In terms of popular culture and religion, then, the most effective applications of medium theory are those that avoid cause-and-effect models and examine technology as it is "woven into the texture of everyday existence," recognizing cultural developments already in place (Winner, 1986, p. 12). Similarly, Wellman and Gulia (1999, p. 167) warn that excessive enthusiasm about technology leaves "little room for the moderate, mixed situations that may be the reality" when assessing the evolving nature of community. Future applications of medium theory, therefore, are likely to be unproductive unless viewed within the contexts of religious pluralism, economic developments, and the emerging information society (see Schement and Stephenson, 1996). The blurring line between churchgoer and nonchurchgoer discussed in this chapter is an example of how both technology (new interactive opportunities) and social change (evolving pluralism and distrust of institutions) are necessary to a deeper understanding of religion and mass media.

Perhaps the main objective of this article, however, has been to think more about "medium literacy" (Meyrowitz, 1998, p. 103) than media literacy when it comes to religion and popular culture. Religious communities are information environments that cannot be completely understood apart from technology. This implies a new set of research questions, and if medium theorists focus their energies on the dynamics of community processes, research on religion and popular culture has a bright future.

## Notes

1. Joshua Meyrowitz uses the term "medium theory" to distinguish this school from the more broadly based category of "media theory." See Meyrowitz 1985, 1990, 1994.
2. Hunt and Ruben (1993) refer to this body of research as "The Technological School," and Katz (1987) calls it the "technological paradigm."

## References

Abelman, R. and Neuendorf, K. (1985). How religious is religious television programming? *Journal of Communication, 35,* 98–110.

Adam, A. (1998). *Artificial knowing: Gender and the thinking machine.* London: Routledge.

Adams, C. (1996). "This is not our father's pornography": Sex, lies and computers. In C. Ess (Ed.). *Philosophical perspectives on computer-mediated communication.* Albany: State University of New York Press. 147–170.

Alexander, B. (1997). Televangelism: Redressive ritual within a larger social drama. In S.M. Hoover and K. Lundby (Eds.). Rethinking media, religion, and culture. Thousand Oaks, CA: Sage. 117-132.

Balsamo, A. (1996). *Technologies of the gendered body: Reading cyborg women.* Durham, NC: Duke University Press.

Baudrillard, J. (1983). *Simulations.* New York: Semiotext(e).

Beaudoin, T. (1998). *Virtual faith: The irreverent spiritual quest of generation X.* San Francisco: Jossey-Bass.

Bellah, R.N., Madsen, R., Sullivan, W.M., Swidler, A., and Tipton, S.M. (1985). *Habits of the heart: Individualism and commitment in American life.* Berkeley: University of California Press.

Berger, P.L. (1967). *The sacred canopy: Elements of a sociological theory of religion.* Garden City, NY: Doubleday Anchor.

Browning, D.S., Miller-McLemore, B.J., Coutre, P.D., Brynolf Lyon, K., and Frankin, R.M. (1997). *From culture wars to common ground: Religion and the American family debate.* Louisville, KY: Westminister John Know Press.

Campbell, H. (1999). Finding God online. In H. Campbell and J. Mitchell (Eds.). *Interactions: Technology meets film, TV and the Internet.* Edinburgh, UK: Centre for Theology and Public Issues and the Media and Theology Project. 48–58.

Carey, J. (1988). *Communication as culture.* Boston: Unwin-Hyman.

Carter, S.L. (1993). *The culture of disbelief: How law and politics trivialize religious devotion.* New York: Basic Books.

Cobb, J.J. (1998). *Cybergrace: The search for God in the digital world.* New York: Crown Publishers.

Cornwall, M. and Thomas, D. (1990). Family, religion, and personal communities: Examples from Mormonism. *Marriage and Family Review, 15(1–2),* 229–252.

The cyberchurch is coming: National survey of teenagers shows expectation of substituting Internet for corner church (1998, release date April 20). Internet article. http://www.barna.org/PressCyberChurch.htm

The dawn of e-life. (1999, Sept. 20). *Newsweek,* 38–41.

Dobson, J.C. and Bauer, G.L. (1990). *Children at risk: The battle for the hearts and minds of our kids.* Dallas, TX: Word.

Durkheim, E. (1912). *The elementary forms of religious life.* London: Allen and Unwin.

Eisenstein, E. (1979). *The printing press as an agent of change: Communications and cultural transformations in early-modern Europe.* Cambridge: Cambridge University Press.

Ellul, J. (1964). *The technological society.* New York: Vintage Books.

Fischer, C.S. (1982). *To dwell among friends: Personal networks in town and city.* Chicago: University of Chicago Press.

Fore, W.F. (1987). *Television and religion: The shaping of faith, values, and culture.* Minneapolis, MN: Augsburg.

Goethals, G. (1997). Escape from time: Ritual dimensions of popular culture. In S.M. Hoover and K. Lundby (Eds.). Rethinking media, religion, and culture. Thousand Oaks, CA: Sage. 117-132.

Goody, J. (1987). *The interface between the written and the oral: Literacy, family, culture, and the state.* Cambridge, UK: Cambridge University Press.

Hall, M.C. (1990). *Women and identity.* New York: Hemisphere Publishing.

Haraway, D. (1991). *Simians, cyborgs, and women: The reinvention of nature.* London: Free Association Books.

Havelock, E.A. (1976). *Origins of western literacy.* (Monograph Series No. 14). Toronto: Ontario Institute of Studies in Education.

Hoover, S. (1990). The meaning of religious television: The 700 Club in the lives of its viewers. In Q.J. Schultze (Ed.). *American Evangelicals and the mass media: Perspectives on the relationship between American Evangelicals and the mass media.* Grand Rapids, MI: Academie. 231–249.

Hunt, T. and Ruben, B.D. (1993). *Mass communication: Producers and consumers.* New York: Harper Collins.

Hunter, J.D. (1991). *Culture wars: The struggle to define America.* New York: Basic Books.

Impact (1997, March). Television program "Impact" broadcast by the Cable News Network.

Innis, H.A. (1950). *Empire and communication.* Toronto: University of Toronto.

Innis, H.A. (1951). *The bias of communication.* Toronto: University of Toronto.

Katz, E. (1987). Communication research since Lazarsfeld. *Public Opinion Quarterly, 51,* S25–S45.

Kaufman, J. (1997, March 29). Tuning in to God. *TV Guide, 45(13),* 33–35.

Leonard, A. (1999, Sept. 20). E-mail is here to stay. *Newsweek,* 58–61.

Lundby, K. and Hoover, S.M. (1997). Summary remarks: Mediated religion. In S.M. Hoover and K. Lundby (Eds.) *Rethinking religion, media, and culture.* Thousand Oaks, CA: Sage.

Marty, M. (1994). Public and private: Congregation as meeting place. In J.P. Wind and J.W. Lewis (Eds.). *American congregations, volume 2: New perspectives in the study of congregations.* Chicago: University of Chicago Press. 133–166.

McLuhan, M. (1964). *Understanding media: The extensions of man.* New York: Signet.

McQuail, D. (1994). *Mass Communication theory: An introduction.* London: Sage.

Medved, M. (1992). *Hollywood vs. America: Popular culture and the war on traditional values.* New York: HarperCollins.

Meyrowitz, J. (1984). The adultlike child and the childlike adult: Socialization in an electronic age. *Daedalus 113(3),* 19–48.

Meyrowitz, J. (1985). *No sense of place: The impact of electronic media on social behavior.* New York: Oxford University Press.

Meyrowitz, J. (1990). Using contextual analysis to bridge the study of mediated and unmediated behavior. In B.D. Ruben and L.A. Lievrouw (Eds.). *Mediation, information, and communication: Information and Behavior, Vol. 3.* New Brunswick, NJ: Transaction. 67–94.

Meyrowitz, J. (1994). Medium theory. In D. Crowley and D. Mitchell (Eds.), *Communication theory today.* Stanford, CA: Stanford University Press. 50–77.

Meyrowitz, J. (1997). Shifting worlds of strangers: Medium theory and changes in "Them" versus "Us." *Sociological Inquiry,* 67(1), 59–71.

Meyrowitz, J. (1998, Winter). Multiple media literacies. *Journal of Communication.* 48(1): 96–108.

Moore, R.L. (1994). *Selling God: American religion in the marketplace of culture.* New York: Oxford University Press.

Mumford, L. (1934). *Technics and civilization.* New York: Harcourt, Brace.

Mumford, L. (1986). The monastery and the clock. In D. Miller (Ed.). *The Lewis Mumford reader.* New York: Pantheon Books.

Niebuhr, G. (1995, April 18). The minister as marketer: Learning from business. *New York Times,* A1, A20.

Olasky, M. (1988). *Prodigal press.* Westchester, IL: Crossway.

Ong, W.J. (1982). *Orality and literacy: The technologizing of the word.* London, UK: Methuen.

Park, R. (1915). The city: Suggestions for the investigation of human behavior in the urban environment. *American Journal of Sociology, 20,* 577–612.

Postman, N. (1982). *The disappearance of childhood.* New York: Delacorte.

Postman, N. (1985). *Amusing ourselves to death: Public discourse in the age of show business.* New York: Penguin Books.

Postman, N. (1992). *Technopoly: The surrender of culture to technology.* New York: Alfred A. Knopf.

Ramo, C. (1996, Dec. 16). Finding God on the Web: Across the Internet, believers are reexamining their ideas of faith, religion, and spirituality. *Time, 149(1),* 60–67.

Rohter, L. (1999, June 25). Can a melodic priest be good for the church? *The New York Times,* A4.

Roof, W.C. (1999). *Spiritual marketplace: Baby boomers and the remaking of American religion.* Princeton, NJ: Princeton University Press.

Schement, J.R. and Stephenson, H.C. (1996). Religion and the information society. In D.A. Stout and J.M. Buddenbaum (Eds.). *Religion and mass media: Audiences and adaptations.* Thousand Oaks, CA: Sage. 261–289.

Schultze, Q.J. (1991). *Televangelism and American culture: The business of popular religion.* Grand Rapids, MI: Baker Books.

Shils, E.A. and Janowitz, M. (1948). Cohesion and disintegration in the Wehrmacht in World War II. *Public Opinion Quarterly, XII,* 280–315.

Silk, M. (1995). *Unsecular media: Making news of religion in America.* Urbana, IL: University of Illinois Press.

Stout, D.A. (1998). Marketing and missionary work: Religious advertising in the United States. Paper presented at the annual meeting of the International Communication Association (ICA), Jerusalem.

Stout, D.A. and Buddenbaum, J.M. (Eds.) (1996). *Religion and mass media: Audiences and adaptations.* Thousand Oaks, CA: Sage.

Thigpen, D.E. (1995, May 22). Leaving little to chants. *Time, 45(21),* 72.

Turkle, S. (1997). *Life on the screen: Identity in the age of the Internet.* London: Phoenix-Orion Books, Ltd.

Weber, M. (1963). *The sociology of religion.* Boston: Beacon.

Wellman, B. (1979). The community question: The intimate networks of East Yonkers. *American Journal of Sociology, 84,* 1201–1231.

Wellman, B. (1988). The community question re-evaluated. In M.P. Smith (Ed.) *Power, community and the city.* New Brunswick, NJ: Transaction.

Wellman, B. and Gulia, M. (1999). Virtual communities as communities: Net surfers don't ride alone. In M.A. Smith and P. Kollock (Eds.). *Communities in cyberspace.* London: Routledge. 167–194.

Wind, J.P. and Lewis, J.W. (1994). Introducing a conversation. In J.P. Wind and J.W. Lewis (Eds.). *American congregations, volume 2: New perspectives in the study of congregations.* Chicago: University of Chicago Press. 1–20.

Winner, L. (1986). *The whale and the reactor: A search for limits in an age of technology.* Chicago: University of Chicago Press.

Zaleski, J. (1997). *The soul of cyberspace: How new technology is changing our spiritual lives.* New York: Harper Collins.

# PART II

Institutional Perspectives on Religion and Popular Culture

CHAPTER 6

# Christian Perspectives on Mass Media

## JUDITH M. BUDDENBAUM

O n one thing Christian church leaders and commentators agree: the mass media undermine morality, threaten traditional beliefs, and, in general, pose a threat to the faith. For decades, they have been saying that the media, and particularly television as the most popular medium, have usurped the role of the church (Newman, 1996).

From the Roman Catholic perspective:

> [W]hat has done the most damage to organized churches, and particularly the Roman Catholic, is not so much the intellectual questioning and doubt of enlightenment or existentialist provenance, which have so little interest for the average secular tribesman in any event. It is the substitution of secular mass culture for previous popular Christianity. (Phelan, 1980, p. 148)

Similarly, William F. Fore (1987, pp. 11–12), former president of the National Churches of Christ, writes:

> [T]oday television is beginning to usurp a role which until recently has been the role of the church in our society, namely, to shape our system of values, embody our faith, and express our culture essence. This shift, from a religious center to what I call a technological center, is ominous.

And the more conservative Methodist minister and founder of the American Family Association/Federation for Decency, Donald E. Wildmon (1985, p. 5), adds:

[T]he organized church in America faces the greatest threat to its existence since our country was founded. . . . [T]here is an intentional effort among many of the leaders of our media to reshape our society, to replace the Christian view of man as our foundation with the humanist view of man.

In order to learn more about the attitudes of Christian churches toward the mass media and their teachings about media use, students in my fall 1994 freshman seminar on religion and the media sent questionnaires to the leaders of 209 Christian churches listed in the *Yearbook of American and Canadian Churches* (Bedell, 1993). Results revealed that leaders from all branches of Christianity share a general concern about media practices and the effects they have on individuals and on society.

Fewer than one-fourth of the respondents gave mass media entertainment a passing grade. The average grade for entertainment was a D; the D+ they gave the media for news coverage wasn't much better (Buddenbaum, 1997).

Although the 65 useable replies are neither a census nor a truly random sample of all Christian churches, they did come from both very large and very small churches from all Christian traditions. The grades church leaders gave the media did not depend on how much contact the leaders had with representatives from the media or on how much or how well they believed their church was covered in news or portrayed in entertainment.

Leaders from all Christian traditions complained that the news media miss, mangle, and generally sensationalize and trivialize important stories. Entertainment media, they said, give too much emphasis to sex and violence while ignoring and denigrating religion and the value it holds for many people and for society. In that widespread antagonism toward the media, many find confirmation of what sociologists such as James Davisson Hunter (1991) have described as a culture war. Although that war has often been portrayed as a "struggle for America's soul" being led by Christians who feel their deeply held values are under attack from a secular, areligious, or even antireligion information and entertainment industry, describing it that way overlooks the diversity that exists within Christianity.

Although leaders from all Christian traditions said it is more appropriate for members of their faith to use information media than it is to use the entertainment media and that print media are more appropriate than other kinds, there were significant differences among Christian traditions. None of the mainline leaders said movies are an inappropriate form of entertainment; only one called television inappropriate. However, more than four-fifths of the Pentecostal and other fundamentalist leaders called movies inappropriate, and about one-fifth said the same for television.

These differences are, of course, related to leaders' understandings of appropriate and inappropriate media messages and their perceptions of what may typically be available through different media. Responses to a series of questions asking how much legal protection various kinds of expression should have indicate that, again, mainline leaders were more tolerant and more likely to support full legal protection for messages that could be construed as sacrilegious or as portraying sinful behaviors than were Catholics or conservative Protestant leaders.

Although Mainline Protestant leaders were more likely than leaders from other traditions to say music videos showing drug use and music with satanic lyrics should be protected by the First Amendment, leaders from all Christian traditions were generally less supportive of those kinds of music than they were of other kinds of potentially offensive media fare. Again, Pentecostal and other fundamentalist leaders were least likely to believe offensive music should have any First Amendment protection. They were also significantly less likely than leaders from other traditions to want First Amendment protection for X-rated movies, nudity in magazines, and portrayals of homosexuality on television (Buddenbaum, 1997; see also Rimmer, 1996).

Although all Christians share a belief in the same God and consider the Bible an authoritative source for learning about God and God's commands, they have very different understandings of what it means to be a Christian. Those understandings, rooted as they are in theology, explain differences in church leaders' opinions about the mass media, media content, and use. While it would be impossible to explore fully what each of the more than 200 Christian churches, denominations, and sects teach, some attention to church teachings can help explain the very real differences among Catholics, Mainline Protestants, and more conservative Protestants that emerged from the survey data.

## The Roman Catholic Perspective

Although many people equate the Catholic approach to concerns about the media and media use with the *Index of Forbidden Books,* Catholic theology vests ultimate authority with the individual. That responsibility stems from the Catholic understanding of natural law. As Jelen (1996) points out:

> Catholic doctrine on proper use of communications media begins with the premise that objective truth exists and is accessible to humans. In the Augustinian framework, "natural law" is that portion of God's eternal law made available to humans through divine revelation and human reason. . . . As creatures created in God's image, we are placed in charge of the earth and of ourselves.

From this perspective, "the ultimate appeal is to human reason." But people are not God; human reason, left to its own devices, can fail. Because reason must be guided by an informed conscience, God also reveals himself through scripture and through his church (Jelen, 1996; McHugh, 1976).

For Catholics, the Bible is one source of revelation, but its message must be understood in light of what particular passages meant to their original, intended audience and what they mean for contemporary society. Thus, the Church must take seriously its right and responsibility to guide and instruct so that the faithful will develop the properly informed conscience that will allow them to use their reason to apprehend God's truth and live in perfect freedom in accordance with his will. This right and responsibility stems from Christ's charge to Peter:

> And I say also unto thee, that thou art Peter, and upon this rock I will build my church, and the gates of hell shall not prevail against it. And I will give unto thee the keys of the kingdom of heaven; and whatsoever thou shalt bind on earth shall be bound in heaven; and whatsoever thou shalt loose on earth shall be loosed in heaven. (Matthew 16:18–19, *New Catholic Bible*)

It is this understanding of natural law, the nature of scripture, and the authority of the Church that led to the creation of the *Index of Forbidden Books* as a way to warn Catholics of the dangers to their faith inherent in the proliferation of Protestant writings during the Reformation. Originally, then, works were listed because they challenged Catholic doctrine and practices. However, over time, works were added to the list if they were seen as tempting people to sinful behaviors.

Through the cooperation of secular authorities, books listed as unacceptable could not be printed or sold in Catholic countries. In the United States, the National Office for Decent Literature and the National Legion of Decency were able to limit the availability and use of print media and movies respectively, even though they never had official government backing. From its founding in 1930 through the 1950s, National Legion of Decency ratings of "partly objectionable" or "condemned," for example, could spell financial disaster for a Hollywood movie. Therefore, studios voluntarily subscribed to the legion's Hollywood Production Code, which spelled out moral guidelines for film plots and images (Walsh, 1996; Soukup, 1989, pp. 7–8).

However, *Inter Mirafica,* a relatively short statement issued in December 1963 at the end of the Second Vatican Council, signaled a more tolerant and open approach toward communications that might be objectionable on theological or moral grounds. In 1967 the Church stopped publishing its *Index of Forbidden Books.*

Since then, the Church has reiterated its support for freedom of public opinion, the right of access to the means of communication, and the right to communicate in *Communio et Progressio* and *Aetatis Novae,* issued by the Pontifical Commission on Social Communication, as well as in Pope Paul VI's 1976 papal encyclical *Evangelii Nuntiandia* and Pope John Paul II's encyclical *Redemptoris Missio.* The 1971 statement *Communio et Progressio* also states that governments have the duty to avoid censorship and to promote freedom of speech, press, and religion (Baum, 1993; Soukup, 1993).

Since the 1970s, Catholic publications intended for both clergy and lay audiences have carried thoughtful, nuanced critiques of the mass media and media content. Consistent with Catholic social teachings, this criticism is as likely to be aimed at commercialism with its attendant lack of concern for issues of justice for the poor and oppressed as it is at sex and violence per se. Catholic commentators often criticize things that other Christians praise; they may also find value in books, movies, or television programs that others find appalling.

Writing for the Jesuit publication *America,* Aline Wolf (1998), for example, singled out the stereotypes and historical inaccuracies found in Disney's animated movies in order to illustrate ways in which "corporate America" dictates inappropriate and unwholesome "interests, choices and values to our children." In a piece for *U.S. Catholic,* Patrick McCormick (1998) described the proliferation of gay and lesbian characters on prime-time television shows as generally beneficial. In the May 2, 1998 issue of *America,* columnist Thomas J. McCarthy used viewing of the *Jerry Springer* show as an excuse for critically examining his own motives and relationships; with some caveats, James Martin recommended *The Simpsons, King of the Hill,* and *South Park* for creativity and insightful social commentary.

Such commentaries are, of course, aimed at adults, but the Church also promotes media literacy programs, such as the Media and Values one created by Sister Elizabeth Thoman. Instead of discouraging media use, these programs are designed to help parents and church leaders guide children toward developing the kind of moral reasoning that will lead them to question what they read, see, or hear and ultimately to make informed decisions. These twin emphases on media criticism and media literacy represent a change in strategy for the Catholic Church rather than a change in the underlying theology (Jelen, 1996). But old ways die hard.  Some Church leaders and clergy in the United States still argue for government censorship (McHugh, 1976) or attempt to prevent distribution of media content they consider objectionable, as occurred in 1998 with the television program *Nothing Sacred.* Some lay members long for the "good old days" when the Church told them what they could or could not read and what movies or television programs they could or could not watch. Most, however, prefer the new approach over the older reactive approach of placing items on lists of forbidden material.

## The Mainline Protestant Perspective

With at least 100 churches that are traditionally classified as "mainline" or "old line," it is difficult to say with any certainty what these moderate to liberal Protestants believe about the media or, for that matter, almost anything else (Buddenbaum, 1996). There are differences among mainline churches, denominations, and congregations and differences within them.

Although these differences mean that the mainline approach to the media is less uniform than the Catholic perspective, superficially, at least, it is quite similar. However, it has different philosophical and theological underpinnings.

In contrast to Catholic teachings, Mainline Protestants reject the church as sole authority on matters of conscience. Although only about 3 percent of all Americans are Lutheran, like Martin Luther most Mainline Protestants could say:

> Unless I am convicted by Scripture and plain reason—I do not accept the authority of popes and councils, for they have contradicted each other—my conscience is captive to the Word of God. I cannot and I will not recant anything, for to go against conscience is neither right nor safe. (Quoted in Bainton, 1952, p. 61)

But for Mainline Protestants, "being captive to the word of God" does not mean that they take the Bible as literally true. In fact, some such as the Quakers do not consider it the sole or even primary source of God's word, for they believe that God can and does reveal himself in other ways. Almost all Mainline Protestants believe that proper understanding of Bible passages requires a sensitivity to their context within the Bible itself and to the meaning they had for their original audience.

If Mainline Protestants do not see the Bible as literally true, neither do they take media messages as literally true. Thus, media criticism by Mainline Protestants is as thoughtful and nuanced as that found in contemporary Catholic publications. They are as likely to complain about stereotypes and instances of injustice as about violence and more likely to complain about both than about sexually oriented content (Charry and Charry, 1998; National Council of Churches, 1992, 1993; Rebeck 1990).

Instead of focusing on individual passages or episodes, they look to context and purpose as keys to meaning just as they do when reading the Bible. For them, good and bad often come in the same package so that "from the 'human side' it is often difficult to distinguish God's so-called friends from God's so-called enemies" (Van Til, 1959, p. 197; see also Newman, 1996).

The question for Mainline Protestants, then, is not so much whether the media or media use is sinful. Rather, the important questions are: How did the content come to be the way it is and how and why are people attending to it?

Because they see the media producing an overabundance of shallow and sensational content in response to commercial pressures, they are among the leading proponents of government regulations that would open up the marketplace to more meaningful fare (Budden-baum, 1996, 1998). In general, they support government funding for the arts and for public broadcasting. They have also been leaders in movements to require television networks and stations to produce and air more educational programs for children and to reduce commercials on children's programs or at least distinguish them more clearly from program content.

Although they do call for government action and some also support mandatory warning labels and the V-chip, most Mainline Protestants do not support censorship. Neither are they inclined to support boy-cotts of material they personally find offensive (Fore, 1987). As the Quaker writer Jessamyn West put it, writers and journalists

> should be the eyes of the public, [seeing] as much as possible and [report-ing] as fully and as meaningfully as [their] talents permit. Otherwise soci-ety is wasteful. . . . When the artist is made to scamp his proper work by the pressure of the community, it is as if the community willingly lopped off a finger or bound up one eye. (1959, pp. 169, 174)

Instead of arguing from natural law and church authority as Catholics do, Mainline Protestants are more likely to quote Milton, whose defense of the marketplace of ideas was essentially a religious one:

> He that can apprehend and consider vice with all her baits and seeming pleasures, and yet abstain, and yet distinguish, and yet prefer that which is truly better, he is the true warfaring Christian. I cannot praise a fugitive and cloistered virtue, unexercised and unbreathed, that never sallies out and sees her adversary, but slinks out of the race, where that immortal garland is to be run for, not without dust and heat. (Quoted in Patrick, 1968, pp. 287–288)

The key for Mainline Protestants is taking personal responsibility for choosing what to produce, what to read or watch, and then how to understand and act or refrain from acting (Marino, 1999). Toward that end, they support media literacy programs, although they have been less active in developing and promoting them than have Catholics. They look to church leaders for guidance, but they do not consider them the final authority. Ultimately it is up to the individual, for God has given people his Word and blessed them with the gift of reason.

Trusting individuals to make their own decisions is, from the Mainline Protestant perspective, at least as safe as trusting popes, councils, and kings who also err so long as there is a true marketplace of ideas (Buddenbaum, 1996).

## The Conservative Protestant Perspective

Conservative Protestants have a love-hate relationship with the mass media (Schultze, 1986, 1990b, 1996). They see the media as the "magic multiplier" that makes it possible for them to fulfill the Great Commission to make disciples of all nations. At the same time, they see the media as presently constituted as representing and promoting an "apostate culture of despair" that can only undermine faith and promote immorality.

These conflicting views of the media flow naturally from the religious beliefs that are widely shared by fundamentalist Protestants and the more moderate Evangelicals who make up the conservative wing of Protestantism. Conservative Protestants place greater emphasis on being personally saved or "born again" and on saving others. For them, being saved means accepting Jesus as savior, but it also means avoiding temptations to sin. And, in contrast to other Christians, conservative Protestants are much more likely to accept the Bible as literally true. Therefore, they are also more inclined to make sharp distinctions between the sacred and secular, good and bad, right and wrong.

From this perspective, conservative Protestants quite naturally see the mass media as sinful; quite naturally they also want to use media technologies in the service of their faith. They have been leaders in creating parallel media—Christian radio, television, and newsmagazines—to promote their worldview and genres ranging from Christian romance novels to Christian rap to provide entertainment fare more compatible with their beliefs (Bendroth, 1996; Gooch, 1996; Nord, 1985; Schultze, 1990a, 1996). But because they must, of necessity, live in a world they consider sinful, conservative Protestants also support efforts to remake the mass media in their image. Marvin Olasky (1988) has, for example, argued that all journalism should be "Christian journalism." Toward that end, they promote efforts to train conservative Protestants for media careers and place them in positions where they will be able to influence media content (Fisher, 1998; "Rarity," 1981).

That is, however, a long-term strategy that leaves unresolved the problems associated with material that is currently available. Therefore, some, particularly from the Evangelical wing of conservative Protestantism, take an approach that is quite similar to that of Roman Catholics and Mainline Protestants. Quentin Schultze, who writes both for scholarly audiences and for the Christian market, for example, finds much in the media that is valuable and even supportive of Christian values. Instead of advising people to shun the media, he encourages them to understand and evaluate media content (1986, 1990b, 1990c). But where Schultze argues that material that people find personally distasteful can perform a "prophetic function" by alerting them to real-world problems and dangers, the tendency within conservative Protestantism is to equate "coverage of" or "attention to" with "support for" lifestyles and behaviors they consider sinful (Buddenbaum, 1998).

Where Catholics and Mainline Protestants are as likely to see sin in structural arrangements that promote injustice as in the behaviors of individuals, conservative Protestants more often see sin in personal behaviors, particularly sexual ones. At the individual level, they usually recommend avoiding using the mass media or at least shunning its more problematic offerings. In making recommendations about content to avoid, their literal reading of the Bible often leads them to focus on individual, isolated instances of objectionable content (Fackler, 1990).

As a result, recommendations are often rule-based. The Church of Jesus Christ of Latter-day Saints, for example, now counsels that all R-rated movies are objectionable; members should not watch them, and they cannot be shown at LDS schools such as Brigham Young University (Stout, 1996). In advocating a kind of media literacy, *American Family Association Journal* editor Randall Murphree (1998) proposed a "three-strikes-and-you're-out" strategy that makes no provision for the game itself or for the number of "at bats":

> When a program offends your family's Christian values (with profanity, crude language, unacceptable behavior, illicit sex, etc.) turn it off immediately.
>
> Then discuss why you did so. . . .
>
> Use a three-strikes-and-you're-out rule to rate the series. For example, if "Program A" has to be turned off this week, that's strike one. If you watch it again in two weeks and it has to be turned off again, that's strike two. When it gets the third strike—whether it's the third week or the thirteenth—it's permanently off the family viewing list.

Occasionally conservative Protestants call for outright government censorship. In an interview with Michael Cromartie (1999) published in *Christianity Today,* former U.S. Supreme Court nominee Robert H. Bork, for example, argues that "The original meaning of the speech clause was the protection of ideas and circulation of ideas, not the protection of self-gratification through pornography and other stuff."

Sometimes, they engage in political activism intended to elect leaders who support their views (Liebman and Wuthnow, 1984; Fowler, Hertzke, and Olson, 1999, pp. 137-156).

More often, however, they encourage and organize letter-writing campaigns, protests, and boycotts aimed directly at producers, distributors, and corporate sponsors (Fackler, 1990; Swatos, 1988; Liebman and Wuthnow, 1984). Equating television content with cancer, the Reverend Donald E. Wildmon has led conservative Protestant efforts to prevent people from contracting that "cancer" by ridding the media of objectionable content (Abelman, 1990; Wildmon, 1985). Over the years, more than a hundred television programs ranging from *Alf* to *The Wonder Years* have come under attack (Fackler, 1990).

## Conclusion

All Christians churches are concerned about media content and its potential effects on individuals, on the faith, and on society. But because Christianity is not monolithic, members of Christian religious traditions perceive the problem differently. They also recommend quite different approaches to ameliorating what they see as very different threats. Those differences are rooted in the variant understanding of God, his Word, and his commands that gave rise to divisions within Christianity itself.

Thus, any emphasis on a culture war between religion and the media, as an exemplar of secularism, is at least partially misguided. As sociologist Robert Wuthnow (1989) points out, the war is as much one among proponents of varying religious understandings and forms of moral reasoning as it is a war between religion and secularity.

Church leaders are rightly concerned. Media messages do have their effects. But religion is also a powerful force, with its own influences. That is particularly true in the United States, where freedom of religion has forced each to act as an interest group. Historically, as the contending factions within Christianity have jockeyed for legitimacy and dominance, they have shaped the way their members use the media and respond to their messages (Stout and Buddenbaum, 1996). They have also exerted their influence on messages and the media (Sloan, 1999; Buddenbaum and Mason, 1999).

# References

Abelman, R. (1990). In conversation: Donald E. Wildmon, American Family Association. In R.A. Abelman and S.M. Hoover, Religious television: Controversies and conclusions (pp. 275–280). Norwood, NJ: Ablex.

Bainton, R.H. (1952). The Reformation of the sixteenth century. Boston: Beacon.

Baum, J. (1993). The church and the mass media. In J. Coleman and M. Tomka (Eds.), Mass media (pp. 63–70). London: SCM Press.

Bedell, K.B. (1993). Yearbook of American and Canadian Churches. Nashville, TN: Abingdon Press.

Bendroth, M.L. (1996). Fundamentalism and the media, 1930–1990. In D.A. Stout and J.M. Buddenbaum (Eds.), Religion and mass media: Audiences and adaptations (pp. 74–84). Thousand Oaks, CA: Sage.

Buddenbaum, J.M. (1996). Mainline Protestants and the media. In D.A. Stout and J.M. Buddenbaum (Eds.), Religion and mass media: Audiences and adaptations (pp. 51–60). Thousand Oaks, CA: Sage.

Buddenbaum, J.M. (1997). Reflections on culture wars: Churches, communication content and consequences. In M. Suman (Ed.), Religion and prime-time television (pp. 47–60). Westport, CT: Praeger.

Buddenbaum, J.M. (1998). Media influence on traditional values. In W.D. Sloan and E.E. Hoff (Eds.), Contemporary media issues (pp. 24–38). Northport, AL: Vision Press.

Buddenbaum, J.M. and Mason, D.L. (1999). Readings in religion as news. Ames: Iowa State University Press.

Charry, D. and Charry, E. (1998). The crisis of violence. Christian Century, 115, pp. 668–679.

Cromartie, M. (1999, May 19). Give me liberty, but don't give me filth. Christianity Today, pp. 28, 30.

Fackler, M. (1990). Religious watchdog groups and prime-time television. In J.P. Ferré (Ed.). Channels of belief: Religion and American commercial television (pp. 99–116). Ames: Iowa State University Press.

Fisher, M. (1998, March). Pat Robertson's J-school. American Journalism Review, pp. 45–54.

Fore, W.F. (1987). Television and religion: The shaping of faith, values, and culture. Minneapolis, MN: Augsburg.

Fowler, R.B., Hertzke, A.D., and Olson, L.R. (1999). Religion and politics in America: Faith, culture, and strategic choices. Boulder, CO: Westview Press, 2nd ed.

Gooch, C.R. (1996). Rappin' for the Lord: The uses of gospel rap and contemporary music in black religious communities. In D.A. Stout and J.M. Buddenbaum (Eds.), Religion and mass media: Audiences and adaptations (pp. 39–50). Thousand Oaks, CA.: Sage.

Hunter, J.D. (1991). Culture wars: The struggle to define America. New York: BasicBooks.

Jelen, T.G. (1996). Catholicism, conscience and censorship. In D.A. Stout and J.M. Buddenbaum (Eds.), Religion and mass media: Audiences and adaptations (pp. 39–50). Thousand Oaks, CA.: Sage.

Liebman, R.C. and Wuthnow, R. (Eds.) (1984). The New Christian Right. New York: Aldine.

Marino, G.D. (1999). Remote control: The ethics of watching. Christian Century, 116, pp. 57–58.

Martin, J. (1998, May 2). A tale of three cities. America, pp. 21–22.

McCarthy, T.J. (1998, May 2). From this clay. America, p. 6.

McCormick, P. (1998, April). Out of the closet and into your living room. U.S. Catholic, pp. 45–48.

McHugh, J.M. (1976). Morality and the mass media. New York: Vantage Press.

Murphree, R. (1998, July–August). A winning game. Plain Truth, pp. 50–53.

National Council of Churches. (1992). Global communication for justice. New York.

National Council of Churches. (1993). Violence in electronic media. New York.

Newman, J. (1996). Religion vs. television: Competitors in cultural context. Westport, CT: Praeger.

Nord, D.P. (1985, May). The Evangelical origins of mass media in America. Journalism Monographs, No. 88.

Olasky, M. (1988). The prodigal press: The anti-Christian bias of the American news media. Westchester, IL: Crossway Books.

Patrick, J. (Ed.). (1968). The prose of John Milton. New York: New York University Press.

Phelan, J.M. (1980). Disenchantment: Meaning and morality in the media. New York: Hastings House.

Rarity in the news: A TV station takes religion seriously. (1981, Nov. 20). Christianity Today, pp. 52–53.

Rebeck, V.A. (1990). Recognizing ourselves in the Simpsons. Christian Century, 107, p. 622.

Rimmer, T. (1996). Religion, mass media, and tolerance for civil liberties. In D.A. Stout and J.M. Buddenbaum (Eds.), Religion and mass media: Audiences and adaptations (pp. 105–122). Thousand Oaks, CA: Sage.

Schultze, Q.J. (1986). Television: Manna from Hollywood? Grand Rapids, MI: Zondervan.

Schultze, Q.J. (Ed.) (1990a). American Evangelicals and the mass media (pp. 23–46). Grand Rapids, MI: Academie.

Schultze, Q.J. (1990b). Keeping the faith: American Evangelicals and the media. In Q.J. Schultze (Ed.), American Evangelicals and the mass media (pp. 23–46). Grand Rapids, MI: Academie.

Schultze, Q.J. (1990c). Television drama as sacred text. In J.P. Ferré (Ed.). Channels of belief: Religion and American commercial television (pp. 3–28). Ames: Iowa State University Press.

Schultze, Q.J. (1996). Evangelicals' uneasy alliance with the media. In D.A. Stout and J.M. Buddenbaum (Eds.), Religion and mass media: Audiences and adaptations (pp. 61–73). Thousand Oaks, CA: Sage.

Sloan, W.D. (Ed.). (1999). Media and religion in American history. Tuscaloosa, AL: Vision Press.

Soukup, P.J. (1989). Christian communication: A bibliographic survey. New York: Greenwood Press.

Soukup, P.J. (1993). Church documents and the media. In J. Coleman and M. Tomka (Eds.), Mass media (pp. 71–79). London: SCM Press.

Stout, D.A. (1996). Protecting the family: Mormon teachings about mass media. In D.A. Stout and J.M. Buddenbaum (Eds.), Religion and mass media: Audiences and adaptations (pp. 85–100). Thousand Oaks, CA: Sage.

Stout, D.A. and Buddenbaum, J.M. (Eds.) (1996). Religion and mass media: Audiences and adaptations. Thousand Oaks, CA: Sage.

Swatos, W.A. (1988). Picketing Satan enfleshed at 7-Eleven: A research note. Review of Religious Research, 30(3) pp. 73–82.

Van Til, J.R. (1959). The Calvinist concept of culture. Grand Rapids, MI: Baker Books.

Walsh, F. (1996). Sin and censorship. New Haven, CT: Yale University Press.

West, J. (1959). Readers and writers. In H.M. Lippincott (Ed.), Through a Quaker archway (pp. 166–176). New York: Sagamore.

Wildmon, D.E. (1985). The home invaders. Wheaton, IL: Victor Books.

Wolf, A.D. (1998, Aug. 1). Advertising and children. America, pp. 13–18.

Wuthnow, R. (1989). The struggle for America's soul: Evangelicals, liberals and secularism. Grand Rapids, MI: Eerdmans.

# CHAPTER 7

# Mass Media in the Jewish Tradition

## YOEL COHEN

The question of Jewish thinking about mass media has taken on practical relevance in the modern state of Israel. Contrasting perceptions among the Israeli population about the nature of mass media—for the nonreligious, a Western-style free media, and for the religious, one subservient to Jewish values—has had an impact on the media marketplace in Israel. As an ethical religion, Judaism regulates man's relationship with God and with his fellow man. While not rejecting the "good life," the Jewish weltanschauung is that man should raise his stature to emulate the characteristics of the infinite God. Judaism does not preach asceticism or social isolation but encourages social participation and, therefore, communication between men. This chapter article examines whether a view of the nature and social role of mass media may be extrapolated from the Jewish tradition.

The question of the nature of the relationship of the new state to the Jewish religion has occupied leaders on both sides of the political spectrum, the nonreligious and the religious, since the Israeli state was founded in 1948 as each sought to impose their own mold on the national fabric. Much of the religious-versus-secular debate takes place on the pages and across the airwaves of the news media. The nonreligious wish to create a modern, secular, social democratic state. They see Israel as a national home for Jews, serving a vital role for those fleeing from persecution. The nonreligious are broken down between the strictly secular and the traditional, though not strictly religious, population. The number of secular Israelis is less than is generally assumed. A survey on religious behavior among the Israeli Jewish population found that only 21 percent of respondents said they are totally nonobservant; added to this number is a middle gap of 41 percent who while not religious are somewhat observant of Jewish tradition (Liebman and Katz, 1997).

The religious communities have swelled in numbers in Israel. Of Israel's 4.9 million Jewish population, 430,000 Jews belong to the ultra-Orthodox or Haredi community and 170,000 to the modern Orthodox community. Twenty-eight of the 120 seats in Parliament, the Knesset, are held today by Jewish religious parties.[1] For the religious, the state-religion dilemma should be reconciled in the form of a democratic theocracy of sorts. The "religious" are broken into two main groupings: modern Orthodox and ultra-Orthodox, or *Haredim* (Hebrew for "pious ones"). Both religious communities wish the Jewish state to be Jewish in substance, and not just in symbolic nature. For the modern Orthodox, the creation of the state of Israel was seen as a positive juncture on the path toward Jewish messianic redemption. To them there is no conflict between modernity and Jewish goals. Their members participate at all levels, including carrying out national army service and engaging in university study. The new state entity should be run along democratic lines as long as this does not clash with Jewish law. For the Haredim, the independent Zionist state of Israel is premature; only the Jewish Messiah can bring Jewish statehood into being. The new state was not recognized. While today the Haredi Jews vote for their party factions, in order that their institutional and religious interests are defended in the Knesset, some of their parties are not prepared to accept ministerial portfolios in the coalition-style government.

Little academic research on media and religion in Israel has been conducted. This contrasts with religion-state relations that have become an important area of sociological research in Israel. Research questions on media and religion in Israel that require attention include content analysis of the media's image of religion; the influence of the mass media in constructing communal images; audience survey research; religion leaders' usage of the media; and religious public relations.

# The Torah and Mass Media

Given that the Five Books of Moses, or Torah, and later Jewish law works like the Mishnah, Talmud, and such codifiers as Maimonides necessarily predated the mass media age, it is necessary, in determining the "Jewish view of mass media," to locate points of overlap between Judaism and mass media behavior. The extent to which Judaism should intrude into social life is unclear. Some Jewish theologians argue that, with the exception of specific subjects including family law and the Sabbath, Judaism has nothing to say about much of human activity. But others define Judaism as an entire way of life with something to say about all spheres of life.

Whether narrowly or widely interpreted, much of the overlap between media behavior and Judaism appears conflictual. Areas of conflict to be discussed include sexual exposure in the media, biblical prohibitions on social and political "gossip"; and the functioning of the electronic media on the Sabbath day. Where there is a confluence of interests between Judaism and mass media—such as the provision of information about events and societies that contributes to understanding and reduces conflict—it is not generally identified as a peculiarly religious goal.

## Sexual Modesty

Although the Jewish tradition is critical of sexual exposure in the news media, notably in film and in photographs, this is less obvious than it appears. Both physical pleasure from sexual relations within marriage, as well as female beauty, are regarded in a positive light in Judaism. Rabbinical discussion of modesty (tziniut) as an ethical value concerns mostly the manner a person behaves in his or her social relations. Yet the Israelite camp in the Wilderness in "which God walked shall be holy ... that God should not see anything unseemly and turn Himself away from you" (Deuteronomy 23:15) is an allusion to nudity being looked on negatively. A concern of Jewish sources is that as a result of his exposure to images alluding to sex a man could be sexually aroused to masturbation or "improper emission of seed" (onanism) (Genesis, Chap. 38). Different branches of Judaism interpret sexual modesty differently. Orthodox Judaism forbids a man to look on a female immodestly attired; in the Haredi community it includes the uncovered hair of a married woman. Similarly, they forbid a man to listen to a woman singer lest he be sexually aroused; the modern Orthodox community permits this if the song is prerecorded. The same prohibition on men does not apply to women. These restrictions raise profound artistic questions of how love can be portrayed and expressed in a manner that is religiously acceptable. Conservative and Reform Judaism take a more liberal attitude, but the latter, in defending women's rights, takes a stand on the sexploitation of women in the media.

## Political and Social Gossip

The major innovation of Jewish theology in mass media behavior concerns the divulging of previously unknown information. Leviticus (19:16), in warning against not being "a talebearer among your people, or standing idly by the blood of your neighbour," imposes substantial limits on the passage of information. The rabbis have divided types of information into a number of categories. Most severe is divulging secret information to the wider public that is intended or has the effect of damaging somebody's reputation (*lashonhara*). When Miriam spoke ill of Moses for "the Cushan woman he married," she was smitten with leprosy (Numbers, Chap. 12). Also forbidden, but with lesser severity, is the disclosure of even positive information about somebody (*rehilut*) (Israel Meir Ha-Kohen, 1873).

While in modern society, the right to privacy is subservient to the right to know, in Judaism the right to know is subservient to the right to privacy. In Judaism the only right to know is the right to know Jewish knowledge (i.e., the Torah, national laws, and information that if kept secret would cause damage to somebody). Modern society permits everything to be published apart from that which personally damages somebody's reputation. This includes a large middle category of information that is not of vital importance to know. Judaism does not acknowledge an automatic right to this middle category of information.

These restrictions in Judaism profoundly affect the work of the professional journalist in disclosing previously unpublished information. The journalist draws much of his or her information from sources who disclose selectively often in order to weaken a political opponent.

However, once the information is known to three people, it is no longer forbidden but becomes permitted to hear it. As the Talmudic Tractate *Erachin* (16a) notes, once the information is known to three people, it is the same as announcing it to the world. Information, therefore takes on a relative value. The journalist and his informant have carried out a most heinous act in making the information public, but that same information may be heard by other people.

Yet the Torah says that it is not only permitted to publish information that if kept unpublished would damage society but it is obligatory. That the same verse that prohibits the disclosure of secret information continues "do not stand idly by the blood of your neighbour" suggests that if somebody, including a journalist, hears of information, such as corruption committed by a government minister or an official, he or she has an obligation to take steps to rectify the situation. The Bible acknowledges the fourth estate role, or societal watchdog, fulfilled by the media (Korngott, 1993). If the matter can be dealt with by other means than press disclosure, this is preferred. If not, media disclosure is necessary. Thus, Judaism distinguishes between the large flow of otherwise interesting information disclosed by the media that does not come under this category, disclosure of which it prohibits, and the much smaller category of information of social value (Shevat, 1995).

A related question that has occupied some rabbis today concerns the disclosure of information concerning inappropriate behavior of rabbis, such as corruption or sexual improprieties. Such disclosures defame the religion and even God. Over the years rabbis have generally favored covering up rather than disclosure even if it may be in the social interest for people to know. Yet the Bible was not averse to publishing details of the sins of the righteous as a means toward moral teaching. One of a number of examples is Moses' sin in smiting the rock instead of speaking to the rock to bring forth water, which would have otherwise publicized a miracle—a means toward moral teaching.

## The Sanctity of Communication

Knowledge and information also possess Jewish ethical dimensions in terms of copyright ownership, accuracy, and usage of God's name. Jewish law recognizes a prohibition of stealing knowledge. Material, such as a book or song, which is the exclusive property of one person may not be copied without his or her permission. News coverage of events that are publicly known cannot claim to copyright ownership. But investigative journalism in which one news organization is the exclusive source of the information may claim exclusivity. "News borrowing" of information in the latter category is, therefore, only permitted where such permission has been obtained. In the case of

Bible-related material—such as sermons and related material in religious media—some rabbis argue that since the Bible is not the exclusive property of one party, no copyright stipulation exists for Bible-related materials.

Information reported in the media has to be accurate to avoid the audience being deceived. The requirement for accuracy is problematic when a news organization, under tight deadlines, faces news sources that do not wish to give their account of events. The problem of deception is acute in advertising, such as persuading a customer to buy a product that he or she would not otherwise do if they knew all the facts.

An extension of the Jewish law prohibition to pronounce the Holy Name, the Tetragrammaton, Jewish law regards as sacrilegious the destruction of texts with other names of God. To overcome the problem, texts such as prayer books are by tradition buried in a cemetery. Some religious newspapers print sermons and other religious material. The preferred means of the religious media is to use God's name in an abbreviated form (for example, G—d). Some rabbis limit the prohibition to the printing of full scriptural verses and not to other types of references to God such as in the media. With the introduction of computers and Internet, rabbis have addressed the question of the name of God appearing on screen and have ruled that the prohibition on erasing God's name occurs in print, not when in electronic form.

## Media Functioning and the Sabbath

The prohibition of work on the Sabbath day, as enjoined by the fourth of the Ten Commandments (Exodus, 20:8), has implications for the Jew's exposure to the media on the Sabbath and other holy feasts. Work is not only defined as employment but embraces over 39 categories of work (stipulated in the biblical description of the Israelites' building of the Sanctuary in the Wilderness). It includes lighting fire, the source for the prohibition to turn on electricity on the Sabbath and holy days. Given the prohibition on activating electricity on the Sabbath, television and radio cannot be switched on (Auerbach, 1996). Reform Judaism, however, does not rule against using the electronic media.

Certain types of information in newspapers may not be read, such as advertisements or economic and other articles directly related to an individual Jew's work lest he or she comes to make even a mental decision regarding work. A Jew may not benefit on the Sabbath from work carried out specifically for him or her, such as having a newspaper delivered to his or her house or from news provided by a journalist who is Jewish. In modern Israel the electronic media function on the Sabbath and holy day, with the single exception of the Yom Kippur fast day, but newspapers are not published. The subject of Sabbath observance in the modern technological age is one that occupies rabbis today. Amongst media-related questions are whether a religious Jew may give an interview to a broadcast journalist on the weekday in the knowledge that it will be broadcast on the Sabbath and whether a Jew living in Israel may listen or see a rebroadcasting of a program first broadcast by Jews on the Sabbath.

The Sabbath day is not only characterized by restrictions on work but also as a spiritual experience of prayer, study, and rest on the holy day. Mundane activities such as media exposure, including newspapers, take away from the Sabbath atmosphere. Thus, even though a radio or television set could theoretically either be left on from before the Sabbath or be turned on automatically by a time-clock (the device by which many Jews have heating and lighting on the Sabbath), it would distract from the Sabbath experience, unless the program is of a religious nature.

## Media Events

No research attention has been given to examining media events involving Israel and the Jewish people in the context of being divinely influenced actions. The Bible is not just a book of laws and ethics but the revelation of the seeds of a 4000-year-long relationship between God and his chosen people; the entire book of Genesis does not contain one law. According to Jewish theology, God is an activist god both for the Jewish people as a whole and in the life of individual Jews. In chronicling often-dramatic events such as the early Israelite history in Egypt, the crossing of the Red Sea, the giving of the Ten Commandments at Mount Sinai, and the capture of the promised land of Canaan, the Bible is not very different from the news media. The Bible may have been one of the earliest messengers.

But since the end of Jewish prophecy in the fourth century BCE, the hidden divine meaning to events cannot be extrapolated. Prophecy was replaced by faith as the staple ingredient of the relationship between the Jewish people and God.

The creation of the State of Israel together with such latter events as a series of dramatic wars, the reunification of Jerusalem, and historic peace agreements since suggest to some a divine force. But in the absence of prophecy, any Jewish theological study of media events is reduced to belief (*emunah*).

## The Structure of Media and Religion

In order to examine the influence of Jewish theology on journalistic practice, media coverage of religion in Israel may be divided into three community categories: the media of the ultra-Orthodox or Haredi community, the media of the modern Orthodox community, and the general Israeli media coverage of religion.

Religious newspapers belonging to the first two categories have long existed in Israel and in most cases are sponsored by political parties or religious organizations. In the first category, the major daily newspapers are *Hamoadia,* published by the Agudat Israel political party, representing the Ashkenazi, or European, Haredi hassidic community, and *Yetad Neeman,* the voice of Eliezer Shach, a leading rabbinic force in the Ashkenazi Haredi nonhassidic or Lithuanian community. Shas, the Sephardi, or Oriental, Haredi party, recently founded *Yom Yom.* Other Haredi communities also sponsor weekly or monthly magazines. In 1983 *Yom Shishi,* an independent newsweekly, characterized by investigative journalism, popular interest articles, and modern graphic format, was successfully launched (Micolson, 1990). For their party sponsors the media fulfill an important role in political recruitment, and for their readers they are an alternative to the general media. The extent to which the latter is true may be seen in that 67 percent of Haredim surveyed read *Hamoadia* (37 percent) or *Yetad Neeman* (30 percent). Only 14 percent read secular papers or those belonging to the general Israeli press. Thirty-two percent of Haredim read no newspaper (Israel Advertisers' Association, 1995).

A similar pattern of Haredi exposure to the electronic media was found. Twenty-six percent listened to Arutz-7, a pirate nationalist-religious–orientated station, according to the 1995 survey. Only 25 percent listened to the two major radio stations in Israel, Israel Radio, and the Galei Zahal military radio. Forty-six percent said they did not listen to any radio. In 1996, 12 licensed regional radio stations were established, one of which, Radio Kol Chai, is intended for the religious communities. This, and the mushrooming of a large number of pirate Haredi stations, fill the information vacuum for the Haredi community. Television is banned by the spiritual leaders of the Haredi community both because much of its content is regarded as morally inappropriate and because entertainment is regarded by them as a waste of time that should otherwise be spent in religious study.

The modern Orthodox community is exposed to the general media, including television. This community's main political party, the National Religious Party, publishes *Hatzofe,* but its circulation is small. In addition to listening to the Arutz-7 radio station, many in this community—which identify with nationalist goals of strengthening the Jewish presence in the biblical homelands of Judea and Samaria and oppose the transfer of these territories to the Palestinians—read a variety of nationalist media including a quality weekly, *Mekor Rishon.*

The Orthodox communities are not exposed to the electronic media on the Sabbath and most religious holy days when some of the best programming is broadcast. Twenty-two percent of respondents surveyed said they do not watch television or turn on the radio on the Sabbath (this correlates with 20 percent of the Israeli population belonging to the Haredi and modern Orthodox communities) and a further 5 percent and 4 percent who "often" and "sometimes" refrain from turning on the television or radio (Levy, Levinsohn, and Katz, 1993).

Coverage of religion in the general Israeli media may be divided between news reporting on religion-related news stories and religion-related content not concerning the daily news. The former include controversial subjects like religious conversion, government funding for yeshivot (talmudical educational institutions of higher religious learning), army exemptions for yeshiva students, and Sabbath observance in public institutions. The latter include feature programs on radio and television, mostly coinciding with the Sabbath and religious festivals. Since the religion departments of Israel radio and television are managed by journalists who identify with the religious political parties whose representatives sit on the plenum of the umbrella broadcasting authorities, program content has an Orthodox accent. One result is that religion-related broadcasting does not take place on the Sabbath itself, given the religious prohibition on broadcasting, even though broadcasting itself functions then and audience interest among the general viewing and listening audience in religion matters is at a peak.

## Religion Content

The media whose content is most influenced by Jewish principles are those published in the Haredi sector. Its mandate reflects less what reality is and more what it should be. Drawing on the biblical edict that the Israelite camp shall be holy (Leviticus, Chap. 19), the media see themselves as sharing responsibility to build the model society. Thus, there are no reports on entertainment, singers, or women. There are no photographs of women. Sex, crime, sports, and leisure go unreported. When the Starr Report on President Clinton's infidelities with Monica Lewinsky was published, not a word was published about it in *Hamoadia* or *Yetad Neeman* (13.9.1999), despite the question mark over the future of the Clinton presidency. The major story was the crisis in Serbian-controlled Kosovo. The major Haredi organs, including *Hamoadia* and *Yetad Neeman,* have their own "censors" or rabbis trained to cast an eye on all material to ensure content does not clash with Jewish rulings or family values (Levi, 1990).

The Haredi media have few reporters, relying heavily on news agencies. Most of the material produced in-house comprises analyses, op-eds, and interpretations of news developments, according to the Haredi worldview. Drawing on Jewish social responsibility as an ideal, Israelis or Jewish heretics need to be rescued. Parallel to the press, wall posters plastered in religious neighborhoods in Jerusalem and Bnei Beraq act as conduits for rabbinical edicts including castigation or excommunication of political personalities. Secular people are described in the Haredi press as Israelis, not Jews. Official Israeli institutions are the target of criticism. In particular, the judiciary is criticized for not basing its decisions on Jewish religious teachings; court decisions are not described as rulings, instead "the court decided" is written.

The Israeli Army is often attacked. Accidents are explained as resulting from individuals' sins.

The secular press is often the butt of criticism and is pictured as being permissive, antiestablishment, and atheistic. One example of the intermedia tensions was the case of the Radio Chai station licensed by the government to serve the entire religious population. Its early founders included journalists from a modern Orthodox outlook who broadcast songs with women singers. In order not to upset Haredi sensitivities, these were limited to broadcasting women singers in the morning when most Haredi men were at work or in religious study. Later, two of the station's journalists who identify with the modern Orthodox community resigned on the air when a station journalist with a Haredi background stopped them from playing songs sung by a woman singer.

The modern religious media are less restrictive. Photographs of women are printed as long as they do not show women's flesh uncovered above the knee or elbow or beneath the neck. In its coverage of the Starr Report, for example, *Hatzofe* focused coverage on the political aspects of the crisis.

The religious media have failed to fulfill the prohibition against reporting social and political gossip. While none run gossip columns, their reporters are often the targets for leaking, notably by the political party sponsoring the publication.

In its coverage on religion, the general Israeli media do not reflect specifically religious values but rather the Western, social democratic ones underlying the modern Zionist state of Israel. One exception is patriotism for the modern state founded in the ancient biblical homeland of the Jews. The media are not ideologically against the values of religious communities but rather are hostile to attempts by the Orthodox to impinge on the lifestyles of modern Israelis.[2] Media essayists use language about the battle against "the blacks," an allusion to the distinctive black garb worn by Haredi men. Television and newspaper photo images of the ultra-Orthodox convey an image of them as primitive and generally fail to penetrate their inner world. Biased images of the wider population painted within the Haredi media presenting secular Israelis as lesser, sinning Jews add to the communication gap (Sasson-Levi, 1998). The assassination in 1995 of Prime Minister Itzhak Rabin by a religious nationalist exacerbated the secular-religious tensions. So has the demographic trend of the Orthodox toward large families and the greater political clout they possess today. Up to 1993 Israel's single television and civilian radio station had an important role in social agenda setting. But as a result of media diversification since, both in licensed television and radio and in the new pirate Haredi stations, public discourse has become more populist, with each audience listening to its "own" station, exacerbating yet further secular-religious tensions.

## Media Technology: Threats and Challenges

Future major developments to the media-religion matrix in Israel are likely to occur in spheres of new media technology. Media technological innovation has been either welcomed by different Jewish religious communities, or seen as a potential threat to Jewish moral values, or both. Improvements in information storage and transmission have contributed to Jewish religious education. Jewish learning, previously the enclave of rabbis and a select few, is more accessible to large numbers of people. One of many examples is that leading Israeli rabbis present weekly religious lessons by satellite simultaneously to thousands of people in different towns of Israel and overseas. Another is the Bar-Ilan University CD Rom Responsa Project, a database of the most comprehensive collection of traditional texts from the Bible, biblical commentaries, Mishnah, the Babylonian and Jerusalem Talmuds, and later Jewish law codes, covering 4000 years of Jewish written scholarship.

Some media technology is seen by the Orthodox communities as threatening religious and family values. The case of video and the Haredi community is illustrative. When Israel Television was established in 1968, Haredi rabbis banned their followers from watching television because its content was considered inappropriate and it was not possible to control watching. But when video cameras were produced—with many Haredi families using them to record family celebrations—no rabbinical ban was introduced initially because its usage could be controlled. However, after it was discovered that television programs could be seen if videos were plugged into computers, Haredi rabbis in 1993 declared a public ban on videos.

The introduction of the Internet raised similar fears. Computers are widely used in the Haredi world, but no statistics are available. An earlier attempt by some of their spiritual leaders to place a ban on them was dropped after the ruling was not widely accepted. Leading rabbinical sages in the Haredi community in 2000 declared a public ban on accessing the Internet because of its pornographic sites. But the ban was limited to using the Internet at home, a recognition of the fact that computers and the Internet are widely used in the Haredi business world. A number of computer filtering programs have been attempted. In 1997 a Haredi Jew established Toranet, which provided access to sites of a Jewish religious nature and those of more general information including educational sites, history, geography, and consumer information. No access to a site was allowed until it had been vetted. Its committee of rabbis met weekly to approve which sites could be accessed.

These concerns ignore the wider challenge that transocietal data flows pose to maintaining Jewish religious identity. Even the Haredi community is less insulatory than it was. Community identification is ensured less and less by information censorship. The future challenge for educators will be to strengthen understanding of beliefs and practices rather than censor—affording the Jew, in turn, a more solidly based and integrated, intellectual worldview.

## Notes

1. The Conservative and Reform religious movements, which make up the majority of the Jewish community in the United States, have had little impact so far in Israel, where only the Orthodox possess official recognition.

2. A different case concerns Reform and Conservative rabbis appearing infrequently in the religious programming of the first and second publicly controlled channels owing to pressure from Orthodox political parties to exclude the former.

## References

Auerbach, S.Z. (1996). Shidurei Radio B'Shabbat [Hebrew: Radio Broadcasts on the Sabbath], Alon Shevut, *Tehumim* (16).

Israel Advertisers' Association (1995). *Seker Hasifa L'Emtzoei Tikshoret: Haredim* [Hebrew: Survey of Exposure to Mass Media: Haredim] Tel Aviv.

Israel Meir Ha-Kohen (1873). *Hafez Hayyim,* Vilna. For an English edition: Z. Pliskin (1975). *Guard Your Tongue: A Practical Guide to the Laws of Loshon Hara Based on the Chofetz Hayim,* Jerusalem, Aish Hatorah.

Korngott, E.M.H. (1993). *Or Yehezkel* [Hebrew: The Light of Ezekiel: Contemporary Issues in Jewish Law], Petach Tiqva, pages 329–366.

Levi, A. (1990). The Haredi Press and Secular Society. In C. Liebman (ed.): *Religious and Secular: Conflict and Accommodation between Jews in Israel,* New York, Avi Chai Foundation.

Levy, S., Levinsohn, H., and Katz, E. (1993). *Beliefs, Observances and Social Interaction among Israeli Jews,* Jerusalem, Guttman Institute of Applied Social Research, B-14.

Liebman, C., and Katz, E. (1997). *The Jewishness of Israelis: Responses to the Guttman Report,* New York, State University of New York Press, page 3.

Micolson, M. (1990). Itonut Haredit B'Yisroel [Hebrew: The Haredi Press in Israel], Tel Aviv, *Kesher* (8).

Sasson-Levi, O. (1998). *Hishtakfut Ha-Hilonim B'Itonut He-Haredit* [Hebrew: Secular Israelis as Reflected in the Haredi Press], Ramat Gan, Am Hofshi.

Shevat, A.I. (1995). Itonim V'HadashotMitzva O Isur [Hebrew: Newspapers and News: Religious Obligation or Prohibition], Elkana, *T'Lalei Orot*.

# CHAPTER 8

# Islam and Western Culture: Navigating Terra Incognita

ALLEN W. PALMER

ABDULLAHI A. GALLAB

Islam's relationship with the West, though it goes far into antiquity, has been overburdened with rivalries and marred by conflicts. From the Christian crusades of the Middle Ages to the *fatwa* on Salman Rushdie at the close of the millennium, the predominantly Christian societies of Western Europe and North America have been suspicious and fearful of Muslims. Conversely, Muslim adherents of Islam find much in Western social values and practices antithetical to their tradition.

The arena of conflict between these communities is changing rapidly, primarily due to the technological innovations of the information age and the confrontation of cultures. No longer are geographical boundaries adequate to separate these cultures. Western values are propagated by TV programs via satellite into the Islamic nations of the Middle East, Asia, and North Africa. At the same time, Muslims of the diaspora are creating religious and cultural enclaves using Arabsat and the Internet, as well as traditional channels.

Yet recent Islamic migrants to Western nations face the dilemma of finding their authentic voice in popular Western culture balanced against their fears of cultural assimilation and loss of identity. Muslims as a group have had less success compared with other religious or ethnic minorities, like the Jews or African Americans, in opening "a window on the multidimensionality of what can be called cultural ecology" (Mowlana, 1996, p. 178). They seek to know how it is possible to move toward the center of Western culture without compromising deeply held religious beliefs and traditions.

Navigating the cultural conflicts between Islam and the West is not a trivial challenge given sharply contrasting worldviews; the two domains of knowledge are poorly matched. Islam offers a totalized worldview encompassing all spheres of community intercourse, such as political, economic, and social. The West isolates the spheres of knowledge and action and enshrines the individual. Despite overtones of "civic religion" in Western societies, they are extrinsically *secular;* traditional Muslims are overtly committed to the *sacred* as the cornerstone of community and family life.

The clash that arises from conflicting worldviews leaves emotional and psychological scars. Among recent migrants to Europe and North America, many Muslims agree with American Islam scholar Yvonne Haddad (1991) in their "frustration and dismay as they continue to experience prejudice, intimidation, discrimination, misunderstanding, and even hatred" (p. 3). Yet, in the midst of these uncertain encounters, Islam and Western society are finding ways to adapt, if incompletely, to each other's worldviews and values.

## Islam's Struggle for Acceptance in the West

Muslims compatibility with Western cultural values taps into the broader question of how they have adapted to conditions historically in all their respective host nations. The Islamic world consists of diverse ethnic, cultural, and geographic populations and faces the challenge of uniting diverse national cultures.

There are 30 countries, mainly in Asia and Africa, with a total population of about 900 million, in which Muslims have an overall majority; many more countries have sizable Muslim minorities. The total Muslim world population is close to 1.5 billion, one-quarter of the total world population (Hoogvelt, 1997).

The Muslim population has grown rapidly in Europe and North America in the past two decades. There is a growing Islamic presence in the United States, although it is concentrated primarily in a dozen major urban centers (El-Badry, 1994). At the close of the century, there are approximately 35 million Muslims in Europe and North America, with about 1,250 mosques and Islamic centers in the United States.

Adaptation of Islamic peoples into a secular society depends on their resourcefulness. In the recent analysis of Islam in diaspora there is evidence of a "tentative ascent" into Western society (Haddad, 1991; Esposito, 1992; Haddad and Smith, 1993; Lebor, 1997; Haddad and Esposito, 1998; Haddad, 1997). Arabs in general find acculturation to be somewhat more difficult than other immigrants, especially those who are more distinctly identified as Muslims (Gordon, 1964; Tavakoliyadzi, 1981; Naff, 1983; Abou, 1997; Gans 1997; Faragallah, Schumm, and Webb, 1997.)[1]

No longer satisfied to be strangers in a strange land, some Muslims are beginning to claim a kind of cultural ownership in America. They point to black African slaves who held Islamic beliefs until as late as the early part of the twentieth century. Earlier, migration of the Melungeons came to North America prior to the 1600s. Scholars assert that Muslim groups may have preceded the Plymouth and Virginia settlements on the shores of the "new world." Moors who were expelled from Spain made their way to the islands of the Caribbean, and from there to the southern United States. The first waves of Arabic immigrants from Lebanon and Syria occurred in the 1870s and 1880s (Haddad, 1997).

Even though Muslims embrace different religious traditions (i.e., Sunni and Shi'ite) within the broader Muslim community (*umma*), they share, to a significant extent, a common textual language (i.e., Arabic) and common religious beliefs based on the Koran, with their basic duties expressed in the five pillars of Islam: profession of faith, prayer, almsgiving, fasting, and pilgrimage. Traditional Muslims affirm, as did Pakistani anthropologist Akbar S. Ahmed, one of the leading interpreters of Islamic values for Western audiences: "Islam is essentially the religion of equilibrium and tolerance; suggesting a breadth of vision, global positions and fulfillment of human destiny in the universe" (Ahmed, 1992, p. 48).

# The Challenge of Islamic Universalism

More than two decades ago, Edward Said (1978) argued that Western values were dominating the Arab and Islamic worlds by a curious twist of global consumerism: Arabs exchanged their oil in the open world marketplace for a foreign and antagonistic Western culture. Said argued: "The Arab and Islamic world remains a second-order power in terms of the production of [global] culture, knowledge, and scholarship" (p. 323).

Muslim adherents disagree about the power of Western values to secularize Islamic culture. Traditionalists argue either for severance of Islamic nations with Western institutions or for globalization of Islamic values. Among a new class of Muslim neofundamentalists—a group Oliver Roy (1994) calls "*lumpen* intelligentsia" or "Islamic new intellectuals"—there is concerted effort to counter Western science and ideology with equivalent concepts drawn from the Koran and Hadith or Sunnah, the most widely accepted authoritarian guides to the Islamic canon.

Some Islamic intellectuals are ambivalent, too, about the desirability of a "public sphere" for common discourse and the role of democracy from which Western societies derive their base for rationalized public action. At best, Muslims have deep ambivalence about their role as "cocitizens" in the West (Hofmann, 1997). At worst, Islam's defensiveness amounts to what has been described as "a holding operation against modernity" (Sivan, 1985, p. 3).

Simultaneously, the West has been reluctant to embrace Muslims at or near the "cultural center." Those who distrust Islam's collective motives point to the uneven treatment of outsiders (*dhimmi*) in mixed populations where Islam has been dominant (Ye'or, 1985). The history of Muslim-Christian dialogue includes periods of great hostility and open war, as well as times of uneasy toleration, peaceful coexistence, and even cooperation toward shared goals (Kimball, 1991). A growing consensus, however, suggests Islamic-Western tensions may be growing with the expanding information society (Yamani, 1994).

Among those most fearful of Islam's designs for global expansion are writers like noted French-Catholic historian Jacques Ellul (1985), who cautioned: "Whether one likes it or not, Islam regards itself as having a universal vocation and proclaims itself to be the only true religion to which everyone must adhere. We should have no illusions about the matter: no part of the world will be excluded" (p. 28).

Some Islamic leaders do promote the goal of internationalization and globalization. Such designs have been circulating in the Islamic world at least since the days of early Islamic modernists Gamal Al-Din

Al-Afagani (1839-97) and Mohamed Abdu (1849-1905). More recently, Egypt's Sunni leader, or Mufti Nasr Fareed Wasil, affirmed that Islam should not be reticent in developing its case for globalization. He argued that Muslims should not fear globalization and should seek to benefit from all the means of progress in science, economics, and wealth. In his opinion, Muslims should be careful to protect themselves from the negative effects of this kind of expansion, remaining aware of the danger of being dissolved in the world and losing their identity ("Interview with Egypt's Mufti," 1998).

The dialogue between Islam and the West over fundamental disagreements in worldviews has occurred quietly, behind the controversies (Lewis, 1996). In the short term, whether Muslims find a voice in Western culture depends on the success they achieve in developing strategies to blend two radically different "cultural ecologies" (Mowlana, 1993). The Western secular model privileges a rational, reasoning mind in the pursuit of individual and collective fulfillment; and Islam's model emphasizes justice and tradition as the basis of a legitimate community and family life.

## Demonization of Muslims in the Western Mass Media

Muslims are critical of Western media because of their invasiveness. Within Arab nations with controlled borders, the deluge of messages and images conveyed by communication technologies from around the world is perceived as a "cultural invasion" (Ghaffari-Farhangi, 1998). As Ahmed (1992) assessed, the average Muslim is "as disgusted as he is confused with his own sense of impotence in shaping reality around him; he can no longer challenge what is real or unreal, no longer separate reality from the illusion of the media" (p. 3). (See also Schlesinger, 1993.)

Others have observed the struggle to develop a comprehensive theory for mass communication to compete with Western theories of communication (Hussain, 1986; Pasha, 1993; El-Affendi, 1993; Khawaja, 1995; Al-Hajji, 1998). It is not widely appreciated, however, that very few efforts have been advanced—West or East—pertaining to the role of media in acculturation of ethnic groups (Kim, 1988, 1995; Korzenny and Ting-Toomey, 1992; Hwang and He, 1999).

Ahmed (1992) has been especially outspoken about the role of

Western media creating an inverse version of Islam's worldview: "By their consistently hammer-headed onslaught, [mass media] have succeeded in portraying a negative image of it. They may even succeed in changing Muslim character" (p. 38). The Western media offend Muslims at two levels: first, Muslims are often demonized in media programs as fundamentalists, terrorists, or religious zealots, and second, many Western cultural practices, including drinking alcohol, gambling, and permissive sexual activities are too offensive for Islamic moral-ethical tradition.

Growing more astute to political action, Arab and Islamic action groups now address the imbalances in the negative images that have been used in media programming for at least two decades (Al-Disuqi, 1994; Ghareeb, 1983; Kamalipour, 1995). American movies that Muslims interpreted as particularly offensive were Arnold Schwartzenegger's *True Lies,* 20th Century Fox's *The Siege,* Hanna-Barbera's *Arabian Nights,* Disney's *Aladdin,* and the MGM's movie and video *Not without My Daughter.*

Television has been condemned most frequently because of its invasiveness. It conveys the modernist message in the most enticing forms directly to Islamic homes. This amounts to a "destructive campaign [of] ideas diametrically opposed to Arab and Islamic concepts, encouraging loose morality and immediate satisfaction, placing love and life and its pleasures over everything else, totally oblivious of religious belief, and of punishment and reward in the hereafter" (Sivan, 1985, p. 4).

Islamic parents are offered a wide range of guidelines on American customs, mix-gendered activities, and media use. In the book titled *Parents' Manual: A Guide for Muslim Parents Living in North America* (Women's Committee, 1976), Islamic parents are offered a wide range of guidelines designed to avoid conflict. Muslims are urged not to celebrate birthdays, for example, because they are an expression of an unacceptable selfishness. Even though most American holidays, such as Christmas and Easter, have essentially been secularized, they are "one more element in the mass culture which each year enables manufacturers and merchants to take in millions of dollars through an elaborate system of gift exchange" (p. 117). Mixed-gender activities, such as dating, dancing, and swimming, are regarded as sexually permissive.

Muslim attitudes toward the invasiveness of American television and movies are especially harsh:

Many [TV] programs are downright harmful and vicious in their effects. Among the harmful programs, which should be strictly avoided by Muslim children and adults, we would list the following: shows depicting illicit sex or center around sex themes, including comedies, and shows depicting crime, violence, sadism, depravity, and anything which can be considered degrading to religion, moral values or human dignity. (Women's Committee, 1976, pp. 139–140)

Of particular worry to conservative Muslims are the romantic sub-plots and vivid violence in many media programs.

Alternatives to such entertainment have been scarce until recently. One of the first in a series of Muslim-friendly productions was the children's cartoon *Salam's Journey,* a 40-minute U.S.-produced animated movie created by Hollywood-trained artists and producers. Using fictional characters, the film weaves a story from the Koran about the adventure of a young boy in an Ethiopian kingdom. The avowed goal was to sell at least 100,000 copies of the film. The creators sought to create a plot based on friendship, trust in God (Allah), and family values. The production scrupulously avoided un-Islamic images and messages.

Missing in the dialogue over accommodation of Islamic values in Western culture, however, are the voices of young Muslims who find new ways to invent religious traditions in a modern milieu. Perhaps their adaptation was best described by Carla Power, a *Newsweek* magazine journalist, in a portrayal of Islamic youth who are caught between competing values: "American Muslims, wealthy, wired and standing on the fault line between cultures, are well positioned to bring a 13-century-old faith into the next millennium" (1998, p. 35).

Living in a cultural/religious island within American society, young Arab Muslims find America is what the consumer magazine called "a laboratory for re-examination of their faith." They are finding ways to balance many of the tensions over traditional thought and religious practices, as well as racial and ethnic politics, economic opportunities, and religious traditions.

## Organizing Political Action to Fight Negative Media Portrayals

Islamic resistance to offending media portrayals is also achieved by increasingly well-organized political groups. Among the advocacy groups organized to protest negative stereotyping in media are the American-Arab Affairs Council, American Arab Anti-Discrimination Committee, and the Council on American-Islamic Relations (CAIR).

CAIR has organized 20 local chapters in major American and Canadian cities to train volunteers as monitors of local media programs and to report ethnic-religious slurs. In turn CAIR publishes national "action alerts" about media problems, such as topics on radio talk shows, magazine articles, and books.

In its response to the movie *The Siege,* CAIR distributed hundreds of "community response kits" to challenge the unfair portrayal of negative Arab stereotypes. CAIR suggested: "There are two kinds of Islam in America, Hollywood's version and the real thing. We are inviting moviegoers to local mosque open houses so they may learn more about the reality of the American Muslim community" (CAIR Action Alert No. 191, Nov. 5, 1998).

Management of broadcast and news operations have been targeted in order to change the persistent negative images. In a widely distributed "Know Your Rights" pocket guide distributed to Muslim activists, instructions were offered about how Muslims can approach newspaper editors and media managers to get favorable response:

> React quickly to news of the day of negative coverage. If possible have the letter in the hands of an editor on the same day in which the negative coverage appears. Be authoritative. Speak on behalf of an organization, even if you have to create that organization. Be passionate or even controversial, but avoid rhetoric and defamation.

More abstractly, Muslim outrage over negative images can be traced historically to prohibitions in early Islam against graphic images of all types. Those most severely punished on the Day of Judgment—along with the murderer of a prophet and the seducer from true knowledge—will be the maker of images or pictures (Boorstin, 1992).

## Who Should Speak for Islamic Values?

The diversity of the American Muslim community is a distinct obstacle to effective organized political and social action. One factor that contributes to this diversity is the absence of a cultural leader or spokesperson, one clearly identified as a defender of Islamic values and worldview in the mainstream media.

Among the media personalities who are variously identified as representative of the Islam cultural tradition are numerous professional athletes who have changed their names (i.e., boxer Muhammad Ali).[2]

One of the famous "crossover" Islamic personalities recognized by both popular Western culture and traditional Islam is former singer-songwriter "Cat" Stevens, who is a respected leader in Britain's Islamic community. A popular recording artist and folk singer in the late 1960s and early 1970s, Stevens changed his name to Yusuf Islam in 1977 after his conversion to the Islamic faith. A written account of his religious conversion outlines his emerging awareness of the incompatibility of his religious convictions with Western cultural identity:

> I wanted to be a big star. All those things I saw in the films and on the media took hold of me, and perhaps I thought this was my God. I decided then that this was the life for me; to make a lot of money, have a great life. Now my examples were the pop stars. I started making songs. So, what happened was I became very famous. I was still a teenager, my name and photo were splashed in all the media. They made me larger than life, so I wanted to live larger than life and the only way to do that was to be intoxicated with liquor and drugs. (Islam, 1999)

Upon embracing an Islamic worldview, Cat Stevens/Yusuf Islam sold his musical instruments and avoided public performances. His faith, he explained, was "religion not in the sense the West understands it, not the type for only your old age. In the West, whoever wishes to embrace a religion and make it his only way of life is deemed a fanatic. I was not a fanatic" (Islam, 1999).

Of particular relevance, Yusuf Islam agreed to act as a spokesperson for the Islamic community in the heat of the ideological battle over Salman Rushie's controversial novel *The Satanic Verses* (1988). Rushdie's fictional version of Koranic history provoked a dramatic response from fundamentalist Islam, particularly among Imamite Shi'ites of Iran. Rushdie tested Muslim resolve with his writings, bringing notice to the collision of cultures in the new mediated global arena. What resulted was both new popular awareness and precedent to deal with such worldview conflicts. Rushdie's offense to Islam arose from the unitary allegiance of traditional Muslims to their family and community, and in turn, the defense of Rushdie's artistic freedom by Western literati was rooted in the liberal values of freedom and self-expression (Palmer and Gallab, 1993).

## Electronic Media and Islamic Life

In order to maintain their identity Muslim individuals and groups, similar to other minority groups in Western society, have created different types of cultural and communicative strategies to maintain their dual cultural citizenship. Muslims have employed cultural and communicative strategies to balance their dual cultural citizenship. Through these strategies, they maintain a life that reinvigorates the religious, cultural, and social heritage with Islam. So it happens that through these processes of communication and interaction, group formation and mutual solidarity (i.e., "cultural enclaves") are formed (Gallab, 1997).

The development of new electronic media have made global pathways even more feasible for the Islamic life, opening the realization to many adherents that Islam can maintain its spiritual center and still extend its geographic reach. To the degree Islamic leaders are committed to globalization, it is clear that they are fearful and apprehensive about the Western colonization of their life, in Habermas' terms. Through colonization of the electronic pathways, Western values can intervene into the religious sphere, which depends on communicative action and dialogical discourse.

One solution to this dilemma is for Muslims to further the processes of enclave building. The dynamic of enclave formation leads to a discourse of constraint and empowerment as an existential strategy to combat U.S. media offenses even while it tends to reinforce the marginalization of the Arab-Islamic voice in American culture.

Even though communication technologies played a powerful role in the globalization of Western values and images, those technologies gained acceptance more slowly in most of the Islamic world. Where they gained a foothold, Islam creates a "highly distinctive" communication system with "considerable influence on the content, production, and distribution of modern communications media" (Mowlana, 1995, p. 406).

Technology may have been an obstacle for Islam at political and management levels. Broadcast systems in Arab countries have operated without general agreement about a philosophy arising from pan-Arabic or pan-Islamic, or even national, goals (Boyd, 1999). Egypt, in particular, has become the leading source of offending programs and publications. Other non-Arab Islamic nations such as Indonesia and Malaysia have moved toward a less defensive global posture but remain uncertain about the future challenge of communication and technology.

Vast distances, language diversity, and lack of central planning inhibited broadcasting from achieving its potential in the Middle East. Others have argued that media technologies were particularly ill-fitted for the social and cultural traditions of the Arab world. Media systems in Arab countries operated for several decades without a philosophy tied to the goals of the countries (Boyd, 1982). Further, Arab broadcasting operations seemed to have no way to accommodate a method of systematic audience feedback or research, contributing to a tradition stressing top-down programming decisions.

The development of electronic networks and individualized media has made new cultural pathways possible for enclave Muslims (Alterman, 1998). Hundreds of World Wide Web sites have been created on Islamic topics, but such initiatives are poorly coordinated and do not contribute significantly to the advancement of institutional Islam like the older television and radio systems.

The information age has created a new communication regime enhancing a mutual process of empowerment among the ranks of Muslims throughout the world. Perceived from within the daily developments in Muslim everyday life, technology is critical to this empowerment process.

The introduction of Arabsat has changed the landscape of Arab and Islamic communication (Amin, 1999). Now, as the third generation of this powerful communication device has been launched in the year 2000, a pragmatic assessment of social, economic, and cultural change is necessary. Most Arab regimes were apprehensive of the negative political impact of direct TV broadcasting. Judging from the bitter conflict that the radio had promoted in Arab political and social life during the 1960s and 1970s, those fears were behind the delay in utilizing Arabsat successfully. Now, satellite broadcasting is the area of pride and competition between different Arab states (Gher and Amin, 1999).

Arabsat has a dual role to play in the communication processes inside and outside the Arab world. The massive regional flows of cultural, religious, and entertainment programs through the different Arab

Satellite TV channels have created a new Arabic showcase of popular culture. New waves of Arab entertainers, newscasters, intellectuals, politicians, religious speakers, and reciters of the Koran, and writers from different Arab countries, have become part of the new public mapping of a new terrain of a complex inter-Arab discourse.

On the other hand, Arabsat has made a significant stride in feeding the Islamic and Arab diaspora with news, information, and entertainment through direct broadcasting. By supporting local Arabic TV stations in the West, like MBC in London or ANA in the United States, and making it easy to receive distant Arabic TV stations, Arabsat facilitated the creation of global information broadcasting that ranks alongside other major electronic media in the West. Such services provide an alternative communication system that empowers Muslims in the West who have been living under the threat of powerful Western media and adverse cultural practices.

Taken as a whole, these social and technological developments that now accompany globalization are significantly changing the long-standing antipathy between Islam and Western nations. Even though tensions are not entirely resolved, the promise of mutual understanding is making inroads in the uncertain relations between Islam as one of the world's great religious traditions and the predominantly Christian West.

## Notes

1. Many Muslims are not Arabic, and conversely, many Arabs are not Muslim, yet the categories persistently and incorrectly overlap in popular Western discourse.

2. Others who have become visible in the Western "star system" of celebrity are tangentially identified more with the Arab-American community and less with Islam. None of these persons, however, claims an overt public Muslim identity as explicitly as Nation of Islam leader Louis Farrakan. Regarded as a national political-religious movement, the black Muslim movement leaves few doubts as to its distinctly Islamic national identity, but members tend to displace traditional Islamic religious discourse in the public sphere with American racial politics.

## References

Abou, S. (1997). "The Metamorphoses of Cultural Identity." *Diogenes,* 177, 3–13.

Ahmed, A.A. (1992). *Postmodernism and Islam: Predicament and Promise.* New York: Routledge.

Al-Disuqi, R. (1994). "Influencing Decisions on Palestine: Muslim Image in Contemporary American Fiction." *The Muslim World League Journal,* 21 (June), 47–55.

Al-Hajji, M.N. (1998). *Egyptian Television and Islamic Revivalism: A Perspective on Islam and the Mass Media.* Unpublished dissertation, Department of Telecommunications, Indiana University.

Alterman, J.B. (1998). *New Media, New Politics? From Satellite Television to the Internet in the Arab World.* Washington DC: The Washington Institute for Near East Policy.

Amin, H.Y. (1999). "Arab Satellite TV." *Middle East Insight,* 14, 33–34.

Boorstin, D.J. (1992). *The Creators.* New York: Random House.

Boyd, D.A. (1999). *Broadcasting in the Arab World: A Survey of the Electronic Media in the Middle East.* Ames, Iowa: Iowa State University Press.

El-Badry, S. (1994). "Understanding Islam." *American Demographics,* 16 (1), 10–11.

El-Affendi, A. (1993). "Eclipse of Reason in the Muslim World." *Journal of International Affairs,* 47 (1), 163–194.

Ellul, J. (1985). "Preface." In B. Ye'or, *The Dhimmi: Jews and Christians under Islam.* (pp. 25–33). Canbury, NJ: Associated University Presses.

Esposito J. (1992). *The Islamic Threat: Myth or Reality.* New York: Oxford University Press.

Faragallah, N.H., Schumm, W.R., and Webb, F.J. (1997). "Acculturation of Arab-American Immigrants: An Exploratory Study." *Journal of Comparative Family Studies* (Autumn), 28 (3), 182–224.

Gallab, A.A. (1997). *The Thread of Conversation: How Do Non-Mormon Individuals and Groups in Utah Maintain Their Cultural Identity.* Unpublished dissertation, Sociology Department, Brigham Young University, Provo, Utah.

Gans, H.J. (1997). "Toward a Reconciliation of Assimilation and Pluralism: The Interplay of Acculturation and Ethnic Retention." *International Migration Review,* 31 (4), 875–918.

Ghaffari-Farhangi, S. (1998). "The Era of Global Communication as Perceived by Muslims." *Gazette,* 60 (4), 267–280.

Ghareeb, E. (1983). *Split Vision: The Portrayal of Arabs in the American Media.* Washington, DC: American-Arab Affairs Council.

Gher, L.A. and Amin, H.Y. (1999). "New and Old Media Access and Ownership in the Arab World." *Gazette,* 61, 59–88.

Gordon, M.G. (1964). *Assimilation in American Life: The Role of Race, Religion and National Origins.* New York: Oxford University Press.

Haddad, Y.Y. (1991). *The Muslims of America.* New York: Oxford University Press.

Haddad, Y.Y. (1997). "Islam in the United States: A Tentative Ascent." (http://usis-israel.org.il/publish/journals/society/march97/hadad.htm)

Haddad, Y.Y. and Esposito, J.L. (1998). *Muslims on the Americanization Path?* Atlanta: Scholars Press.

Haddad, Y.Y. and Smith, J.I. (1993). *Mission to America: Five Islamic Sectarian Communities in North America.* Gainesville: University Press of Florida.

Hofmann, M.W. (1997). "Muslims as Co-Citizens in the West—Rights, Duties, Limits and Prospects." *The American Journal of Islamic Social Sciences,* 14, 87–95.

Hoogvelt, A.M.M. (1997). *Globalization and the Postcolonial World: The New Political Economy of Development.* Baltimore: Johns Hopkins Press.

Hussain, M. (1986). "Islamization of Communication Theory." *Media Asia,* 13(1), 32–36.

Hwang, B. and He, Z. (1999). "Media Uses and Acculturation among Chinese Immigrants in the USA." *Gazette,* 61 (1), 5–22.

Islam, Y. (1999). "How I Came to Islam." (*http://catstevens.com/articles /convert.html*)

"Interview with Egypt's Mufti." (1998). *Asharq al-Awsat Daily* (Nov. 25).

Kamalipour, Y.R. (1995). *The U.S. Media and the Middle East: Image and Perception.* Westport, CN: Greenwood Press.

Khawaja, M.A. (1995). "'Fundamentalism' and International Media." *The Muslim World League Journal,* 23, 8–13.

Korzenny, F. and Ting-Toomey, S. (1992). *Mass Media Effects across Cultures.* Newbury Park, CA: Sage.

Kim, Y.Y. (1988). *Communication and cross-cultural adaptation: An integrative theory.* Clevedon, UK: Multilingual Matters.

Kim, Y.Y. (1995). "Cross-cultural adaptation: An integrative theory." In R. Wiseman (Ed.). *Intercultural Communication Theory* (pp. 170–193). Thousand Oaks, CA: Sage.

Kimball, C.A. (1991). *Striving Together: A Way Forward in Christian-Muslim Relations.* Maryknoll, NY: Orbis Books.

Lebor, A. (1997). *A Heart Turned East: Among the Muslims of Europe and America.* New York: St. Martin's Press.

Lewis, B. (1996). "Islam Partially Perceived." *First Things,* 59, 40–44.

Mowlana, H. (1993). "The New Global Order and Cultural Ecology." *Media, Culture and Society,* 15 (1), 9–28.

Mowlana, H. (1995). "Radio and Television." In J.L. Esposito (Ed.). *The Oxford Encyclopedia of the Modern Islamic World.* Vol. 3 (pp. 405–407). New York: Oxford University Press.

Mowlana H. (1996). *The Global Communication in Transition: The End of Diversity?* Thousand Oaks, CA: Sage Publications.

Naff, A. (1983). "Arabs in America: A Historical Overview." In S. Abraham and N. Abraham (Eds.). *Arabs in the New World: Studies on Arab-American Communities.* Detroit: Wayne State University.

Palmer, A. and Gallab, A.A. (1993). "The Global Mediated Confrontation over Salman Rushdie and *The Satanic Verses.*" Unpublished paper, Conference on Media-Religion-Culture, University of Uppsala, Sweden.

Pasha, S. (1993). "Toward a Cultural Theory of Political Ideology and Mass Media in the Muslim World." *Culture and Society,* 15, 61–79.

Power, C. (1998). "The New Islam." *Newsweek* 131 (March 16), 35–37.

Roy, O. (1994). *The Failure of Political Islam.* Cambridge: Harvard University Press.

Said, E. (1978). *Orientalism.* New York: Vintage Books.

Schlesinger, P. (1993). "Islam, Postmodernity and the Media: An Interview with Akbar S. Ahmed." *Media, Culture and Society,* 15 (1), 29–42.

Sivan, E. (1985). *Radical Islam: Medieval Theology and Modern Politics.* New Haven: Yale University Press.

Tavakoliyazdi, M. (1981). *Assimilation and Status Attainment of Middle Eastern Immigrants in the United States.* Ph.D. Dissertation, University of Minnesota.

Women's Committee, Muslim Students' Association of the United States and Canada (1976). *Parent's Manual: A Guide for Muslim Parents Living in North America.* Indianapolis: American Trust Publications.

Yamani, M.A. (1994). "Islam and the West: The Need for Mutual Understanding." *The American Journal of Islamic Social Sciences,* 14, 88–98.

Ye'or, Bat (1985). *The Dhimmi: Jews and Christians under Islam.* Canbury, NJ: Associated University Presses.

CHAPTER 9

# The Formation of Interpretive Communities in the Hindu Diaspora

## RASHMI LUTHRA

Hinduism has seen a resurgence in the twentieth century, intensifying in the postcolonial era (Hefner, 1998). This revitalization has taken different forms, and the extent to which a more muscular Hinduism should occupy the public sphere has been bitterly contested in India and the Indian diaspora (Hefner, 1998). Apart from the contest between Indian secularists (Hindu and non-Hindu) and Hindu nationalists, there are continuing philosophical debates among devout Hindus about what constitutes Hinduism, the nature of reality, and the stance Hinduism takes on, for example, women, religious minorities, and caste. There are also varying degrees of organization within Hindu communities vis-à-vis the practice of religion and a number of recognized and equally validated approaches to the practice of Hinduism.

In this study I had the opportunity to glimpse two very different forms of Hinduism in the United States—one a very private expression of Hindu devotion within a relatively small Hindu religious community, most of whose members are women, the other a very public expression under the organized rubric of the American Hindus against Defamation set up under the aegis of the Vishwa Hindu Parishad. The two sites allowed me to observe, directly or indirectly, the ongoing process of the formation of two distinct types of Hindu interpretive communities (Lindlof, 1996).[1]

## Strategies of Interpretation within a Hindu Fellowship

First, I will take up the private expression of Hindu religiosity within a group of devotees.

This group of devotees, or fellowship, consists mostly of Hindu women but also includes men.[2] These devotees are united by their allegiance to a particular guru, or spiritual guide, who lives in one of the major metropolitan centers in India.[3] They refer to themselves as *satsanghis*, roughly translated as those who live in the society of pious people. They are constituted of informal groupings in various locations in India, the United States, Canada, Indonesia, and elsewhere. The groups are composed mostly of people of Indian origin, but non-Indians are members as well. These localized and fluid groups of satsanghis are loosely tied to each other through informal networking mechanisms so that a satsanghi in Detroit may know a satsanghi in Delhi or in Virginia. There is a great deal of mobility among satsanghis so that a satsanghi may spend part of the year in Detroit and part of the year in Delhi.

The particular *satsangh*, or community of piety/the pious, I studied is thoroughly diasporic. This particular satsangh is also defined by its emphasis on gaining spiritual knowledge, as opposed to other forms of devotion such as meditation, chanting, and singing devotional songs. Localized groups gather periodically (some gather daily, others once a week or sporadically) to interpret and discuss a *vani*, or the written version of what the guru has spoken during satsangh (used here to mean a spiritual session, a gathering of devotees) on a particular day.[4] The satsangh can therefore be seen as a type of religiously based "textual community" (Stock as cited in Long, 1994).

Some groups receive vanis regularly from India; other groups and individuals receive them sporadically. Often, a group has an informal leader who receives the vanis and makes them available to other members. Although the vani is based on the guru's words, it is considered to be divinely inspired. It is often, but not always, in a question and answer form, with a devotee asking questions of the guru, and the guru answering in simple, easily understood language, weaving together text from sacred scriptures, particularly the Bhagvad Gita, with examples from daily life. Occasionally, the guru draws upon texts and examples from other religions, such as Sikhism, Islam, and Christianity, to illustrate particular points. The belief within this Hindu community, and within Hinduism more generally, is that divine knowledge and inspiration can be gained from various religions. As a result, vanis have a very open, eclectic feel to them. The examples used in them address problems devotees meet in their daily lives. Informal address (the informal "you" and "I") is used, thereby decreasing the distance between guru and devotee.

I conducted nine in-depth interviews with devotees to gain insight into the satsangh, particularly the ways in which the satsangh constitutes an interpretive community. In these interviews, devotees expressed their appreciation for the practical character of the spiritual knowledge they receive from the vanis, saying it is particularly well suited to the spiritual quest of householders, those with an active family life.

One devotee explained that she had been exposed to Hindu philosophy in many forms before, but this satsangh allowed her to put theory into practice. Many said that when they were facing a personal dilemma, the vani seemed to address that dilemma, increasing their faith in the satsangh. Another devotee explained this seemingly mysterious connection between the vani and a devotee's personal problems by saying that the vanis are widely applicable and that any two devotees would take different messages away from a particular vani, depending upon their life situation and where they are on the spiritual path. Many devotees expressed a conscious recognition of the vanis' polysemic nature (Fiske, 1987).

When asked whether the guru or the satsanghis themselves receive or give any instructions on what to read, watch, or listen to, satsangh members said emphatically that the guru does not forbid them from reading, watching, or listening to anything or, for that matter, forbid them from doing any of their daily activities. As one satsanghan put it, you can tell children not to do something, but it doesn't mean they will not do it. They will follow their own will, their own mind. Similarly, she said, there is no use for the guru to tell devotees what not to do. They will follow their own will, their own mind. Another satsanghan pointed out that just as in the Bhagvad Gita Krishna imparts knowledge to Arjun in answer to his questions but never tells him what to do or what not to do, the guru imparts knowledge to the devotee in answer to her or his questions but never tells the devotee what to do or what not to do. The guru encourages them to read particular scriptures such as the Gita as often as they can but does not provide instructions on which popular media to read or avoid.

As a result, satsanghis vary tremendously in their use of media. Some read particular magazines (whether originating in India or the United States) and watch films (whether originating in the United States or in India) fairly regularly. Others spend very little time on entertainment media. Some watch television fairly regularly, and others hardly watch at all. Some read and watch the news daily; others shun the news altogether. And yet all the satsanghis said the *gyaan,* or knowledge, they receive from the vanis or directly from the guru has greatly influenced what they do with their time, including their leisure time.

Many satsanghis said they didn't have time to attend to media because household responsibilities (or in the case of professionals, household responsibilities and jobs) absorbed much of their time. They used the rest to go to satsangh and read vanis and other scriptures. Because they found themselves more and more absorbed in satsangh-related activities and literature, they had less time for popular media. One longtime satsanghi asked what is the need to watch cinema, for example, when the world around us is a veritable cinema, a play. There is enough material in this illusory world to keep us absorbed, she said. Others mentioned watching TV to relax, reading the *New York Times,* or watching CNN to keep up with what's happening in the world, but as a marginal activity. All placed central importance on reading the Gita or the vanis. The media were peripheral by comparison.

Referring to their guru's guidance to move toward the positive in all things and actions and to avoid the negative, the satsanghis also indicated that they tended to select TV programs that are "positive," that offer some possibility of upliftment. When probed, they said "positive" content gives them insight for living according to the gyaan they receive and takes them farther on their spiritual path rather than distracting them from it.

The influence of gyaan was even clearer in the general strategies of interpretation (Fiske, 1987) adopted by the satsanghis. A more complete understanding of those strategies would require asking satsanghis how they interpret specific programs in an actual viewing situation, which I did not have the opportunity to do. But the interviews suggested a general approach to media interpretation that satsanghis indicated would be applicable across programming content because it has to do with how the gyaan has profoundly influenced their way of being in the world. The satsanghis indicated that the gyaan they receive has changed everything—their whole perception. One satsanghan expressed it as wearing a new set of glasses so that everything looks entirely different. Another satsanghan expressed it as entering a new state of being, a new existence, which influences everything you do. Regarding media, they said that they used to get involved in the content, perhaps even identifying themselves with one or more of the characters in particular TV shows, but now they take a distanced, detached view of the content. It appears to them like the chirping of birds, going into one ear and coming out the other.

They made frequent analogies between attending to media and other leisure activities such as going to parties. They said they do not avoid parties or especially seek them out, just as they do not avoid particular media content or especially seek it out. They are indifferent to these things. At a party, they listen to people chatter, they are pleasant and enjoy the company, but they do not participate in useless talk or gossip. Similarly, when they watch TV programs, they enjoy and relax, but they do not get involved in the content emotionally. They do not allow the content to manipulate their thoughts and emotions.

Further, satsanghis indicated that when the program allows it, they use it for spiritual education, to further their gyaan. As an example, one satsanghan said that if she were watching a TV program that showed someone's house on fire, and one person was shown grabbing their material possessions and being in a state of panic, and another was shown gathering their material possessions but in a much calmer manner, she would use this as a lesson for how different people relate to the world, with some being completely identified with material possessions and others not seeing the possessions as being part of who they are.

The stance toward media expressed by the satsanghis suggests that to fully understand the strategies of interpretation adopted by particular communities it may be important to understand not only their differing locations in the social structure, such as gender, race, and class (Press and Cole, 1994; Lewis, 1991), as related to their material interests, but also how their belief systems, including religious beliefs, centrally inform their perception of the world, including their interpretations of media. With people like the satsanghis interviewed, religious belief appears to be a central anchor in their perception of the world and therefore has a determining influence on strategies of media interpretation.

The interviews also suggest that the nature of media interpretation is not adequately captured by the notion of dominant, negotiated, or oppositional reading positions (Hall, cited in Storey, 1996). Neither is the duality of active and passive audience adequate to capture the potentially more complex relations between the viewers/readers/listeners and the media. Consider, for example, the satsanghis' expression of the media as a "play," as an "illusion," in the same breath as they allude to the world around us also as a "play," as an "illusion." It is not that the real world is being distinguished from the media world, with the media world easily dismissed as illusory. Rather, the gyaan satsanghis receive encourages them to gradually detach themselves from the material world even while being in it, to gradually come to understand that the world itself as we perceive it is *maya,* or illusion, with the real truth being God, the infinite, the soul.[5]

In this scheme of things, media content is just another form of maya, a play within the larger play of life; when we come to see the illusion for what it is, media become as inconsequential as the rest of the world. Understood in this way, the stance of the satsanghis toward media is not quite resistance or accommodation. Rather, it is a distanced view of the media, and the exact nature of this "distant" or "detached" perception cannot be fully understood without using concepts from within the audience's own religious cosmology, such as "maya" and "detachment."

With regard to where the locus of power in the audience-media relationship lies, once again the situation is considerably complicated. From the way the satsanghis describe themselves as selecting and utilizing particular media content, and at other times neither avoiding nor seeking out particular content, it appears that the media's power is relatively diminished. The audience member actively uses the media in service of her spiritual (not political) goals. And yet to speak of the "power" of the audience in this context may be misplaced because the devotee is using the media to further her spiritual goal of diminishing her self, of diminishing or erasing her own ego completely in order to awaken her true self, the soul. Thus, empowerment in the narrow sphere of media interpretation contributes to spiritual empowerment in the broader sphere of life, which paradoxically entails the disempowerment of self as ego.

At any rate, the interviews suggest that it is possible to speak of an interpretive community based on religious beliefs. It is remarkable that in the absence of any specific instructions or guidance from the guru regarding the media, the satsanghis exhibited, in separate interviews, very similar stances toward the media. This suggests a common strategy of interpretation based on shared religious belief. The interviews also suggest a conscious use by the satsanghis of the polysemic possibilities offered by both the vanis and media content in service of their spiritual goals. Further, there is clear evidence of intertextuality here, with the satsanghis using the vanis as a lens to interpret media content.

## Media Activism and the Formation of a Hindu Interpretive Community

The second and completely different context I used to gain further insight into the interpretive processes within Hindu communities included various Hindu newsgroups on the World Wide Web. Through an iterative process, made possible by the hyperlink feature of the Web, I was able to do an exhaustive search of the archives of the "alt.Hindu" newsgroup, the Vaishnava Internet News Agency (VINA) site, the Hinduism Today site, and the Bhakti (a society for Hindu Cultural Awareness) site. From each of these sites, I carefully read all articles pertaining to mainstream U.S. media. In all, I found 43 articles relating to U.S. media. In my Web wanderings I also stumbled upon the AHAD (American Hindus against Defamation) site. Although I could only access two articles from this site, the organization is mentioned in many of the other articles and is a lynchpin organization in antidefamation activity within Hindu communities. Therefore, I will spend some time discussing the organization in this section.

The majority of articles focused on depictions of Hinduism that were considered objectionable on particular grounds. Chief among the media controversies discussed in the articles was one centered around an episode of the television program *Xena, Warrior Princess,* which depicted Krishna as a fictional character. Therefore, I will focus on the *Xena* episode "The Way" and make references to other media controversies as necessary. I will then draw implications from the controversies for the general process of the constitution of a particular kind of Hindu interpretive community focused on mainstream media depictions of Hinduism. Finally, I will contrast this process with the much looser and yet far-reaching interpretive process engaged in by the satsanghis discussed in the earlier section of the article.

On February 28, 1999, the press secretary of the World Vaishnava Association (WVA)[6] received a fax outlining the basic story line of an episode of *Xena* soon to be aired by TV stations in New Zealand, Canada, the United States, and elsewhere. Realizing that Lord Krishna was part of the plot, the press secretary contacted other WVA members to get consensus on whether to approach the producers of the show. Next, he contacted members in New Zealand to get their opinion. A member in New Zealand then spoke with the media liaison for Pacific Renaissance Pictures, which produces the show in New Zealand, to enquire about the plot, but the liaison said details could not be revealed. The press secretary of the WVA followed up with a call from the United States to the same media liaison in New Zealand but received no information on the plot. The press secretary also conferred with the spokesperson for American Hindus against Defamation (AHAD), which is based in the United States but has working alliances with Hindu groups in other countries. Together, the WVA and AHAD representatives decided it was alright if a lead player was shown praying to Krishna or seeing him in a vision, but it would be unacceptable to show Krishna engaged in fictionalized activities or to put words in his mouth.

Even before the airing, the WVA and AHAD formulated a platform against the episode, detailing the grounds on which it should be protested, defending their stance against Hindu critics, and instructing devotees (Vaishnava and non-Vaishnava Hindus alike) on how to protest the upcoming depiction of Krishna, including the actual "talking points" to use in protest letters. Articles listed the following grounds for protest:

1. Krishna is real, and depicting him as a fictional character makes light of his position and is offensive to all sincere devotees.
2. It is insensitive and offensive to use Krishna in this manner for cheap entertainment purposes.
3. The show openly promotes homosexuality, and having a fictionalized Krishna help Xena save her girlfriend will give the false impression that homosexuality is condoned or even promoted by Krishna and the Vedic scriptures (Universal Studios, 1999).
4. Portraying Krishna as fictional or mythical casts His worshipers as superstitious, uneducated persons (Krishna das, March 3, 1999).
5. The portrayal of Krishna as fictional is discriminatory against Hindus—the producers would never portray Allah, Jesus, Abraham, or Moses as a fictitious character (Krishna and Xena, 1999).

6. The portrayal of Krishna in this manner creates further hardship for Hindus in places such as Eastern Europe and the Middle East where they already face severe discrimination and oppression.
7. Portraying Krishna as fictional reinforces the notion that Hinduism is the cause of India's economic backwardness, providing justification for the cultural, religious, and economic imperialism increasingly taking place in India.
8. Such portrayals provide justification for missionary efforts in India to convert Hindus to Christianity.
9. Such portrayals will set back the image of Hinduism, India, and Hindu politicians and political parties a hundred years (Krsna das, March 6, 1999).

Although the Global TV Network in Canada pulled the *Xena* episode in response to what a VINA press release called "a snowballing worldwide protest" (Canadian stations, 1999), stations in the United States aired the episode as scheduled. After the airing, WVA articles confirmed the fears expressed beforehand, adding specific critiques of the plot to more general objections regarding the fictionalization of Krishna. According to WVA officers, Vedic culture is treated very lightly, as a "treasure chest" for fictional plots and characters (Krsna das, February 28, 1999). That concern is linked in the articles with the more general concern that the growing interest in yoga and Eastern mysticism in the West is being exploited by producers such as Renaissance Pictures, who wrap themselves in the "cloak of Indian spirituality" (Krishna and Xena, 1999) for the sake of profit.

The WVA and AHAD continued the protest effort after the airing of the episode, culminating with a peaceful demonstration by hundreds of Hindus at the Universal Studios Theme Park on March 29, 1999. Renaissance Pictures finally relented and agreed not to distribute "The Way" to foreign markets, although it left open the possibility of distributing a modified version.

The protest against *Xena* is part of a larger effort by Hindu organizations based in the United States, but with worldwide reach, to organize the Hindu community into a self-conscious, united entity ready to defend itself against, among other things, defamation by non-Hindus and against the distortion of Hindu history, philosophy, and image more generally. Glimpses of this larger effort were seen in other controversies, such as the one surrounding the use by Madonna of a Hindu facial marking called a "Vaishnava tilak" while wearing see-through clothing and performing a sexually suggestive dance at the MTV Music Video Awards in September 1998.

Led by the WVA, the protest against the performance centered around the accusation that by combining Eastern mysticism with Western hedonism Madonna undermined the principles of purity the markings represent. This was seen as another instance of the use of Hindu spirituality for a crass commercial purpose (Hindus Outraged, 1998). The protest was joined by the Meditation Retreat Center, the Chaitanya Mission, the Hindu Religious Freedom Foundation, and AHAD, among others.

The AHAD web site showcases other instances of anti-Hindu defamation and calls upon Hindus and non-Hindus everywhere to participate in letter writing, calling, or faxing prominent persons or media that "maliciously assail Hindu dharma"[7] (http://www.hindunet.org/anti_defamation/). One incident revolved around the use of pictures of Shiva[8] and Krishna adjacent to pictures of women in revealing clothes displayed on the walls of Club Karma, a Chicago nightclub. Another centered around the cover of the compact disc *Nine Lives* published by Sony, which used an altered version of an ancient Hindu painting showing Krishna conquering the serpent Kalinag, replacing Krishna's face with the head of a cat and his male chest with a female's.

The antidefamation campaigns organized by AHAD and the WVA are part of an ongoing effort to unite the Hindu community internally so that it may present a particular face to non-Hindu people all over the world. I would also contend that the antidefamation efforts constitute the formation of a particular type of religiously based interpretive community—one focused on the critique of mainstream media appropriations of Hindu gods, demigods, and symbols for commercial purposes. Through the campaigns, members of the Hindu diaspora are being instructed on how to understand mainstream media depictions of Hinduism, what to focus on, and what to consider objectionable and why.

This interpretive community is narrowly focused in the sense that it is directed only toward mainstream portrayals of Hinduism, particularly its gods and symbols, and not toward media content in general. Much of the antidefamation activity is centered around preserving the sanctity of Hindu gods and symbols by preventing their association with profanity and sexuality, considered to be a perversion by those involved. It is also centered around defending the status of Hindu scriptures and gods as real and historically based rather than mythical. This defense is considered necessary in light of what is seen as a long-standing effort by Western scholars and more recently by Western media to denigrate Hinduism and the history of Vedic civilization (Frawley, 1994; Gokhale, 1994; Dasa, 1993).

The sense of being besieged is expressed in the term "anti-Hindu onslaught" used on the AHAD web site as the rationale for all Hindus to join forces (http://www.hindunet.org/anti_defamation/). One gets the sense of a Hindu community taking up cudgels against those who would denigrate and belittle it, in a newfound consciousness of its own worth in the context of the larger world. And this Hindu community is clearly global in its dimensions.

## Interpretive Communities, Interpretive Politics in the Postmodern Age

Through a study of the satsangh on the one hand, and Hindu web sites on the other, I was able to view two very distinct processes of the formation of Hindu interpretive communities.

Whereas the satsanghis engaged in a very private form of devotion involving varied local interpretations of a globally disseminated religious message, the AHAD and WVA web sites are very public attempts to disseminate a particular interpretation of Hinduism. Whereas the satsanghis were purposely open and eclectic in their use of spiritual knowledge to inform every aspect of their lives, the AHAD and WVA endeavors attempted to mandate a particular use of Hindu gods and symbols in the mainstream media. Whereas the satsanghis consciously used the notion of polysemy to make use of both the vanis and mainstream media to further their spiritual growth, the antidefamation project tried to fix a single definition of Hindu symbols and scriptures in order to build an interpretive community around that single definition.

The satsangh and the antidefamation activity can be viewed as two very different responses to the "absence of belonging" (Ahmad, cited in Grossberg, 1996) experienced in the postmodern age, a sense created by the gradual erosion of national-cultural identities (Hall, 1997), among other forces. The antidefamation activity can be seen as a taking of refuge in an "excess of belonging" (Ahmad, cited in Grossberg, 1996), in an attempt to build a diasporic "virtual [Hindu] neighborhood" (Appadurai, 1996). Further, the antidefamation activism harbors within itself a multitude of contradictions, perhaps because it is advancing on a terrain of globalization that is itself contradictory (Hall, 1997). While it sees itself as the defender of a historically maligned Hinduism, positioning itself as marginal outside of India (in the United States, in Canada, in the Middle East, in Eastern Europe, etc.), its project is connected to a larger one to advance religious nationalism (most often in the form of Hindutva) within India, in this form becoming the purveyor of a multiplicity of oppressions[9] (van der Veer, 1996; Suresh, 1998). The satsangh, on the other hand, while also using the Hindu religion as a resource and also being thoroughly diasporic, works in and through the spaces created by the postmodern condition, embracing difference and polysemy in the constitution of a spiritually based private identity.

Although to some extent both the satsangh and the antidefamation activity can be seen as "culturally congenial way[s] of asserting identity while avoiding the issue of race" in the U.S. context (Rajagopal, 1997, p. 58), the more public and assertive Hinduism of AHAD and the WVA makes it a more amenable partner for an "aggressive Hindu nationalism" in India (Rajagopal, 1997, p. 58). Here, only a beginning can be made in looking at the complexities spawned when religion is used as a resource in the formation of interpretive communities in the postmodern age.

## Notes

1. I am greatly indebted to my mother who introduced me to the satsangh for my research and provided her own insights on the satsangh, and Hinduism in general. I am also greatly indebted to all the satsanghis who agreed to speak to me, and particularly to one satsanghan who opened up her network to me and enabled me to get in touch with interviewees. I am not mentioning their names out of respect for their privacy. I would also like to thank Sangeeta Kumar for sending me material related to the research.

2. My sense from interviewing nine satsanghans (the feminine form of the word "satsanghi") is that this community is particularly appealing to women because it addresses itself to day-to-day living, translating the Bhagvad Gita (The Song Divine, the most sacred source of spiritual knowledge within Hinduism), and other sources of divine knowledge into practical terms that provide a guide to living within this world as a householder. I also sense that the informal, nonhierarchical, and egalitarian ethos of this religious community is very appealing to the women involved. The guru of this satsangh is currently a woman, but I am not sure that members would find this significant. I do

know that they find her egalitarian and personal approach, her approachability, inviting. It became apparent from initial questioning about this aspect that the whole duality of "man" and "woman" itself is rejected within the Hindu belief system espoused by the satsangh, with "man" and "woman" being simply transient, and in a sense unreal, manifestations of soul. So the specifically feminine aspects of the satsangh were not seen as significant by the satsanghans themselves.

3. I have not named the city here, again out of respect for the group members. This is a very private religious community, and I have made every effort to preserve this privacy without compromising the scholarship or presentation of information. This fellowship started more than 40 years ago, although satsanghis could not place the exact year. It has more than a thousand, or even thousands, of devotees, although satsanghis could not place the number. They mentioned that it has grown tremendously since its beginning, and especially in the last several years.

4. *Vani* literally means "voice" or "speech" or "language" in Hindi. The vani used by the satsanghis is literally the transcription of the spoken words of the guru. The guru usually speaks these words in the daily satsangh held in India. The words are originally written in Hindi by attending devotees, then translated by satsanghis into various languages such as Gujarati, Marathi, Sindhi, and English in different parts of the world.

5. The concept of *maya* is central to Hindu philosophy as expounded in the Bhagvad Gita and elaborated in other scriptures and texts. The vanis often refer to the concept of maya as well. Other phrases used to describe it are "panorama" and "veil." According to this philosophy, our desires and attachments to things and people are based on this grand illusion. We can only escape the cycle of reincarnation when we arrive at a state of detachment, fully realizing ourselves as soul and not as body.

6. Although Krishna is revered as a god by the majority of Hindus, he holds an even more central place for Vaishnavas, who can be considered a subset of the Hindu religion. Vaishnavas have as the center of their practice and philosophy personal devotion to Krishna, the Supreme Personality of Godhead. Krishna is considered to be the ultimate reality, with worldly reality being the pastimes of Krishna as we perceive them. Because Krishna's image and status as the supreme reality was at stake in the *Xena* episode, the World Vaishnava Association took the lead in this antidefamation effort, with American Hindus against Defamation getting involved because this was another instance of defamation of Hindus in the mainstream U.S. media.

7. "Dharma" is so central to Hindu philosophy that it has multiple meanings in Sanskrit and, by extension, Hindi. Here, "Hindu dharma" can be roughly translated to mean "the Hindu religion."

8. In the Hindu trinity, Lord Shiva is the Destroyer, or the god of destruction. He holds a central place in Hindu cosmology.

9. The notion of Hindutva, or the formation of a Hindu nation in place of the currently secular Indian nation, has been propagated by the Vishwa Hindu Parishad in close alliance with the Rashtriya Swayamsevak Sangh (RSS) and the Bharatiya Janata Party (BJP). The VHP operates in at least 20 countries, including the United States, Canada, and India. It is also the backbone of AHAD. The Hindutva movement has contributed to the oppression of various minority groups in India, including the Muslim minority, and its ideology undercuts the work done by secularly based women's movements in India.

# References

Appadurai, A. (1996). Modernity at large: Cultural dimensions of globalization. Minneapolis: University of Minnesota Press.

Canadian stations cancel Xena (February 26, 1999). Press Release issued by Vaishnava Internet News Agency. Retrieved May 12, 1999, from the World Wide Web: http://www.fina.org/articles/canadian_stations_cancel_xena.html.

Dasa, S. (January/February 1993). World views: Vedic vs. Western. Back to Godhead Magazine. Retrieved May 13, 1999, from the World Wide Web: http://www.hindunet.org/alt_hindu/1994/mgs0514.html.

Fiske, J. (1987). Television culture. London: Methuen.

Frawley, D. (1994). The myth of the Aryan invasion of India. Retrieved May 24, 1999, from the World Wide Web: http://www.hindunet.org./alt_hindu/1995_Jul_2/msg00087.html.

Gokhale, P. (August 10, 1994). Mahabharat: A myth or a reality? Retrieved May 13, 1999, from the World Wide Web: http://www.hindunet.org/alt_hindu/1994/msg00582.html.

Grossberg, L. (1996). Identity and cultural studies: Is that all there is? In S. Hall and P. du Gay (Eds.), Questions of cultural identity (pp. 87–107). Thousand Oaks, CA: Sage.

Hall, S. (1997). The local and the global: Globalization and ethnicity. In A. McClintock, A. Mufti, and E. Shohat (Eds.), Dangerous liaisons: Gender, nation and postcolonial perspectives (pp. 173–187). Minneapolis: University of Minnesota Press.

Hefner, R.W. (1998). Multiple modernities: Christianity, Islam, and Hinduism in a globalizing age. Annual Review of Anthropology 27: 83–104.

Hindus outraged by Madonna. (September 14, 1998). Calgary Sun. Retrieved May 13, 1999, from the World Wide Web: http://www.vina.org/news/madonna_calgary_sun.html.

Krishna and Xena: Behind the scenes. (February 23, 1999). Retrieved May 13, 1999, from the World Wide Web: http://www.vina.org/articles/krishna_and_xena_behind_the_scenes.html.

Krishna das, T. (March 3, 1999). Xena's message to the Viewers. Retrieved May 13, 1999, from the World Wide Web: http://www.vina.org/articles/xena's_message_to_the_viewers_html.

Krsna das, T. (February 28, 1999). Xena, after the airing. Retrieved May 13, 1999, from the World Wide Web: http://www.vina.org/articles/xena_after_the_airing.html.

Krsna das, T. (March 6, 1999). Communication to the Indian community. Retrieved May 12, 1999, from the World Wide Web: http://www.vina.org/articles/communication_to_the_indian_community.html.

Lewis, J. (1991). The ideological octopus: An exploration of television and its audience. New York: Routledge.

Lindlof, T.R. (1996). The Passionate Audience: Community inscriptions of The Last Temptation of Christ. In D.A. Stout and J.M. Buddenbaum (Eds.), Religion and mass media: Audiences and adaptations (pp. 148–168). Thousand Oaks, CA: Sage.

Long, E. (1994). Textual interpretation as collective action. In J. Cruz and J. Lewis (Eds.), Viewing, reading, listening: Audiences and cultural reception (pp.181–212). Boulder: Westview Press.

Press, A. and Cole, E. (1994). Women like us: Working class women respond to television representations of abortion. In J. Cruz and J. Lewis (Eds.), Viewing, reading, listening: Audiences and cultural reception (pp. 55–80). Boulder: Westview Press.

Rajagopal, A. (1997). Transnational networks and Hindu Nationalism. Bulletin of Concerned Asian Scholars 29(3): 45–58.

Storey, J. (1996). Cultural studies and the study of popular culture: Theories and methods. Athens: University of Georgia Press.

Suresh, V. (December 6, 1998). Minority baiting. The Hindu, p. 25.

Universal Studios offends Vaishnavas, casts Krishna in fictional plot (February 22, 1999). Retrieved May 13, 1999, from the World Wide Web: http://www.vina.org/articles/universal_studios_offends_ vaishnavas.html.

van der Veer, Peter (1996). The ruined center: Religion and mass politics in India. Journal of International Affairs 50: 254–277.

# PART III

## Empirical Studies, Essays, and Case Studies

CHAPTER 10

# The Role of Religion and Culture in Tolerance for First Amendment Freedoms in a Southern California Vietnamese Community

TONY RIMMER
JEFFREY BRODY

An appreciation for the civil liberties of others is deeply embedded in the American polity. Political rhetoric and judicial evaluation continually endorse these values, and children are socialized in them from an early age. Public opinion polls suggest that the liberties of freedom of speech and press are valued by the populace, at least on a general level, though poll respondents tend to more conservative postures when more specific examples are offered.

We owe thanks to the following: Yen Do, Publisher, *Nguoi Viet Daily News* of Westminster, California, for translation services and moral support; Michael Halberstam and Francine Carfachia, Interviewing Service of America (ISA) of Van Nuys, California, for giving us more interviews than we could afford; and Cal State Fullerton's Intramural State Minigrant Program for financial support.

But how are these values transmitted to and held by new immigrant communities, particularly those from cultures where such aspirations might not be valued? The immigrant community considered here is that of the Vietnamese, whose immigration to the United States for the most part reaches back just twenty years to the end of the Vietnam War, and whose emigrating circumstances raise intriguing questions on how new constitutional freedoms might be held and inculcated.

The study discussed in this chapter builds on a body of research that describes the relative influences of social institutions such as education, religion, and mass media in evaluating tolerance for the civil liberties of speech and press. The study tests the relevance for the Vietnamese of a tolerance model developed from data on the general U.S. population. Factors unique to the Vietnamese, for example those of religion and political/historical experience, are incorporated in the model. Our expectation was that the political history and culture of the Vietnamese would have a significant impact on their perceptions of the American conceptions of freedom, and on the tolerance that the Vietnamese demonstrate for the civil liberties of others. These ideas were expected to have important implications for the socialization of new immigrant communities.

The data for this study come from a telephone survey executed in the Vietnamese language in the summer of 1995 from a sample drawn in Orange County in Southern California. The county has a Vietnamese population of some 100,000, arguably the largest concentration of Vietnamese outside of Vietnam. The Orange County cities of Garden Grove and Westminster, in particular, have seen a tremendous influx of Vietnamese immigrants in the last two decades. Many of these people are political refugees from the aftermath of the Vietnam War. Since they were forced to flee their homeland, most may not have been willing travelers to the United States. Some may not be comfortable with their new political lot. Their opinions about U.S. political freedoms suggest a potent test for the received model of how civil liberties are valued by a new immigrant community from a third world country. It should be noted, however, that this community is not a microcosm of Vietnam. It more likely represents a unique and relatively homogeneous class of Vietnamese society: those from government, military, and social elites.

This chapter first reviews the literature on tolerance for civil liberties and identifies some of the key variables considered important in predicting tolerance. A received model is derived from this literature, and some argument is offered to support the idea that the Vietnamese immigrant community's political history, religion, and culture may follow a different tolerance model. The survey and its data are described in both univariate and bivariate form, and then the two multivariate prediction models are tested. Following a review of the results of these tests, some ideas are then offered for further research in the promotion of tolerance of other's speech and press freedoms in new immigrant communities.

# Review of Literature and Argument

## The Received Model

For more than two centuries the American political tradition has promoted free speech and tolerance of varying, even abhorrent, political views. The U.S. Constitution's First Amendment guarantees regarding freedom of speech and freedom of the press, particularly in this century, have generally been upheld by the U.S. Supreme Court. Respect for the Constitution and for First Amendment values is taught to children as part of the education process. From an early age, Americans are socialized into democratic values and freedoms.

Yet Americans often behave contrary to what might be expected from their civil liberties education and socialization experiences. The proportion of people participating in the national electoral process has declined over the years, with only about a half of voting-age Americans taking part in the 1996 elections. When asked in public opinion polls how they feel about their civil liberties, Americans generally report agreement with the principle that freedom of speech should be granted to everyone. Yet when they are offered more specific situations, such as allowing a communist to speak at a local meeting, or making books containing unpopular ideas available at a local library, these same poll respondents qualify their responses such that they demonstrate little tolerance for other's civil liberties (von Elten and Rimmer, 1992). Polls surveying political tolerance show that Americans oppose extending free speech guarantees to dissenters, nonconformists, and extremist political groups.

If the general American population shows this kind of reticence regarding the civil liberties of others, whither new Americans? The present study examines tolerance of First Amendment rights among one new immigrant group in the United States: that of the Vietnamese who emigrated here in 1975 after the Socialist Republic of North Vietnam, a communist government, conquered the U.S.-backed Republic of South Vietnam, an authoritarian regime (Karnow, 1983).

More than one million Vietnamese have settled in the United States since 1975, with the largest concentration in Southern California. It might be reasonable to expect that factors that predict tolerance among native-born Americans may not be true for the Vietnamese because of the unique sociohistoric experience of the Vietnamese. Vietnam, for example, has never had a democratic government or a free press (Buttinger, 1967). These factors are presumed here to outweigh any acculturation toward First Amendment values that the refugees might have received in the relatively short time (approximately two decades) that they have lived in the United States.

Tolerance is defined here as not just a lack of prejudice but rather when a person shows support for the constitutionally guaranteed civil liberties of individuals or groups, whether or not that person approves of those individuals or groups (Rimmer, 1996).

In their review of research on the concept of tolerance that drew on the earlier work, for example, of Stouffer (1963), Allport (1966), Nunn, Crockett, and Williams (1978), and McCloskey and Brill (1983), von Elten and Rimmer (1992) identified three key variables that seem to be associated with tolerant attitudes: education, age, and religion.[1] Education was found to have a positive effect and presumed to be operating through the cognitive sophistication higher education is assumed to bring. Age and religion were seen in the literature to be negatively associated with tolerance. Older people, for example, were more likely to report less tolerant attitudes, and religion, whether measured as a behavior (e.g., participation in religious activities), or as an attitude (e.g., perception of self as religious), was shown to be negatively associated with tolerance.

In a secondary analysis of a 1987 national probability sample of 4,200 respondents, von Elten and Rimmer (1992) found support for the arguments offered in the literature and for their own notion that media reliance should also show a positive association with tolerance. Rimmer (1996) further explored the role of religion by considering an argument that ideology might be confounding religion variables, especially in public opinion data. Given the interests of their sponsors (e.g., mass media), so this argument goes, contemporary public opinion polls tend to focus on the attitudes and behaviors of the religious right. So religion variables in these kinds of data are bound to freight in a lot of political ideology. Rimmer (1996) found some support for this ideology/religion argument, though religion was still found to play a negative role in predicting tolerance. Age was no longer identified as a factor, and media reliance, presumed to be operating in an educational role, continued to show a weak association with tolerant attitudes.

The received model, then, predicts a positive role for education, liberal political ideologies, and media use, especially that of newspapers, and less so for radio and television use. The model further predicts a negative role for religion, age, and conservative political ideologies.

## Should the Received Model be Modified Here?

The questions considered in the present study were twofold: first, how will the received model fare in a recent immigrant community, and second, how might that immigrant community's history impact the model? Our particular interest here was with the second question. We assumed education would play the liberalizing role found in the earlier studies, though this role might be reduced. We expected that religion would play a different, more entangled, role for the Vietnamese community. Religious traditions involving Buddhism, animism, and Catholicism were expected to play a small role in predicting tolerance, but the major influence for religion was expected to arise from its interaction with ideology and the community's political history. We believed that the historic experience of the Vietnamese, who had not seen democracy or a free press until they arrived in the United States, and who experienced a war that made them refugees from communism, would report unique, and likely intolerant, perspectives toward freedom of speech and of the press.

The Vietnamese have little historical experience with freedom of expression (Smith et al., 1967a). Their experience is more with repression than with the expression enjoyed by the general American population. Further, a high percentage of the Vietnamese immigrant community was forced to flee its homeland after the communist takeover in 1975 because of close ties to the American government (Baldwin, 1982). A high proportion of Vietnamese refugees settling in the United States were among the one-third to one-half of the South Vietnamese population imprisoned in re-education camps after the war (Sardesi, 1988).

It was expected then, that the Vietnamese community would report little tolerance for freedom of expression or for the institutions that promote such tolerance. Refugees who have fled communism or suffered under communist rule would presumably have little tolerance for extending free speech rights to communists or those perceived to be sympathetic with the views of the communist government of Vietnam. While the refugees might have a strong ideological bias against communism, their children who were raised in the United States and/or were educated in the American school system, might exhibit more tolerance. Given the short time frame available, however, our data might not have been sensitive to this latter question.

There is strong anecdotal evidence, judging from the number of attacks on Vietnamese-immigrant journalists in the United States, that a segment of the Vietnamese-American community has little tolerance for freedom of the press. Since 1981, five Vietnamese-immigrant journalists have been killed in the United States by purported anticommunist extremists, and many other editors and reporters have been attacked (Brody, 1994b). The pattern for these murders and attacks suggests that the journalists have angered extreme anticommunist members of the Vietnamese immigrant community who aim to set the political agenda for all Vietnamese living in the United States. The murders, which are all unsolved, have had a chilling effect on the Vietnamese-immigrant press. The editor of the largest and most influential Vietnamese-language newspaper in the United States, Yen Do of the *Nguoi Viet Daily News* in Westminster, California, was forced to step down because of red-baiting (Brody, 1994a). Like newspapers in Vietnam at the height of the war, the Vietnamese-language newspapers in the United States have found themselves imposing self-censorship and backing away from printing articles that favor peaceful reconciliation with Vietnam (Brody, 1994a). Although the Vietnamese have resettled in a democratic country that promotes freedom of the press, the Vietnamese-immigrant press operates as if it were still in Vietnam where newspapers were subject to censorship.

From the time of French colonialism in the latter half of the nineteenth century to communist rule at the end of the twentieth century, the Vietnamese have lived under regimes that have repressed civil liberties and dissent (Buttinger, 1967). Even when the country was divided from 1954 to 1975, the two regimes—in communist North Vietnam and in authoritarian South Vietnam—censored the press and used media as a propaganda tool (Smith et al., 1967a, 1967b). Both regimes had no tolerance for traditional First Amendment values, and each repressed religious and political dissent. For example, in 1957, the government of Ngo Dinh Diem issued orders for newspapers to deliver to the Ministry of Information two copies of each newspaper before publication. Furthermore, mobs attacked offices of newspapers known to be critical of the government (Brody, 1997). It became common to see large blank spaces on the pages of many Vietnamese-language newspapers because the censors removed the stories. In North Vietnam, the Communist Party has historically used the press as a propaganda tool and an organ in the fight to reunite the country (Brody, 1997). Communist ideology viewed the press as an instrument to serve the party. The party thus exercised tight control over all forms of media, including newspapers, film, and radio broadcasts. Only information approved by party censors is disseminated to the people.

At the end of the war, Professor Jacqueline Debarats of the Australian National University reported that the first significant act of repression after the fall of Saigon was the burning of four million works in the Khai Tri publishing house (Brody, 1997). Religious institutions also came under attack. Buddhist, Catholic, and Protestant leaders have been arrested, sent to re-education camps, or confined by house arrest.

Ironically, we assumed that media use can also have a liberalizing influence on attitudes regarding tolerance for the civil liberties of others. The evidence in the received model suggests media have this educating influence, although the effect identified in the multivariate context is small.

## The Research Questions

In summary, the arguments offered here suggested two research questions for this study:

1. Will the Vietnamese immigrant community follow the received model in the prediction of its tolerance for the speech and press freedoms of others?
2. To what extent is the religious, cultural, and political history of the Vietnamese immigration experience associated with the community's tolerance for the speech and press freedoms of others?

# Method

## The Data

The data considered here were developed from a 20-minute telephone survey of 164 Vietnamese-surnamed residents aged 18 years and older, of Orange County in Southern California.[2] Respondents were offered a language choice for the interview, and all elected to have their interviews conducted in Vietnamese. The sample was drawn and executed from a countywide population listing of Vietnamese-surnamed residents developed by Interviewing Service of America (ISA) of Van Nuys, California. ISA specializes in the surveying of ethnic groups. ISA has expertise in over 60 languages ("from Armenian to Zulu," ISA, 1995) and executes surveys worldwide, 24 hours a day, from its Van Nuys offices. Cultural counsel and translation services were provided by a local Vietnamese newspaper publisher. One other "cultural affinity" control mechanism was provided by the first author of the study. He is a 15-year veteran newspaper journalist whose beat included the local Vietnamese community, and he has visited Vietnam in the course of his work.

The survey was in the field for 13 days, from July 11 through July 24, 1995. President Clinton announced the restoration of diplomatic relations between the United States and Vietnam on July 11, and the survey's introduction into the field was scheduled to take advantage of the announcement. Our assumption was that the announcement heightened the salience of the issue of contact with Vietnam in the Vietnamese-American community.

Margins of error for a sample of this size might be considered as follows: for scaled questions (e.g., four- or five-point agree/disagree questions) ±3 percent at the 95 percent confidence level, and for dichotomous questions with close to a 50/50 split in responses, ±8 percent at the 95 percent confidence level.

## The Measures

*The Dependent Variables.* Two dependent measures were considered: first, a single item that asked for perceptions of freedom in America and, second, a formally developed multiple-item scale that encompassed a variety of responses to questions on tolerance of speech and press freedoms. The first item allowed a preliminary exploration of the roles of education and media use—in this case newspaper use. The question was a four-point agree-disagree response to the question "There is too much freedom in America."

The second measure was part of a larger test of the forces at play in tolerance for speech and press freedoms. A principal components factor analysis with varimax rotation was run on responses to a battery of 13 five-point agree-disagree questions involving respondent perceptions of freedoms in the United States. These included questions on speech and press freedoms and on extreme ideas being introduced into the community (e.g., "Books containing bad ideas should be banned from the library" and "Pornographic books and movies are harmless"). A 20-point scale (*intolerance* scored high) incorporating six questions was developed. Its reliability (Cronbach's alpha = 0.65) was somewhat lower than Carmines and Zeller's (1979) suggested 0.70 for ad hoc scales of this type.[3] The six questions making up the factor (ranked by factor loading, which might be seen as the correlation of an item with the underlying factor), were "The press in America is too free" (factor loading = 0.79), "Americans have too much freedom of speech" (0.74), "The American media turned the American public against the Vietnam war" (0.59), "The news media should be free to report on any stories they feel are in the national interest" (0.45), "The Vietnamese-language press in America should be free to report whatever it wants about the Vietnamese community *here* in America" (0.32), and "The Vietnamese-language press in America should be free to report whatever it wants about *Vietnam*" (0.30).

*The Independent Variables.*    The independent variables accommodated three arguments. The first argument involved variables and indexes developed for the received model. These included education, religion, ideology, age, and media use. The second is two indexes we call history and culture that attempt to capture our argument involving the influence of the Vietnamese's social history on their civil liberties perceptions. The third argument involved three "categorizing" variables, offered in the manner of covariates in the sense that they are not considered central to the model, yet they offer interesting categorizing opportunities.

1. From the received model:
    a. Education. There were three dimensions to education. First, a ratio-level response to the question "highest school year com-

pleted" that ranged from fourth through seventeenth grade (graduate school); second, a nominal-level measure that identified whether the respondent was educated in Vietnam or the United States or both countries; and third, whether the respondent had studied U.S. history, and the freedoms being studied here, beyond citizenship application requirements.

b. Religion. Religion involved two dimensions: religious affiliation (e.g., Buddhist or Catholic, a nominal-level measure) and religiosity (perception of self as religious). Originally we had data on three dimensions: denomination label (religious affiliation), perception (e.g., "Prayer is important in my life"), and behavior (i.e., frequency of attendance at temple or church). Preliminary testing gave us two unique measures of religion: one a denomination label, the other a perceptual measure we called "religiosity"—how religious respondents considered themselves to be. This involved a factor analysis across seven agree-disagree questions (e.g., "I am a religious person," "I never doubt that God/Buddha exists"), the resulting five-question religiosity index (range 15 points) obtained a reliability of 0.77 (Cronbach's alpha).

c. Ideology. Ideology was a six-point index (from strong conservative to strong liberal) assembled from a series of questions that asked for personal ideology and then probed for salience ("strength of commitment") and valence (direction or "lean").

d. Age. Age was a ratio-level measure derived from a "year of birth" report indicating age in years.

e. Media Use. Three indexes were built to indicate TV news and newspaper use:

(1) Two additive indexes of two variables for each of TV news and for newspapers, namely, "days per week read the newspaper" (or watch TV news) and "attention paid to newspapers (or TV news) regarding news about the Vietnamese community."

(2) A nominal-level media reliance variable that identified respondents as either newspaper or TV "reliers" depending on which of their scores on the media use measure in item (1) above was greater.

2. History and Culture:

a. History. Two indexes identified here as "Vietnam is ruined" (an additive index of agree/disagree questions like "The Communists have ruined Vietnam" and "Communists and non-Communists can live together") and "No contact with Vietnam" ("Those doing business with Vietnam are traitors" and "The U.S. should restore diplomatic relations with Vietnam") were developed to operationalize our historical influence argument. Although we place them here under the labels of history and culture, these anticommunist measures might also be seen as a second ideology dimension. We therefore had two perspectives on ideology available: first, personal ideology, where respondents tended to see themselves as liberal; second, anticommunist, where extremely conservative views were expressed. The two measures were orthogonal (i.e., uncorrelated).

b. Culture. An attempt was made to tap the multicultural studies concepts of "cultural influence" attributed to Hofstede (1979) and his associates. Two questions that appeared to tap an individualistic/collectivist cultural dimension ("There is too much freedom in America" and "Vietnamese is a nurturing culture") were summed to form an intuitive culture index. A third variable, which might be seen as tapping acculturation ("I feel more Vietnamese than American"), rounded out our cultural component.

3. Categorizing variables. Three variables were offered to accommodate anticipated arguments proposing alternative plausible explanations:

a. Whether the respondent was a U.S. citizen, on the assumption that the commitment to citizenship, plus the education on constitutional freedoms associated with the citizenship application process, might have some impact.

b. How long the respondent had lived in the United States (in years), on the assumption that some socializing in speech and press freedoms may have occurred even in the short period this community has been in the United States.

c. Whether the respondent had been jailed in Vietnam for "reeducation" following the war, on the assumption that being jailed might be associated with intolerance.

## Results

The sample data are first described with some comparisons with data from the general U.S. population, a goodness of fit for sample-population representativeness is reported, then bivariate associations between the tolerance variable and its predictors are reported and compared with data from an earlier study. Finally the multivariate tests associated with the study's two research questions are reported.

## A Profile of the Sample

There were 164 respondents in the sample, 86 (52 percent) males and 78 (48 percent) females. A one-way chi-square goodness of fit revealed no significant difference between this gender distribution and a theoretical 50/50 gender split (chi-square = 1.65, df = 1, $n$ = 164, $p$ > .05), suggesting a reasonable fit with the population with regard to gender. A quarter ($n$ = 40) reported language fluency in both Vietnamese and English, though most (70 percent, $n$ = 114) reported fluency in Vietnamese only, with their ability in English sufficient only "to get by." There was substantial diversity in age in the sample, ranging from 19 to 76 years (mean = 39, sd = 13.6). A median time lived in the United States of 10 years was reported, meaning half of the sample had lived in the United States from one to 10 years, and the other half from 10 to 20 years. The sample was relatively well educated, reporting a median education level of one to two years of college education. About half of the respondents reported they had acquired this education in Vietnam. Thirty-nine people (24 percent) reported they had been imprisoned by the communists after the war, for a median time of three years. Fourteen reported prison time of less than one year, and two reported 10 and 13 years in prison in Vietnam, respectively.

With regard to media use, the community appeared to rely more on TV news than on newspapers, but either way they reported a high interest in news about their community. Respondents reported watching TV a median of two hours a day, a median of seven days per week watching TV news, and three days a week reading a newspaper. A possible explanation for this difference between TV news and newspaper use might have to do with the "language" demands of newspaper reading. Television news may be more readily accessible to subjects who report English as their second language. When asked on a five-point scale (1 = a little, 5 = a lot) how much attention they paid to news about Vietnam or the Vietnamese community in Southern California, respondents reported a median attention score of four for TV news and 4.5 for newspapers.

The portrait of the sample is a confusing one with regard to ideology. An extended seven-point "personal ideology" measure developed here (strong conservative-low, to strong liberal-high) showed a normal distribution across the sample, with the mean ideology reported as "lean liberal." Respondent reports on individual questions, however, showed a consistently conservative posture throughout the survey, and this contrasted sharply with the general U.S. population data from the 1987 Times Mirror poll ($n = 4,244$) reported by Rimmer (1996). For example, 82 percent ($n = 123$) agreed with the statement that books containing dangerous ideas should be banned from local schools and libraries. For the U.S. population in 1987 the percentage was 51 percent ($n = 2,170$). Nearly 60 percent of those responding to the question (20 percent, $n = 32$ declined to answer) agreed that freedom of speech should not be extended to communists. Thirty-eight percent ($n = 1630$) of U.S. respondents reported similar sentiments in 1987. Ninety percent ($n = 145$) of our Vietnamese-American respondents agreed with the statement that the U.S. press was too free, and about the same proportion agreed with the more general question that there was too much freedom in America. Seventy-seven percent ($n = 92$) agreed with the statement that the U.S. media had turned the population against the war.

Questions involving contact with Vietnam did not evoke as conservative a reaction. Fifty percent of the sample ($n = 65$) agreed with the proposition that the United States should restore diplomatic relations with Vietnam. About the same proportion (47 percent, $n = 64$) agreed with the question that people doing business with Vietnam were traitors. Sixty percent ($n = 76$) said they would return to live in Vietnam if the country were free, and 29 respondents (18 percent) said they had visited Vietnam recently.

This community is religious. On a six-question religiosity index (e.g., "Prayer is important in my life" and "I never doubt the existence of God/Buddha"), a median score of 22 was reported on a 24-point scale.[4] Fifty percent of the sample reported attending church or temple twice a month or more often. Religious affiliations included Catholic ($n = 74$, 46 percent) and Buddhist ($n = 61$, 38 percent), and 16 respondents (10 percent) reported belonging to the animist religion referred to as Ancestor religion.

## Some Associations with Tolerance

Bivariate relationships between our tolerance variable and the predictors developed in our argument were evaluated with Pearson corre-

TABLE 10.1.    ZERO ORDER PEARSON CORRELATIONS WITH TOLERANCE
FOR SPEECH AND PRESS FREEDOMS (WITH CORRELATIONS FROM AN
EARLIER STUDY)

| Variable | Tolerance | |
| --- | --- | --- |
| | Vietnamese Americans (*in*tolerance high) (1995, $n$ = 164) | General U.S. population (tolerance high) (Rimmer, 1996, $n$ = 2,700) |
| Education | −.04 ns | .42** |
| Religiosity | .25** | −.49** |
| Church/temple attendance | .16* | −.22** |
| Ideology (liberal high) | −.21* | .29** |
| Age | .13 ns | −.18** |
| Newspaper use/attention | .06 ns | .07** |
| TV news use/attention | .22** | −.10** |
| History[1] ("no peace") | .05 ns | |
| History[2] ("no contact") | −.14 ns | |
| Culture ("nurture > freedom") | .10 ns | |
| Feel Vietnamese > American | .09 ns | |
| Imprisoned in Vietnam | .01 ns | |
| Years lived in United States | −.09 ns | |

*Note:* ns = no significance.
*$p$ < .05, **$p$ < .01

lations. In Table 10.1, these correlations are reported, and a comparison is made of the present study's data with that of an earlier study reported by Rimmer (1996).

The Vietnamese data offered just four significant weak bivariate associations with tolerance. This suggested that there would be even fewer significant predictors revealed in the multivariate context—a problem for the received model. These four relationships, however (religiosity, $r$ = .25; TV news use, $r$ = .22; ideology, $r$ = −.21; church attendance, $r$ = .16), were in the directions expected from the literature. Note that our tolerance measure scored intolerance high and that the ideology measure scored liberal high.

Religion appears to be a key variable associated with tolerance. Religiosity ($r$ = .25, $p$ < .01) and church/temple attendance ($r$ = .16, $p$ < .05) showed weak, positive relationships with tolerance. We interpret this finding as suggesting that as respondents report higher levels of religiosity and frequency of church/temple attendance, so they also report higher levels of intolerance. This is consistent with prior research in the general American literature. Previous studies with the general population tended to report negative relationships between tolerance and religion variables, and the correlations from Rimmer (1996) reported in Table 10.1 confirm this. Religiosity there was negatively associated with tolerance ($r = -.49$, $p < .01$) and, further, showed the strongest correlations in the analysis. In both studies then, the more religious a respondent reported they were, the less tolerant they were.

Of the two media use measures considered, only TV news use showed a significant correlation with tolerance ($r = .22$, $p < .01$). High levels of TV news use and attention were associated with high levels of intolerance. Newspaper use did not show a significant association with tolerance. From Table 10.1 it can be seen that this finding is consistent with that found in previous research. Rimmer (1996) found newspaper use to be positively associated with tolerance and TV use to be negatively associated with tolerance. The TV measures are somewhat different across the two studies, with the Vietnamese study asking more specific questions associated with TV news. The 1987 U.S. survey reported general TV use, while the 1995 Vietnamese-American data reported TV news use and asked about attention paid to TV news about Vietnam and the Vietnamese community. Rimmer (1996) argued that education was likely acting as a surrogate for media use in his 1996 study, and this would appear to be the case also in the Vietnamese community.

Table 10.1 shows no significant associations between tolerance and the history and culture arguments we had developed.

Through the use of two-way boxplots, Figures 10.1–10.3 offer an alternative perspective of some of the relationships. They report on one of our categorizing variables (time lived in the United States) and on religious preference and media reliance. We do not report our other two categorizing variables since bivariate analyses (and plotting) showed that tolerant attitudes were not related to U.S. citizenship or whether our subjects had been imprisoned in Vietnam after the war.

Figure 10.1 illustrates the relationship between tolerance and time lived in the United States. The bivariate analysis reported in Figure 10.1 shows no significant relationship between the two measures. However, the boxplots in Figure 10.1 suggest a finding consistent with what we had expected. Our assumption was that time in the United States might be an acculturator promoting tolerance. The longer our subjects lived in the United States, we assumed, the more tolerant they would become. The data show such a tendency. Those living in the United States from one to five years showed higher median tolerance scores than did those who had lived in the United States longer. Living in the United States longer also means being older, however, and there

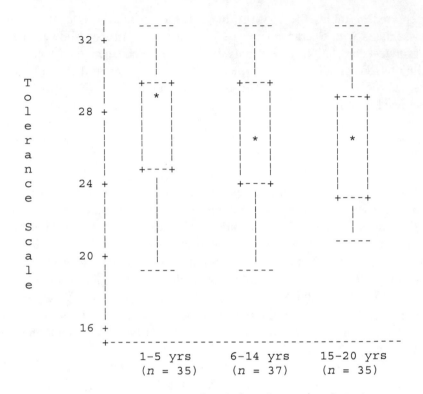

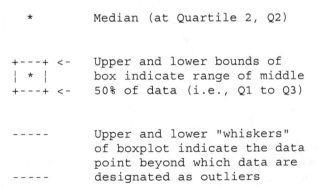

**Figure 10.1 Two-way Boxplots of Tolerance for Speech and Press Freedoms by Time Lived in the U.S. (High Scores = Intolerance)**

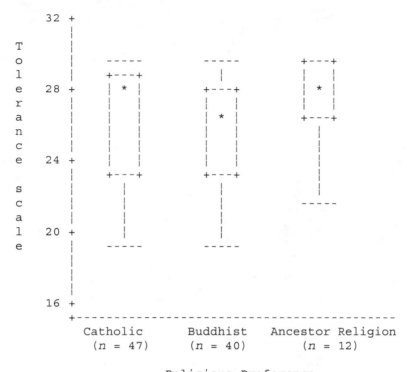

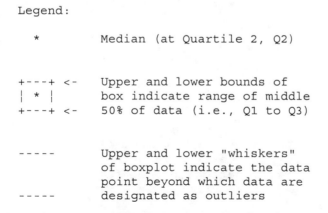

Figure 10.2  Two-way Boxplots of Tolerance for Speech and Press Freedoms by Religious Preference (High Score = Intolerance)

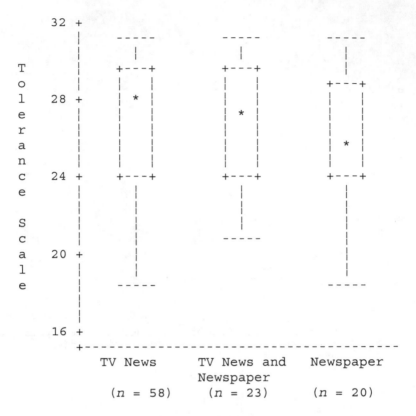

Figure 10.3 Two-way Boxplots of Tolerance for Speech and Press Freedoms by Media Reliance (High Score = Intolerance)

is a hint in the data that older respondents tended to report less tolerant attitudes.

Figure 10.2 partitions tolerance by religious preference. Catholics showed a slight tendency to higher median intolerance levels than did Buddhists. This despite the fact that Buddhists were perhaps persecuted more than were Catholics during the Vietnam War, which we assumed might have led to lower levels of tolerance for speech and press freedoms on the part of Buddhists. Figure 10.3 partitions tolerance by media reliance. It can be seen that the median tolerance scores distribute by medium as proposed by the correlations in Table 10.1. TV news reliers tended to show higher levels of intolerance than did newspaper reliers. This tendency is consistent with our expectations derived from the literature where we assumed that newspaper use would be more closely tied to tolerance than would TV use. It should be reiterated that the differences found here are tendencies only. They were not statistically significant differences.

Education may be operating as a surrogate, or third variable, insofar as general TV use is usually associated with lower levels of education, while TV *news* use is associated, as is newspaper use, with higher levels of education. If this holds in the context of the present study, then we might expect TV use and TV news use to be inversely associated with tolerance, and newspaper use to be positively associated. There is some support for this idea insofar as Table 10.1 reports a correlation ($r = .22, p < .01$) between TV news use and *in*tolerance while newspaper use does not show a significant relationship with tolerance.

## The Research Questions

The first research question proposed that the Vietnamese community's tolerance of speech and press freedoms would follow the received model that had been developed in earlier work in the general American population. Rimmer (1996), for example, developed a model incorporating education, religion, ideology, and media use and found it accounted for 33 percent of the variation in his dependent tolerance measure.

This first question was evaluated in two phases: first, a preliminary model was evaluated with two- and three-way cross tabulations (education by perception of freedom in America, controlled by level of newspaper reading), and second, the fit of the received model was evaluated using stepwise multiple regression techniques.

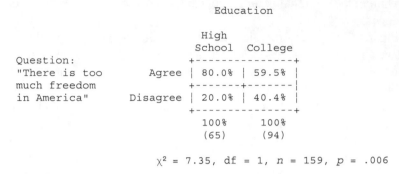

$$\chi^2 = 7.35, \text{ df } = 1, \; n = 159, \; p = .006$$

**Figure 10.4 Two-way Crosstabulation of Perception of Freedom by Education**

First we review the cross tabulations. The premise here was that there would be a significant relationship between level of education (high school versus some college) such that education would be associated with higher levels of tolerance. The expectation was sustained (chi-square = 7.35, df = 1, $n$ = 164, $p$ < .05).

Figure 10.4 shows this two-way cross tabulation. Twenty percent of the less well-educated respondents (high school education or less) disagreed with the statement that "there was too much freedom in America" whereas 40 percent of the more highly educated (some college or more) disagreed with the statement. Newspaper reading was then offered as a control in a manner that allowed the evaluation of newspaper use as a promoter of tolerance. Support for this idea should be demonstrated by the sustaining of the null hypothesis in the high newspaper reading figure (Fig. 10.5B). A finding of no difference in Figure 10.5B suggests that less well-educated respondents who report high levels of newspaper reading will show similar tolerance levels to those who are more highly educated. The hypothesis was supported (chi-square = 2.05, df = 1, $n$ = 77, p > .05). Both education and newspaper reading appear to be associated with high levels of tolerance. An inspection across A and B in Figure 10.5 shows a further intriguing phenomenon. While Figure 10.5B shows no difference overall in tolerance levels between less well-educated and more highly educated respondents under conditions of high newspaper readership (sufficient to deliver the null hypothesis and support our hypothesis), the movement that appears to "power" the shift in significance across the two tables comes not from the less well-educated but from the more highly educated respondents. Those reporting a high education showed a sub-

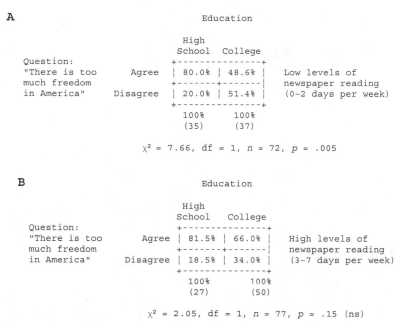

```
A                                    Education

                          High
                          School  College
  Question:              +---------------+
  "There is too    Agree | 80.0% | 48.6% |   Low levels of
  much freedom           +-------+-------|   newspaper reading
  in America"    Disagree | 20.0% | 51.4% |   (0-2 days per week)
                          +---------------+
                           100%    100%
                           (35)    (37)

              χ² = 7.66, df = 1, n = 72, p = .005


B                                    Education

                          High
                          School  College
  Question:              +---------------+
  "There is too    Agree | 81.5% | 66.0% |   High levels of
  much freedom           +-------+-------|   newspaper reading
  in America"    Disagree | 18.5% | 34.0% |   (3-7 days per week)
                          +---------------+
                           100%    100%
                           (27)    (50)

              χ² = 2.05, df = 1, n = 77, p = .15 (ns)
```

**Figure 10.5 Three-way Crosstabulation of Perception of Freedom by Education, Controlling for Level of Newspaper Reading**

stantial movement in the direction of *in*tolerance in the high newspaper use condition. This can be seen by reading across A and B in Figure 10.5. The percentage of highly educated respondents who disagree with the question (i.e., report tolerant opinions) changes from 51.4 percent in Figure 10.5A to 34 percent in Figure 10.5B. The less well educated show virtually no change across the two tables. This apparent anomaly for our premise that education and newspaper use are liberalizing influences will be addressed in the discussion section.

The second test associated with the first research question is reviewed next. The test involved an evaluation of the received model using stepwise multiple regression techniques. The attempted fit was spectacularly unsuccessful. None of the variables and indexes (e.g., education, age, personal ideology, religiosity, church/temple attendance, media use) that had shown significant multivariate associations with tolerance in earlier studies in the general population showed any support here in the Vietnamese data. When the history and culture arguments we had posed in our second research question were introduced into the model, they too made no significant contribution in accounting for variation in the dependent variable of tolerance. These findings had been suggested by the weak bivariate showings reported in Table 10.1.

# Discussion and Conclusions

## The Research Questions

This study sought to explain tolerance for speech and press free-doms in a new immigrant community in terms defined by a model developed over the past 50 years with data from the general American population. The short answer is that the received (and generally successful) approaches to predicting tolerance for speech and press freedoms apparently do not operate at the multivariate level in our data from the Vietnamese-American community. Earlier assertions in the literature claiming to account for the dimensions of tolerance in the general American population appear now to be found wanting for at least this new immigrant community.

Some elements of the received model *were* demonstrated in the bivariate phase of our analysis. For example, religion was found to be associated with intolerance, both as an attitudinal measure (religiosity) and as a behavioral measure (frequency of church attendance). Liberal personal ideologies were associated with tolerance, and conservative personal ideologies were associated with intolerance. Television news use was associated with intolerance. Education and newspaper use, however, showed no significant associations with tolerance. Our attempts to quantify "history" and "culture" and incorporate them into the model were not successful. None of the bivariate associations identified here were sustained in multivariate testing.

## Philosophy of Science and Falsifiability of Theory

What to do now? An inspection of bivariate relationships in the data revealed several interesting, potentially fruitful, areas for consideration. But this approach also teases us with the notion that we might rationalize that we have partial support for our models. This is something philosopher of science Karl Popper (1963, 1977) would decry. For Popper, theory advances through conjecture and refutation—falsifiability. Theories cannot be supported; they can only be falsified. A good theory, then, might be one that puts itself out to be falsified. We might conclude that this is the case here. A theory about tolerance for civil liberties that appeared to operate in a larger context—that of the general American population—was found not to operate when evaluated in a different, more specific context—that of a new immigrant community. This "falsified" finding clearly puts the received theory on notice in the sense that a particular contingent condition was not accommodated by the theory. It would appear that we have, perhaps inadvertently, stumbled onto one of Platt's (1964) examples of a decisive test, one meeting his Popperian criterion of "strong inference."

## Suggestions for Further Research

Further research is obviously needed before we can acquire more confidence in the present findings. Some specific suggestions follow:

1. Replication of this study's approach is needed in order to validate and test its reliability. The present study was exploratory. Our review of the literature did not identify any similar research in immigrant communities. There is a need to expand this line of research, to generate a better understanding for policy as well as scholarly purposes, of how new immigrant communities acquire the political values of their new country. In particular, all of the measures used here need more refining if we are to capture the concepts we are interested in.

2. The time that an immigrant community has lived in the United States is surely important, despite the lack of any statistically significant showing here. Recall, in Figure 10.1, that our data did tend to operate as we had expected. Acculturation is presumed here to be acquired over a much larger time span than was available to us. A comparative study with another immigrant community of similar origins and conservative tendencies that has lived in the United States longer might usefully be undertaken, if only to evaluate the assumption of time in residence as an acculturator. Two such communities might be the Cubans, whose time in the United States reaches further back to the Castro revolution of 1959, and that of the Hungarians, dating back to 1956.

3. The cross tabulations in Figures 10.4 and 10.5, which identified an association for education and for newspaper reading with tolerance for American freedoms, also pointed to another intriguing phenomenon. The changes in the high newspaper readership condition that delivered the null hypothesis and thus support for our hypothesis involved those reporting a high education *and* high levels of newspaper readership rather than the less well educated. The higher educated showed a substantial movement in the direction of *in*tolerance. This flies in the face of our premise that education and newspaper use are

liberalizing influences! One explanation we offer for this apparent irony is that we might need to rethink causal direction assumptions. Rather than assuming that education and newspaper use are *promoting* tolerant attitudes throughout the population, we might think of the two variables as indicators of hegemony for parts of the community. Given the origins of this community in the political and military elite of South Vietnam, we might usefully consider whether some of our more highly educated respondents are now leaders of the community in Southern California, and their reporting of high levels of media use might be more an indicator of a monitoring of media in the interests of hegemony rather than for education. Attempts to identify these individuals as being more conservative and/or reporting higher levels of anticommunism were not successful.

4. It should be noted that our sample accommodated only those aged 18 years of age and older. Privacy concerns and a desire to replicate prior research from public opinion polls (which draw largely on surveys of the voting-age public) meant we did not attempt to survey persons younger than 18 years. The two-decade life in the United States of the Vietnamese community we were studying meant we were not in a position to consider respondents born and educated in the United States. Future research might usefully consider this first-generation class of respondents.

5. There may be some question as to whether our sample was of adequate size. The economics of our survey restricted us to this sample size. Yet it is surely spurious to call for, say, a doubling of the sample size merely so statistically significant relationships can be delivered. More important than bold assertions about sample size limitations is the issue of statistical power and the sensitivity of statistical tools to detect differences (see, e.g., Cohen, 1992). Sample size is but one issue to be considered in association with statistical power. Effect size is another, and further replication in the present study's interest area will provide more evidence to help identify expected effect sizes such that power analyses can then indicate the sample sizes necessary to identify particular effect sizes of interest.

## Notes

1. Ironically, much of this research on tolerance used as its base American opinions toward the war in Vietnam (see, e.g., McCloskey and Brill, 1983).

Here we are studying opinions on civil liberties of Vietnamese respondents and proposing arguments that these opinions were in large part shaped by the same war.

2. Several questions replicated those in a 1987 Times Mirror survey reported by Rimmer (1996) and von Elten and Rimmer (1992). This allowed a comparison of responses from Vietnamese Americans here with those of the general U.S. population. We acknowledge Times Mirror's generosity in allowing us access to these data.

3. This scale incorporated two intriguing, correlated dimensions: an awareness of American speech and press freedoms while at the same time expressing intolerance for them, perhaps as in "I concede these rights, but I don't care for them."

4. The severe negative skew demonstrated here was characteristic of much of the data in this study. This raises questions regarding the violation of assumptions of the parametric tests employed here. The dependent variable was also severely skewed. A cube transform brought it near normality (as represented by the Shapiro-Wilks-Lilliefors normality test), but this transformation option was dropped due to the difficulty of interpreting such severe transforms, plus a desire to avoid having to follow the same procedure with most of the interval-level independent variables in the study.

# References

Allport, G. (1966). The religious context of prejudice. *Journal for the Scientific Study of Religion, 5,* 447–457.

Baldwin, B. (1992). *Capturing the change, the impact of Indochinese refugees in Orange County: Challenges and opportunities.* Santa Ana, CA: Immigrant and Refugee Planning Center.

Brody, J. (1994a, October 19). Attack on editor of Vietnamese newspaper is an attack on free speech. *The Los Angeles Times,* p. B11.

Brody, J. (1994b). The Vietnamese press under siege. In *Silenced: The unsolved murders of immigrant journalists in the United States.* New York: Committee to Protect Journalists.

Brody, J. (1997). Censorship in Vietnam: From the Colonial Period to the present. In *Ready Reference: Censorship.* Pasadena, CA: Salem Press.

Buttinger, J. (1967). *Vietnam: A dragon embattled.* New York: Praeger.

Carmines, E.G., and Zeller, R.A. (1979). *Reliability and validity assessment,* Sage University Paper Series on Quantitative Applications in the Social Sciences. Beverly Hills, CA: Sage.

Cohen, J. 1992. A power primer. *Psychological Bulletin. 112*(1), 155–159.

Hofstede, G. (1979). Value systems in forty countries: Interpretation, validation and consequences for theory. In L. Eckernsberger, W. Lonner, and

Y.H. Poortinga (Eds.), *Cross cultural contributions to psychology,* Netherlands: Swets and Zeitlinger B.V., Lisse.

ISA. 1995. Our business is data collection. Van Nuys, CA: Interviewing Service of America.

Karnow, S. (1983). *Vietnam: A history.* New York: Viking.

McCloskey, H., and Brill, A. (1983). *Dimensions of tolerance: What Americans believe about civil liberties.* New York: Russell Sage.

Nunn, C.Z., Crockett, H.J., and Williams, J.A. (1978). *Tolerance for nonconformity.* San Francisco: Jossey-Bass.

Platt, J.R. (1964). Strong inference. *Science. 146*(3642), 347–352.

Popper, K. (1963). *Conjectures and refutations: The growth of scientific knowledge.* London: Routledge and Kegan Paul.

Popper, K. (1977). *The logic of scientific discovery.* London: Hutchinson (first published in German, 1934).

Rimmer, T. (1996). Religion, mass media, and tolerance for civil liberties. Chap. 8 in D.A. Stout and J.M. Buddenbaum (Eds.), *Religion and mass media: Audiences and adaptations* (pp. 105–122). Thousand Oaks, CA: Sage.

Sardesi, D.R. (1988). *Vietnam: Trials and tribulations of a nation.* Long Beach, CA: Long Beach Publications.

Smith, B., Bunge, R., and Shinn, T. (1967a). *Area handbook for North Vietnam.* Washington, D.C.: U.S. Government Printing Office.

Smith, H., Bernier, D., Bunge, F., Rintz, F., Shinn, R., and Teleki, S. (1967b). *Area handbook for South Vietnam.* Washington, D.C.: U.S. Government Printing Office.

Stouffer, S.A. (1963). *Communism, conformity and civil liberties.* Gloucester, MA: Peter Smith.

von Elten, K., and Rimmer, T. (1992). Television and newspaper reliance and tolerance for civil liberties. *Mass Comm Review, 19,* 27–35.

CHAPTER 11

# Southern Baptists as Audience and Public: A Cultural Analysis of the Disney Boycott

## HILLARY WARREN

R eligious audiences are not merely media-created entities; they have internal structures that allow members to communicate with one another and support themselves independently of any media program or genre. Religious audiences may, in fact, act in opposition to the media or programming through mechanisms such as boycotts and picketing. Another mode of protest takes the form of interpretation on the part of the audience and, in the case of the Southern Baptist Disney boycott in 1997, that form of individual, private protest was far more effective than the economic impact of the action. Through conversation, interpretation, and teaching, Southern Baptist parents participated in the boycott as individuals, families, and churches, and the primary effect was on what the boycott taught them and their children about their faith and media structures—not Disney.

The author would like to thank Professor D. Charles Whitney, of the University of Texas at Austin, for his advice and support over the course of this study.

In addition, through this audience activity, the conservative Protestant audience formed bonds that created a public of shared interpretation. This transition from audience to public is significant because it forms one way in which media interpretation connects individuals into a larger whole. By foregrounding their communication amongst themselves, I demonstrate the transition between the audience as situated (Anderson, 1995) within the family and conservative Protestant culture to an active, strategic audience that acts consciously as Southern Baptists to reject Disney. To restate this, I see Southern Baptist families as viewing media primarily within the context of day-to-day home/work/family life. I also see their behavior as strategic when they identify themes and issues that spark connections with their religious identities. Placing the primary viewing and decision-making influence within the family makes sense given the fact that, of the factors of official church communication and informal personal discussions, what appear to be most influential are the decisions parents make about Disney products' suitability for their children and their personal reflections about the relative power of the Southern Baptist Convention and the Walt Disney Company. Many parents stopped buying Disney before the boycott and applied their own standards for what was acceptable to buy under the boycott. These choices created a certain tension between themselves, the convention's stance, and their understanding of what is possible in terms of impacting a media conglomerate such as Disney.

## The Conservative Protestant Audience and Public

This study of the conservative Protestant television audience is informed by the work of Stuart Hall and other audience research in the tradition of cultural studies. This research tradition is particularly important in studying the religious audience because of its emphasis on understanding the "meaning of content received and of use in context" and uses ethnographic and qualitative data to "explore perceptions of meaning" in a social and cultural context" (McQuail, 1997, p. 21). This conception of the audience has been developed through research on culturally defined audiences of the series *Dallas* (Ang, 1985), the audience for a particular genre such as romance novels (Radway, 1991), and situationally defined audiences such as homeless men in a shelter viewing *Die Hard* (Fiske and Dawson, 1996) or families at home (Lull, 1990).

Fish's (1982) explication of "interpretive communities" in the creation and maintenance of meaning and the potential inextricability of the individual from the community (p. 14) forms the basis of the connection among individual audience members. Interpretive communities can be constituted through the audience for particular media genres "that share much the same forms of discourse and frameworks for making sense of the media" (McQuail, 1997, p. 19) as in the case of romance readers as explored by Radway (1991). Alternatively, interpretive communities can be seen as arising out of "media use that is typically situation-specific and oriented to social tasks that evolve out of participation in those" communities (McQuail, 1997, p. 19). Fish writes that the "'ways of reading' are extensions of community perspectives" (1982, p. 16) and that an individual's interpretation is inextricable from that of the community's. Interpretation negates the "claims of objectivity and subjectivity . . . because the authorizing agency, the center of interpretive community is at once both and neither" (p. 14). This second example of an interpretive community fits best the religious audience and particularly that audience bounded by denominational or theological lines because that community is not dependent on the media for its creation and maintenance but is constructed as an independent community whose members may hold similar interpretations.

In addition, in accordance with Fish, members of the religious audience are able to perform as members of the same interpretive community while separated from each other. For example, while watching television at home, they may still make similar interpretations as informed by the community membership. This is exemplified through the social structures of organized religion as well as the role of religion in American society in critiquing and/or supporting elements of the culture. The religious audience both reaches in to maintain itself through church services, meetings, and communication such as bulletins and other media and also reaches out through its role as an institution in society, a political actor, and a media audience and critic. This dual role of the religious media audience allows it to form interpretations that inform the personal lives of its members as well as to use those interpretations to exert pressure on not only the media but also on the society that it sees represented in the media.

Recent research on religious audiences for mainstream media finds a conservative/liberal divide in terms of program preferences, interpretations, and approval of programming. This echoes research from other disciplines that finds this divide emerging in terms of both sociologi-

cal indicators such as church attendance and growth and political behavior (Wuthnow, 1988). Through media, religious audiences seek to
position themselves relative to the larger society. Linderman (1997)
writes that in making sense of religion in television "the study of how
audiences understand and use the flow of messages in the mass media
becomes, in part, a study of how people establish their general worldviews and ultimate values" (p. 263). The central role of the media,
then, places it as a site of cultural struggle. Perhaps one reason why
conservative religious audiences continue to use the media they criticize is that media have become ubiquitous and, in some ways, unavoidable. Media occupy the central socializing role that used to be reserved for religion alone. Bendroth (1996) writes in a discussion of
fundamentalism and media from 1930 to 1990 that fundamentalism
previously "helped people negotiate temptations and provide clear
guideposts" for those wishing to live according to fundamentalist values. Media were simply a temptation, not a primary means of cultural
communication. Bendroth found that for fundamentalists media are no
longer simply a detour; the media are unavoidable.

## The Religious Audience as a Public

Scholars in the area of religion, media, and culture have repeatedly
called for the incorporation of religion into the study of culture on the
grounds that religion does connect people to larger elements in society
and provides a means of transition between public and private. Hoover
and Venturelli (1996) write that "[I]t is our view that the status of religion within contemporary mediated discourse has strong implications
for the broader question of public moral discourse, and the fact of the
eclipse of the religious is indicative of a further eclipse, focusing on a
morality, community, and broader public purpose" (p. 260). Wade
Clark Roof also writes that mainstream media programming provides
opportunities for religious audiences to "find expression in secular programming. The media encourage a sense of personal identity that is reflexive, that is a conception of self as constructed and seemingly more
open and protean" (Roof, 1997, p. 65). Others argue that religion is in
itself a bridge between public and private. Cochran (1990) defines the
dynamics essential for institutions (in his examples, religious) that
maintain the criteria for public life and include access to resources, re-
sponsiveness to the larger society, and broad interests. "Religions are

communities of memory, repositories of collective, public traditions, stories, and experiences stretching through time" (p. 54). He contends that this connection of religion between public and private worlds is what provides the physical and spiritual structure and support for organized dissent and protest, "such as Gandhi's campaigns, the civil rights sit-ins, and Operation Rescue" (p. 55). Conservative Protestants, and in this study, Southern Baptists, comprise both an audience and a public; they may be fans of *Touched by an Angel* or *Home Improvement,* but they are also organized through their church, Bible study, and Promise Keepers. One avenue for the maintenance of this public may be the interpretation and adoption or rejection of mainstream media messages as a means of accepting or rejecting the secular world. The conservative Protestant public intersects with the media but is not created by it, nor can it be reduced to an audience; it exists independently of its audience identification (McQuail, 1997, pp. 26, 30).

Distinguishing the audience from the public in this case is important because of the contributions that publics make to civil society; audiences as individuals in their homes do not make such contributions, according to Dahlgren (1995). Dewey also writes that communication, signs, and symbols that create shared experience may create a community or public (1927, p. 142). Habermas emphasizes the indispensability of communication to the public and writes that through communication individuals "come to an understanding with one another about something, that our field of vision changes in such a way that we can see the points of connection for social theory within the theory of communicative action" (1984, p. 337). In a section that applies particularly well to the conservative Protestant public, Habermas writes that the public gathers to debate the rules established by authorities that govern relations, in this case the spheres of commodity exchange and social labor (Calhoun, 1992, p. 9). Writing about religious discourse and transcendence, Habermas (1984) contends that this discourse is created "within communities of the faithful and . . . refers to a common ritual praxis and bases itself in the specifically religious experiences of the individual" (p. 231).

## Method

David Morley (1994) writes that "when it comes to television, the key challenge lies in our ability to construct the audience as both a social and semiological (cultural) phenomenon, and in our ability to recognize the relationship between viewers and the television set as they are mediated by the determinancies of everyday life" (p. 197). With the goal of documenting the role of media in daily life, this project combined in-depth interviews with Southern Baptist parents. Twenty-two couples were interviewed in the fall of 1997; all participating families were members of Southern Baptist congregations with at least one child at home and both parents living in the home. Four Southern Baptist churches participated in this research: one wealthy suburban megachurch, one midtown midsize church, and two smaller and poorer churches.

All of the families had at least one child at home and two parents living together. In 13 of the 22 families both husband and wife worked; in a few cases the wife worked part-time. The parents ranged in age from 26 to 67, and the ages of the children (both in and outside the home) ranged from one month to 36 years. Most families had two or three children. The parents represented a variety of occupations: student, janitor, plumber, homemaker, salesperson, teacher, computer technician, engineer. Annual incomes ranged from $20,000 for a family of three to $130,000 for a family of four; 13 of the families made between $50,000 and $80,000 annually with an overall mean total household income of $56,333.

All the families owned at least one television and approximately half of them subscribed to (but didn't always read) a local daily newspaper. All of the families had one television located in the living room, and over half had second sets in the kitchen and/or the parents' bedroom. None of the parents reported that children had sets in their bedroom(s). Nine of the 22 families had cable—which seems low because of the difficulty in getting any local stations in the town without basic cable. Most families reported listening to Christian gospel music stations, but few listened to Christian talk radio, preferring Rush Limbaugh to Christian hosts. Few families reported receiving Christian-oriented magazines such as *Christianity Today, Focus on the Family,* or specialty Christian magazines, such as the youth-oriented magazine *Brio.* Similarly, few families reported purchasing or borrowing Christian videos for their children either from Christian bookstores or their church library. Of those who did select Christian-oriented videos, they tended to choose either general Bible stories or *Focus on the Family*'s children's series as *Adventures in Odyssey* or *VeggieTales,* both of which are story and song video/audiotape programs. All of the churches had the videos available for parents to check out of the library. This lack of attention to Christian media is interesting given the size of the Christian media industry and the easy availability of magazines, videos, cable programs, and news through mail order, Internet, bookstores, and church facilities.

Interviews with Southern Baptist families echoed media criticism from the Christian media. They showed remarkable consensus on issues of news coverage, potential media dangers, and characterizations of media workers and media conglomerates. However, families didn't seem to know about or pay much attention to this "insider" literature and didn't follow its recommendations to avoid the media or substitute mainstream media with Christian media. This lack of connection between the Christian media and rank-and-file Southern Baptists is perhaps more interesting than a direct top-down dissemination of opinion would be.

## Findings

Interviews with the Southern Baptist families and analysis of Christian media criticism revealed two major related themes in how the leadership and the rank and file interpreted the "threat" of Disney, the convention's response, and the family response to the boycott. Central to the media criticism, the megachurch pastor's sermon, and the rhetoric of others, notably *Focus on the Family,* which joined the boycott, is the language of *betrayal.* Conservative Protestants felt that they were able to count on Disney to portray the cultural ideals with which they agreed and after which they believed the country to be modeled. Disney's representations of happy families, heterosexuality, and reward for virtue made the products safe for family entertainment. The existence of contradictions such as Snow White's evil stepmother and *Fantasia's* magical broom are dismissed by most authors and rank and file, with criticism focused on Disney subsidiaries. While it is possible that Disney seemed the most vulnerable and spectacular of targets because of previous support of Disney by the conservative Protestant community, neither the Christian media criticism nor the families appeared to have considered other potential targets before focusing on Disney. Most seemed to really believe that Disney equaled family entertainment and that a trust that had developed through the parents' own childhood was violated during their children's.

The second theme is *distinctiveness*. Conservative Protestants had been able to embrace Disney and the media when they believed that they shared the same goals. In this, Disney is not much different from other areas of the media. Parents in the study talked longingly about *Leave It to Beaver* and *Gunsmoke*, and those who did subscribe to cable did so, in part, to provide these programs to their children. Without those kinds of programs, parents and Christian media critics have moved to distinguish themselves and their culture from that represented on television. They distance themselves from the media and remind their children that their family's beliefs are opposed by what they see on television. In this way they reinforce their own family's culture by providing a point of discussion and contrast. While families do limit their children's choices to some extent, few appeared to limit actual time in front of the television, which contradicts the teaching of Christian media critics who exhort families to move away from media entertainment. The themes of betrayal and distinctiveness are rooted in a reaction against the culture represented in the media. The first, betrayal, is focused on Disney and the media in general for their products; the second, distinctiveness, is the internalization of media rejection and the reinforcement of the Southern Baptists' own community. As one Southern Baptist messenger at the convention said, "Will a Southern Baptist boycott change The Disney Company? I don't know, but it will change us."

## Betrayal

Both news organization surveys of Baptists after the announcement of the boycott and my interviews with Southern Baptist families revealed an ambivalence about the boycott, although all families were aware of it through either the mainstream media, *The Baptist Standard, Focus on the Family,* or their church. Rank and file understood Disney as a potential threat but were unsure that the boycott was the best way to address the problem. They also demonstrated that their suspicions of Disney came before the convention's consideration of a boycott. However, many families were overwhelmed by the choices to be made and said that they couldn't possibly figure out who owned what when they were trying to make purchasing or viewing decisions. Most opted for a case-by-case basis:

> Disney is so huge and I think to say that we could boycott Disney as a whole was foolish on their part. I think that they [SBC] had motives that

were okay. We don't buy Disney products or watch Disney, not because of the Southern Baptists, but because I think that they went about the Disney boycott all wrong. (Small church family)

All the families articulated the convention's reasoning for the boycott and also understood its voluntary nature:

I think it was based on several things: homosexuality, their acceptance and promotion of it. If it had been any other company . . . but coming from Disney which is supposed to be very family- and children-oriented, they are presenting ideas that go against the Bible and Southern Baptist views. They [Disney] have ABC and there was a lot of programming on that that wasn't very family-oriented. (Megachurch family)

Despite the variety of ways in which families could have supported the boycott or rejected the boycott, they did agree with the reasoning behind it. Many families saw Disney and the interests of the media to be directly counter to their children's and family's interests. One father said, "They [the media and Disney] are after my children. I'm not going to let them have my children." Parents didn't see the issue as a reaction to recent Disney products or actions, but a response to the loss of an ally:

It's been boiling up for some time. The homosexuality was the straw that broke the camel's back. Disney was supposed to be a family-oriented safe place and now here they are and they've bought ABC and they have more "colorful" programs now that push agendas. (Small church family)

Many families highlighted the voluntary nature of the boycott and emphasized that they had made their own choices about whether or not to act against Disney. Others said that they joined not only after the Southern Baptist Convention voted to boycott but also when *Focus on the Family* did as well. Families also emphasized that they had stopped buying Disney before they knew about its policies for gay and lesbian employees and DisneyWorld Gay Days:

I don't believe in their movies for small children. Like the "Hunchback of Notre Dame," we went to see that and it was scary to death. I wouldn't take our son until he was a teenager. They had people with no faces lined up against a wall, spears on the ground and Esmerelda dancing, almost stripping in front of the fire. It was really about the monk's inner sexual desires—and that's a very adult theme. . . . I think that they are masquerading as family entertainment when they are just after money. That's their number one motive-not providing family entertainment. (Small church family)

Another family from a midsize church said that it didn't buy the movies anyway, but now it would also avoid the theme parks after reports from the convention, their church, and their friends. "I know it's dealing with an extreme situation and personally, I wouldn't want to spend $1000 to get to DisneyWorld and I don't want to find homosexuals having a homosexual day." (Midsize church family)

Some families went beyond Disney's perceived unwillingness to stop certain activities in the park or accommodate other groups by claiming that Disney was pushing an agenda that was abhorrent to their values:

They (Disney) openly promote it [homosexuality]. I can see it more and more as their movies come. Not just accepting of it, but pushing it. And I think it's the changes that are gradual, you know Disney's always been doing that. Even the classics and we love them. There aren't many family values anywhere. There's a divorced family or a wicked stepmother. If you look through it, there's not a family unit kind of values happening. Even Walt Disney wasn't. It's not a Christian kind of organization. But we trusted that it wasn't going to really push the kind of lifestyle that it's pushing. I think that Christians somewhere along the line have to draw a line and say, this is it. (Small church family)

Media coverage of the boycott was particularly troubling to clergy and families. They resented the implication that they didn't realize how big the company is or that they thought that they would really be able to change Disney's programming or policies. Many saw the boycott as an opportunity to take a stand and assumed that news coverage would be against them:

The way the media treated the boycott it was like the Southern Baptist Convention did something so stupid, so ridiculous, when there's other causes that do exactly the same thing and it's not going to make any difference. And that's the main point, I don't think the boycott's going to make any difference and it's not going to change Disney's view, but you are raising people's awareness about certain issues and we were treated like it was absurd by the media. (Megachurch family)

Most families said that they would decide on purchases based on individual products, not on brand name. In many ways they seemed frustrated that the convention and the media didn't seem to think them capable of making thoughtful, independent media choices:

> You have to take it on a case by case basis and if Disney's going to make movies that are good for kids to watch, people are going to support it with their money. I heard that Disney's thinking that since the last couple of their movies have been flops they are interpreting that as people don't want family movies, but I don't think that the last string of movies that they have produced have been family movies. (Midsize church family)

Families in the study voiced their concern over representations of family on television, and more than one family said that "the media challenge us as a Christian family" and "the media, they're definitely helping to tear apart the American family." While some Christian media critics have called for conservative Protestants to turn off the media as a way of protecting their children (Schultze, 1994), these families, while willing to limit media by not subscribing to cable or by limiting Disney purchases, did more through discussing media with their children than just turning it off.

## Distinctiveness

The choices made by Southern Baptist parents highlight the way they select media for themselves and their children. Through their continued attention to media while criticizing it, parents showed how they taught their children about the media, the culture, and their own family's values. By selecting shows and by discussing other, more objectionable programs, the parents could create images of acceptable and not acceptable lifestyles while subtly and not so subtly coaching their children to make similar interpretations. In addition, despite the availability of Christian media from cable, church libraries, Christian bookstores, and mail-order media organizations such as *Focus on the Family*, few used these media. As noted previously, fewer than half of the families in the study even subscribed to cable, which would have allowed them, in this market, to receive the *Family Channel* and *Faith and Values/Odyssey* network. This is significant in the context of family and children's viewing because of the lack of programming available for children on network television. Even among the 13 families that did get cable, only a few subscribed to packages including *Nickelodeon* or the *Disney Channel,* which are the only "channels" identified by Wartella et al. (1990) that provide significant media choices for children.

An obvious area for most parents to start in their concern about television is how television families relate to each other. Most parents listed obvious concerns: disrespectful children, idiotic parents, premarital and extramarital sex, and families that just don't appear to be very loving. An area of particular concern is the way fathers on sitcoms are depicted as bumblers and dumber than their wives and children:

> Shows are just trying to be funny and they have things that we don't want the kids to see. Especially kids being disrespectful of the father and like *Home Improvement.* A lot of people like *Home Improvement,* but I think the kids are too disrespectful to their parents and they cut each other down. To me, that's not setting a good example for our kids. I don't think there's anything else (other than *Touched by an Angel* or *Promised Land*) on TV that's family-oriented. (Megachurch family)

In addition to trying to avoid shows that depict negative family relationships, the parents said that it was nearly impossible to not be surprised by commercials that were offensive and had adopted strict policies to manage their children's viewing. Most parents voiced variations on the theme that TV presented the opposite of the values that they wanted their children to have. "We talk with our kids all the time. We try to teach our children and we try to use the shows and lessons as metaphors. [We can't stop it all], though, we watched a football game over the weekend and you have beer commercials and cheerleaders and he's eight, but there are patterns in your mind" (Megachurch family).

In addition to talking with their children, many have policies of what their children can watch and can't watch based on ratings and require that their children be cautious about viewing programs at friends' homes. Other parents tended to only allow their children to socialize within a Christian home-school group or watch television when their parents were in the room, although the second tactic proved difficult for busy parents:

The values it [network TV] has are the exact opposite of what we have. We will watch Lucy almost every night and sometimes we will watch Happy Days—but sometimes it can be a little much, too. . . . We set a very high standard for our children and I'm very proud of that. If it's not G, they don't see it. And if they go to a friend's house and they are going to watch something, they either call here to say we are getting ready to watch something other than G—or they don't watch it. If something comes on now they'll say, Dad, you gotta come change this—it's not G. We probably watch too much, but when you have three kids, you need a little peace. (Megachurch family)

Beyond defining acceptability by ratings and genres (cartoons, sitcoms), most families felt that they had to take each show on a case-by-case basis because of the perceived goal of media producers to sneak in themes about gays and lesbians, sex, or the occult. As previously mentioned, shows that portrayed a gay or lesbian as simply another member of society were particularly problematic. Parents were upset that these characters were portrayed as normal and wished for the programs that either wouldn't depict such characters or that would clearly show that their lives were wrong. "I don't want to sound ugly, but there is also the entire gay lifestyle coming out in the sitcoms. You can't enjoy it with the kids—it's adult TV now" (Midsize church family). Parents of teens were also particularly cautious about sexual themes or shows with extramarital sex. Many of their older children really liked the shows and wanted to watch because their peers did, but the parents claimed that when they realized the themes of the shows, they stopped their children from viewing them:

I think there's just too much violence, sex and cursing. Teenagers especially, they get the ideas from watching the TV for the crimes that they commit. I disapprove of most of the stuff that my daughter watches. They [sitcoms] promote immorality. Most of them never consider the message they are giving to the people that watch them. The other day we were watching and she changed the station and I switched it back and said, "I'm sure that God wants to throw up from that." (Small church family)

In their refusal to go so far as to turn off the set, the families in the study are quite similar to most media users. While their faith creates some differences in interpretation and choices, they are still dependent on the media for information and entertainment. In Ball-Rokeach's

(1985) work describing "individual media-system dependency," she allows for multiple determinants of media dependency including social networks and personal goals. The families in the study watched television to gather information about the weather and upcoming *Xena* episodes. They also watched to gather information that they could use in discussing the plots of shows with friends, the same use that was noted in Morley's family television study (1994). They also watched shows they disagreed with, in part to find out what others were talking about. Their children gained conversational material for connecting with peers in discussions of *Star Trek* or cartoons.

In addition, television provides in the words of one parent, "a little peace," which places them with most parents who use television, to some extent, as a pacifier. The themes and plots of some shows were challenging, however, to the values that Southern Baptist parents were trying to promote to their children, and since they were, for the most part, unwilling to eliminate television, they had to employ other tactics to reinforce their beliefs. In the case of younger children, many parents simply didn't allow their children to watch programs that weren't rated G, and as the children matured, most parents tried to discuss the messages during commercials or during the program. More than one family kept a Bible on the coffee table to refer to during a television show. One parent said that he would watch *Star Trek* with his sons specifically for the Bible study opportunities afforded by the show and its depiction of the future.

## Audience Resistance

Steiner (1988) writes that it is in group resistance to media messages that audiences publicly challenge messages and frameworks within their own "structures, mythologies, and ideology" (p. 3). While the convention scrambled for ways to make its power visible through letter writing and asked families to withhold $100 from Disney, its members acted on the boycott through daily choices and even conversations amongst themselves and those not affiliated with their faith, such as coworkers. The actions of individuals within the group to reject messages are paramount in the maintenance of the group norms and important to their use of media in that they might still view Disney—but balance that viewing with a critique for themselves and their children. As Steiner writes:

Reclaiming and sharing insulting texts may have other purposes besides therapy. Most centrally, the activity gives shape and meaning to group experiences, symbolically marking the group's normative boundaries and reconfirming its convictions and commitments. The group must demarcate its world view from that of the dominant culture. (1988, p. 11)

It is important to note that these parents came up with quite similar interpretations of programs and ways of using those programs to their own advantage without the guidance of Christian media criticism or much leadership from their pastors. Some parents said that they did have the opportunity to discuss these issues in Bible studies on Sunday, and those adult Bible studies are usually organized according to the age of the children, so parents are usually dealing with children at similar stages. It is also likely that since many of the parents have been Southern Baptists or born-again for a while, some since childhood, that they have internalized many of the Christian critiques made of society by conservative Protestants and are applying those critiques to the media.

## Conclusion

By examining the rhetoric of the boycott as promoted by the convention and allied groups such as *Focus on the Family* and juxtaposing that language with the views expressed by the Southern Baptist families, I came away with an understanding of this action that was far more nuanced than had been previously understood. The boycott of the families was a different boycott than that of the convention. The families were more interested in actual programming and its suitability for children than they were in the benefits policies of the Disney corporation. Where Christian media critics called for a total boycott intended to show the might of the conservative Protestant public, Southern Baptist families (and most pastors) saw the fight as futile and limited to simply what they as individuals would get out of such a campaign— not what they might show the world. The boycott's effectiveness came in the reflection of families on the entertainment that they consumed and they provided to their children, in other words, in their actions as an audience and interpretive community.

It is this understanding of conservative Protestants as an interpretive community that connects this group as an audience to this group as a public. Mere audiences can be disconnected groups that might only come together in the same store to make purchases or online in an effort to save a particular show, such as the effort to save *My So-Called Life* from cancellation. They might also "feel" connected to each other, such as the way in which young women might feel kinship with the character of Jamie on *Mad about You*. Interpretive communities, on the other hand, have independent connections with each other outside of any particular medium or genre. The actual program or genre they are viewing is less important than the meaning that they infer from it or the action that they take as a result of their interpretation. The families created meaning from the television, movies, and news that they saw, and that meaning spurred them to reinforce their understanding of the broader culture that they saw reflected in the mass media.

Media and religion are both global and minute in their scope and influence. They are dependent on the people who use and embrace them. They are also powerful and omnipresent. Despite the strongly held beliefs and practices of the Southern Baptists in the study, they were still reliant on media for entertainment, news, and information. On the other hand, the families were also able to be critical of the media and create alternative interpretations of the programming that they saw. Through the practice of their faith, they reflect on the world that they see on television, and when conservative Protestants watch television, they reflect on the values that they embrace as a part of their faith and religious culture.

# References

Anderson, J.A. (1995). The Pragmatics of Audience in Research and Theory. In J. Hay, L. Grossberg, and E. Wartella (Eds.). The Audience and Its Landscape. Boulder, CO: Westview.

Ang, I. (1985). Watching "Dallas." London: Methuen.

Ball-Rokeach, S. (1985). "The Origins of Individual Media-System Dependency: A Sociological Framework." Communication Research 12(4): 485–510.

Bendroth, M.L. (1996). Fundamentalism and the Media, 1930–1990. In D.A. Stout and J.M. Buddenbaum (Eds.). Religion and Mass Media: Audiences and Adaptations. Thousand Oaks, CA: Sage, 74–84.

Calhoun, C. (Ed.) (1992). Habermas and the Public Sphere, Cambridge, MA: MIT.

Cochran, C. (1990). Religion in Public and Private Life. New York: Routledge.

Dahlgren, P. (1995). Television and the public sphere: citizenship, democracy and the media. London: Sage.

Dewey, J. (1927). The Public and Its Problems. New York: Holt.

Fish, S. (1982). Is there a text in this class? The Authority of Interpretive Communities. Cambridge, MA: Harvard.

Fiske, J. and R. Dawson (1996). Audiencing Violence: Watching Homeless Men Watch "Die Hard." In J. Hay, L. Grossberg, and E. Wartella (Eds.). The Audience and Its Landscape. Boulder, CO: Westview.

Habermas, J. (1984). The Theory of Communicative Action. Boston: Beacon.

Hoover, S.M. and S. Venturelli (1996). "The Category of the Religious: The Blindspot of Contemporary Media Theory?" Critical Studies in Mass Communication 13 (September 1996): 251–265.

Linderman, A. (1997). Making Sense of Religion in Television. In S. Hoover and K. Lundby (Eds.). Rethinking Media, Religion, and Culture. Thousand Oaks, CA: Sage, 263–282.

Lull, J. (1990). Inside Family Viewing: Ethnographic research on television's audiences. New York: Routledge.

McQuail, D. (1997). Audience Analysis. Thousand Oaks, CA: Sage.

Morley, D. (1994). Television, Audiences and Cultural Studies. London: Routledge.

Radway, J. (1991). Reading the Romance. Chapel Hill: University of North Carolina.

Roof, W.C. (1997). Blurred Boundaries: Religion and Prime Time Television. In M. Suman (Ed.). Religion and Prime Time Television. Westport, CT: Praeger, 61–68.

Schultze, Q.J. (1994). Winning Your Kids back from the Media. Downers Grove, IL: InterVarsity Press.

Steiner, L. (1988). "Oppositional Decoding as an Act of Resistance." Critical Studies in Mass Communication 5(1): 1–15.

Wartella, E., K. Heintz, and K. Eliza. (1990). "Television and Beyond: Children's Video Media in One Community." Communication Research 17(1): 45–64.

Wuthnow, R. (1988). The Restructuring of American Religion. Princeton: Princeton University Press.

CHAPTER 12

# Critics as Audience: Perceptions of Mormons in Reviews of Tony Kushner's *Angels in America*

DANIEL A. STOUT
JOSEPH D. STRAUBHAAR
GAYLE NEWBOLD

Membership of the Church of Jesus Christ of Latter-day Saints (Mormon) is expanding rapidly (Stark, 1994; Heaton, 1992). As the denomination passes the 11 million–member mark, social science researchers raise a number of questions about the rapid growth of Mormonism. Issues include changing Mormon demographics (Heaton, Goodman, and Holman, 1994; Goodman and Heaton, 1986), cultural tensions of globalization (Young, 1994), as well as the conflicts of Mormon identity and assimilation (Mauss, 1994). Another topic of research focuses on mass media use and the role it plays in the ways Mormons accommodate the larger society (Stout, 1994; Valenti and Stout, 1996). What has not

A version of this chapter first appeared in the journal *Dialogue: A Journal of Mormon Thought,* Winter, 1999.

been examined, however, are the ways mass media such as movies, television, and newspapers tend to describe Mormons.

How religious groups are received by the larger society has much to do with the kinds of information available to citizens. Although messages about Mormons are disseminated through mass media, little is known about what is specifically said and what kinds of media professionals are involved. New research on this issue, however, could expand knowledge about the ways mass media help create the information environments out of which individuals form impressions or make judgments about various religious denominations.

Abbott (1992) argues that society's accommodation of Mormons may be frustrated by recent works of popular literature and drama depicting them as "narrow" and "bigoted." He offers as examples John Gardner's *Mickelson's Ghost,* Edward Abbey's *Desert Solitaire,* John Le Carré's *The Russia House,* and Tony Kushner's dramatic work *Angels in America.* For example, Kushner's Pulitzer Prize–winning play refers to Salt Lake City as a place of "abundant energy; not much intelligence." Abbott fears that these descriptions could make Mormons vulnerable to future stereotyping and biased criticism.

Abbott focuses on literature with admittedly small, elite audiences. The question of whether such portrayals have an impact on larger groups, however, must take into account other intermediary audiences such as newspaper critics, who help disseminate elements of literary portrayal to the larger population. That is, how literary depictions of Mormons in *Angels in America* diffuse into the larger society has much to do with how media organizations filter information through critics, editors, and marketing managers before it is finally conveyed to the public. These individuals are what Kurt Lewin (1947) termed "gatekeepers" who control, shape, and expand information as it flows from one source to another. This chapter investigates what information gatekeepers communicate about Mormons as well as what they discard and examines the mass media as filters of information about religious groups as they integrate within a culture.

## Case Study: *Angels in America*

In order to learn more about how media organizations filter information about religious groups, the authors examine newspaper reviews summarizing the depictions of Mormons in Tony Kushner's play *An-*

*gels in America.* Considered by some to be the major or at least most visible work of the 1990's involving Mormons, *Angels* received both a Pulitzer Prize and Tony Awards for Best Play of 1993 (Part I) and Best Play of 1994 (Part II). Set primarily in New York City, it dramatizes the complex interplay between religion, politics and the AIDS crisis. Although it has a number of themes and subplots, the work revolves chiefly around Prior Walter, a homosexual with AIDS who interacts with three other main characters who are Mormon. At a more general level, the play is about the consequences of the rise of conservative politics and the playwright's views on how well religious institutions offer guidance to society, particularly society's perceived failure to embrace the homosexual community in a time of crisis brought about by the AIDS epidemic.

To say that the main goal of *Angels* is to criticize Mormon theology would not be accurate. Kushner himself asserts that "Mormonism is treated with respect and dignity" (*The Salt Lake Tribune,* November 26, 1995). Yet as Abbott (1992) observes there are scenes in the play, which if taken out of context, could evoke stereotypical notions of Mormons as narrow, superficial, and exclusionary. For example, having heard that Mormons believe in angels, Prior Walter goes to the Mormon Visitor's Center in New York City with some questions. There he strikes up a conversation with Harper Pitt, a valium-addicted, agoraphobic Mormon whose husband, Joe, leaves her to pursue a homosexual affair with Louis Ironson, also a main character.

> PRIOR: Do you believe in angels? In the angel Mormon?
> HARPER: Moroni, not Mormon, the Angel Moroni. Ask my mother-in-law, when you leave, the scary lady at the reception desk, if its name was Moroni why don't they call themselves Morons . . .

Later in the play, when Louis finds out his new lover is a Mormon, he is incredulous:

> LOUIS: But . . . A *Mormon?* You're a . . . a . . . a . . .
> JOE: Mormon. Yes.
> LOUIS: But you . . . *can't* be a Mormon! You're a lawyer! A *serious* lawyer!

The issue here is not so much whether these passages fully capture Kushner's depiction of Mormons in *Angels.* Nor does it matter whether viewers of the play "register Mormonism's presence . . . only as a sort of fanciful local color" (Evenden, 1994, p. 56). The fact is, hundreds of thousands will not see the play firsthand but will rely on the interpretations of critics in the mass media for a summary as well as an opinion about what the play is about. Which depictions of Mormons will critics emphasize in their reviews? Which will they discard? Given that hundreds of major newspapers in the United States have published reviews of *Angels,* such questions are important to those who study the degree to which mass media perpetuate stereotypical notions of particular religious groups.

## Justification for the Study: Media Gatekeepers and Assimilation

This chapter brings together the theoretical concept of *religious assimilation* and the mass communication phenomenon of *gatekeeping.* Given that mass communication researchers and sociologists of religion work in separate fields, these two ideas have been studied in relative isolation with no clear bridge of understanding between them. In order to survive and flourish, all religious groups must be accommodated to some degree by the larger society, and media gatekeepers either facilitate or impede this process by providing the information upon which citizens make judgments about various religious groups. Simply stated, those religious organizations that align themselves most closely with the values and norms of the host society are more likely to receive support and become assimilated, while those whose worldview runs contrary to societal norms usually do not (see discussions in Mauss, 1994; Robbins, 1988; Stark, 1987; Young, 1994). Gatekeepers, whether they be movie critics, editors, journalists, or television program directors, help shape the information environments out of which millions engage in everyday conversations about Catholics, Evangelicals, Fundamentalists, mainline Protestants, Mormons, and other religious organizations.

Scholars and popular writers are divided on the question of how mass media aid the assimilation process. On the one hand, Roof (1993) asserts that recent television programs, novels, and newspaper stories raise the credibility of mainstream religion by giving "serious attention to the spiritual and religious questions" (p. 166). On the other hand, Medved (1992), in his popular book *Hollywood vs. America,* dedicates an entire chapter to how religion is trivialized and degraded in movies and television programs. Similar claims are made by Fore (1987) and Lewis (1977).

Even though important questions are raised by these authors, their work rarely amounts to more than personal speculation about the ability of some artistic works to undermine religious values. What is needed, however, is new research describing how these works are filtered through media decision makers and opinion leaders and passed on to audiences of even greater size. Popular writers often restrict their attention to the actual audience of a movie, play, novel, or television program and forget that first media gatekeepers and then opinion leaders interpret the work for other individuals, many of whom do not experience it firsthand. Of this *two-step flow* of information, Katz and Lazarsfeld (1956) assert that "ideas often seem to flow" from mass media "to opinion leaders and from them to the less active sections of the population" (p. 32). In fact, this idea has been updated by Katz and others to be a multistep flow, in which, for example, *New York Times* gatekeepers decide what they will feature, then television news producers use the *Times* to decide what is most newsworthy, and then the resulting television news reaches a mass audience, even though the *Times* does not. In this case, Kushner creates images and characters about Mormons in a play, and critics decide whether to mention the Mormon characters and themes, which specific characters and themes to cover, and what treatment to give them. Opinion leaders interested in theater may read the reviews and then discuss them with a broader circle of friends, eventually leaving certain images of Mormons with a fairly broad audience. In this study the authors try to expand knowledge about the types of themes and issues gatekeepers focus on when they interpret an artistic work that features a particular religious group, in this case Mormons.

Studies of "gatekeeping" focus primarily on why certain items gain entry to the mass media and why others are rejected. McQuail (1994) argues that there are several factors influencing the decisions of gatekeepers, which include: (1) subjective and arbitrary judgments of writers and editors, (2) personal ideologies and opinions, including views of groups like Mormons, (3) organizational habits and routine, and (4) "news value" or the degree to which the item is perceived to be consistent with the dominant ideologies and values of the audience and the degree to which something is perceived as likely to be interesting to the intended audience. These comprise patterns of what gatekeepers are likely to include or exclude. For example, even though Mormons are prominently featured in *Angels,* will they be as salient to reviewers of the plays as gays or Jews, the other two main groups? Few, if any, researchers have studied the output of media gatekeepers as they interpret artistic works featuring members of particular religious denominations. Therefore, the following general research questions direct the study:

1. Is it possible to identify dominant themes and patterns in the ways Mormons are discussed in newspaper reviews of Kushner's play *Angels in America*?
2. If so, what are the dominant themes and patterns about Mormons?
3. Given the concerns of Abbott (1992) and others, is there a tendency by critics to focus on negative images or themes about Mormons?

At a theoretical level, all three questions address the general issue of how information about religious groups is disseminated to the larger society. By doing so, the study gets beyond the casual and offhanded claims about message effects and provides a more systematic approach to the study of media and the assimilation process.

## Methods

The research method of this chapter is textual analysis of newspaper critics' reviews of *Angels in America*. We analyzed 368 reviews in various newspapers around the country that were available on Lexis-Nexus. That method may have excluded reviews that appeared in smaller papers. We also included two major recent reviews of the Salt Lake production in the two main local papers, the *Deseret News* and the *Salt Lake Tribune*.

As our theoretical perspective reflects, we argue that critics may function as gatekeepers for those who do not see the actual play. Critics' comments about Mormons may function as part of a process of image formation about Mormons for those readers. The critics serve as a second step in a multistep flow of information, which begins with Kushner's creations and flows through various points until images and stereotypes reach a fairly large audience.

However, we realize that textual analysis, like content analysis, is very limited in its scope and generalizability. From the text, we really cannot say much about the intentions of the critics, their opinions about Mormons, or how the plays may have affected those opinions. We can only look at what they have published as a text that newspaper readers will read. We also cannot assume anything about how those reviews will influence readers.

We realize that media texts, like newspaper reviews of plays, have limited effects. Quantitative studies tend to emphasize the importance of the reader in selectively perceiving, remembering, and interpreting such texts (Blumler and Katz, 1974). Qualitative studies about active audiences also tend to reinforce that readers are active and can agree with, negotiate, or reject meanings in such texts (Fiske, 1987; Morley, 1980). However, texts are part of the overall process of sense-making (Shields and Dervin, 1993). So as readers try to make sense of the world, including such relatively low-salience tasks as figuring out who Mormons are, then past or present reading of such texts may well affect their views in at least a modest way.

## Salience of Mormons

Perhaps the most compelling finding is that most reviewers of *Angels in America* did not report anything about the Mormon themes. Despite the salience of Mormon characters in three principal roles, only 68 of 370 reviews mentioned Mormons. It seems that Mormons are not on the cognitive maps of the reviewers, certainly not as much as gay or Jewish cultures, also prominent in the play.

This is a significant example of reviewers acting as gatekeepers. Most of them acted to filter out of their reviews the fact that Mormons were a significant part of the play. In their written texts, most reviewers removed an emphasis on Mormons that Kushner clearly intended. Several interviews with Kushner revealed that he had intended to have Mormons as a significant part of the plays since the beginning, although the two Mormon women characters developed later.

Mr. Kushner told Mr. Eustis he wanted to write a play for five gay male characters, starring Roy Cohn, the Mormons and AIDS. They were sure the N.E.A. would turn the project down. When, to everyone's amazement, they got the $57,000 grant, Mr. Kushner realized that he had proposed a play with five gay men for a theater company consisting of three straight women and one straight man. "I just had to change the story," he remembers.

"That's one of the reasons why the play wound up having eight characters. There's a tremendous amount of accident in all this and that's exciting. I had to write a part for an older actress, too, and the part of Hannah"—the Mormon mother of one of the main characters—"is only there because of that. She is tremendously important to the play and so is Harper, one of the other female parts." Harper, who is married to Hannah's son, "is one of the centers of the play." (*The New York Times,* September 13, 1992, Cheever)

While most theater critic gatekeepers screened Mormons out of their reviews, a number of them did comment on the Mormon characters and the Mormon themes. The following section discusses the themes and characterizations that the critics as gatekeepers and intermediaries in the process of image formation did pass on to their readers.

# General Themes Involving Mormons

## Need for Theories, Laws, and Rules

One of Kushner's larger themes is that the approaching new millennium shows the need for grand theories or religion to guide people. "One of the things the play is saying is that (religious) theory is incredibly important to us and that without it, we don't know where we are going," says Kushner in an interview (*Chicago Tribune,* April 25, 1993, de Vries). Most clearly, at the beginning of the second play, *Perestroika,* the Old Bolshevik character calls for theories to guide us, "not just market incentives."

Most critics seem to like the fact that Kushner addresses such issues. Several see a positive reflection on Mormonism in the fact that Kushner chooses Mormonism as a religion with theories to offer, featured with Judaism and Marxism, even though he doesn't necessarily agree with them.

However, not all critics think Kushner deals well with such material.

Most unsatisfying is Kushner's handling of religion. After divine interventions culminating in a trip to heaven by the dying Prior Walter (Stephen Spinella), we are told that angels and religions have nothing to say about life, only death and the hereafter. That is a rather small perception to serve on so expansive a platter, even for atheists and agnostics in the audience. (Henry, 1993)

Another message noted by some critics is that religious institutions—in this case Mormonism (and Judaism and perhaps even Marxism as a quasireligion)—have outlived their usefulness in today's
world. They see Kushner saying that religion has always provided important guidelines for people, but religions are not keeping up with the
times. "I wanted to show characters struggling to maintain their belief
systems," Kushner said in one interview, "even as those systems were
failing to serve them as useful maps." Their guidelines are no longer
relevant, and the people who continue to try to live by their rules are
"distorting themselves terribly." They are "floundering for guidance"
and "flouting the laws."

> "Millennium" is a juicy adult-themed soap opera with national (and bibli-
> cal and Talmudic) scope. In a chaotic, competitive, plague-riddled world,
> how do you do the right thing for yourself and for your fellow man? Laws
> of Judaism and Mormonism, laws of the government, laws of realpolitik
> (where there are no laws, only winners and losers), and the laws of love are
> all at issue. In a panic, the characters flounder for guidance and flout the
> laws. (*The Washington Times,* May 8, 1995, Pressley )

> "I wanted to show characters struggling to maintain their belief systems,"
> said Kushner, "even as those systems were failing to serve them as useful
> maps." (*The Houston Chronicle,* March 26, 1995, Evans)

> "One of the things the play is saying is that (religious) theory is incredibly
> important to us and that without it, we don't know where we are going,"
> says Kushner. "On the other hand, as systematic approaches to ethics age,
> get passed up by history, the rules and laws which they had laid down be-
> come irrelevant and impossible and we distort ourselves terribly trying to
> adhere to those beliefs. It is a life and death matter to hang onto your be-
> liefs, but it can also be a life and death matter to know when it's time to say
> they aren't working anymore." (*Chicago Tribune,* April 25, 1993, de Vries)

> Indeed, one of the play's main themes—played out as dialectic between Ju-
> daism and Mormonism—is an examination "of how theoretical religion ex-
> ists in a pluralistic society," as one character puts it in "Perestroika."
> (*Chicago Tribune,* April 25, 1993, de Vries)

> The Los Angeles version (which Kushner labels "a mistake") made heaven
> feel more comically political and Cohn, the devil on earth, seem more mag-

ically powerful. The revised Perestroika offers realism with less impact. Kushner even implies that Prior's fevered visions are dreams; he quotes Dorothy's words from The Wizard of Oz on returning to Kansas. Dreams are often sources of revelation in the Bible, but this retreat from the phantasmagorical to the everyday feels like a cheat. If Kushner means that spirituality is no substitute for clear morality and positive mental attitude, he shouldn't need the equivalent of a full working day to get that across. (*Time*, December 6, 1993)

## Mormon Iconography, History, Major Part of U.S. Mythology

Kushner considers both Mormon history and Mormon iconography, or religious symbols, as major aspects of American culture. He gives both prominent space within the play. Kushner uses Mormon iconography, such as angels, buried prophetic books, stone spectacles for translating, and the migration west, even though he repurposes them for his own symbolic ends.

The general feeling we gathered from the critics' reviews is that Mormons were a brave, admirable, and courageous people historically, due to the early pioneers' perilous trek across the country in search of religious freedom. "[H]e envisions another America of truth and beauty, the paradise imagined by both his Jewish and Mormon characters' ancestors as they made their crossing to the new land."

Mormon history and theology are seen as mythic, part of *Angel*'s "spellbinding theater embracing such diverse and compelling native legends as the Army-McCarthy hearings, the Mormon iconography of Joseph Smith, and the MGM film version of *The Wizard of Oz*." Many Mormons may not like having Mormon history and imagery put alongside *The Wizard of Oz*.

Several critics see Mormon themes as aspects of U.S. history and imagery, essentially of American popular culture, more than as reflecting a religion, with a unique religious message. The use of words such as "mythology" may make Mormon readers of such criticism feel that while critics see the early pioneers as people to be admired, the beliefs that drove them west are so much fiction.

And then, even more dazzlingly, come the answers, delivered in three and a half hours of spellbinding theater embracing such diverse and compelling native legends as the Army-McCarthy hearings, the Mormon iconography of Joseph Smith and the MGM film version of "The Wizard of Oz." (*The New York Times,* November 24, 1993, Rich)

Prior's searching pilgrimage is echoed throughout "Perestroika" by the Mormon, Jewish and black characters and implicitly by their pioneer, immigrant and enslaved ancestors. As Prior journeys to heaven, so the Mormon mannequins in a wagon-train diorama come magically to life; Belize is possessed by the ghosts of Abolitionist days while Louis must wrestle with his discarded Jewishness. (*The New York Times,* November 24, 1993, Rich)

This is play writing with a grand design, sometimes written to excess in its wisecracks and philosophizing, but always with an effort to provide historical perspective and political punch to its narrative. In tracing the heritage and odysseys of gays and straights, Jews and Mormons, founding fathers and immigrants, Kushner bridges centuries and cultures for his 20th Century epic, and in so doing he constructs a form and creates a content that in its aspirations and achievements is rare in American drama. (*Chicago Tribune,* May 5, 1993, Christiansen)

But even as Mr. Kushner portrays an America of lies and cowardice to match Cohn's cynical view, he envisions another America of truth and beauty, the paradise imagined by both his Jewish and Mormon characters' ancestors as they made their crossing to the new land. (*The New York Times,* May 5, 1993, Rich)

This two-part, seven-hour "gay Fantasia" explores the AIDS crisis, Mormon mythology and the late sleazy superlawyer Roy Cohn—with plenty of Ronald Reagan/George Bush bashing along the way. (*USA Today,* November 12, 1992, Stearns)

He is the ideal heroic vessel for Mr. Kushner's unifying historical analogy, in which the modern march of gay people out of the closet is likened to the courageous migrations of turn-of-the-century Jews to America and of 19th-century Mormons across the plains. (*The New York Times,* November 10, 1992, Rich)

Director Declan Donnellan proves as adept at integrating the play's oddball styles as he was in Millennium Approaches, which is revived, some-

what recast, in tandem with this new production. When it comes to clari-
fying its meaning, he is understandably less successful. For instance, we
are presumably supposed to contrast the angel who appeared to Joseph
Smith in 1830, and sent him and his Mormon followers bravely across the
American wilderness, with the angel who appears here in black describing herself as a bird of prey. Each of them, we are told, is a "belief with
wings and arms that can carry you." But the demands the newer of the two
is making on Prior remain inscrutable. (*The Times,* November 22, 1993,
Nightingale)

Kushner has said that the story of Joseph Smith's revelation and the Mormon migration west "may be the greatest American story ever told." (*The
Salt Lake Tribune,* November 26, 1995, Melich)

The Angel Moroni led Joseph Smith to the Hill Cumorah, the burial site of
the plates on which the Book of Mormon was inscribed. Smith unearthed,
along with the plates, "bronze bows" with stones set in them. These I take
to have been Bible-era spectacles with rocks for lenses, the Urim and the
Thummim. Before he became a prophet, Smith was known in upstate New
York for his ability to locate buried treasure with use of "peep-stones."
These stones assisted him, as they assist Prior in "Perestroika," in the act
of translating ancient writings. (*The New York Times,* March 27, 1994,
Kushner)

## Mormonism as "Home-Grown" American Religion, Mormon-Jewish Similarities

A few critics reflect Kushner's view of Mormonism, and that of *Angels in America* and *Perestroika,* as a home-grown American religion
that can be respected for its place in America's history and as a major
current force as well. Mormonism is seen as the "home-grown" coun-
terpart to Judaism, the other major religion discussed in the play.

Along with its many historic and pop-culture references (Prior quotes from
films such as "Sunset Boulevard" and "The Wizard of Oz"), Angels is col-
ored by Judaism and Mormonism. The Jewish and Yiddish influences come
from Kushner's Jewish-Lithuanian ancestry. But Kushner also wanted to
depict the influences of a home-grown American religion—hence the presence of Mormon figures such as Joe Pitt and his mother, Hannah. (*The
Houston Chronicle,* March 26, 1995, Evans)

The Mormons I've met have been both right wing and good-hearted, and that, in my experience, is an unusual combination. Mormonism is America's home-grown religion. The Church of Jesus Christ of Latter-Day Saints is notoriously homophobic, as bad in that regard as the Roman Catholic Church. But I do find other aspects of Mormon theology appealing. You're judged by your deeds rather than by your intentions. That's something Mormonism and Judaism share: you have to do good to be good. (The scene above is in the diorama room of the Mormon visitors' center in the play.) (*The New York Times,* March 27, 1994, Kushner)

Hebrew is a language of great antiquity and mystery, and of great compression. Each letter, each word encompasses innumerable meanings, good and evil. The physical letters are themselves totems, objects of power. The Torah, the Book, is to be treated with veneration. Here is another Mormon-Jewish connection: both are People of the Book—only very different books. The aleph is the first letter of the Hebrew alphabet, the seed word, the God letter. This is why, in the play, God is referred to by the Angel as "the Aleph Glyph." The real name of God is, of course, unutterable. (*The New York Times,* March 27, 1994)

## Mormons Key Part of Reagan Era 1980s

Critics note that Kushner uses Mormons as a key and representative aspect of the 1980s, along with AIDS, the fall of Communism, Roy Cohn–style conservatism, and crisis in social institutions like marriage. The typical summary of the play's characters includes several negative characteristics, describing Joe Pitt as a "tightly wound" conservative Republican allied with Cohn and Harper as a Valium-addicted, neurotic housewife.

The reviews contain a number of images using Mormons as examples of 1980s Reagan issues. One is the rise of conservative religions (discussed further below) and the reflection of conservative religions in 1980s politics. Even though Mormons are not as visible politically as groups such as the Christian Coalition, the critics seem to agree that Mormons fit that image. They note the use of a Mormon couple to reflect crises in marriage and, particularly, the effect that has on Harper, who is typically summarized as a pill-popping, neurotic housewife. The critics also pick up on the use of Joe Pitt to reflect contradictions between political conservatism and personal morality crises, as Joe begins to come out of the closet.

When Kushner, now 35, received a commission to write a play five years ago from the small Eureka Theatre in San Francisco, he noted that he wanted to explore three matters in his drama: AIDS, Mormons and Roy Cohn, the Red-hunting aide to Sen. Joseph McCarthy in the '50s who had become a New York attorney of legendary evil powers by the time of his death in 1986. (*Chicago Tribune,* November 13, 1992, Christiansen)

The play—in two parts, "Millennium Approaches" and "Perestroika"—is a seven-hour examination of Reagan-era ethics that addresses such topics as AIDS, Mormonism and the fall of communism. Critics have hailed it as a significant step beyond the usual kitchen sink concerns of much contemporary American drama. (*Chicago Tribune,* April 25, 1993, de Vries)

But the many fantastic flights of "Angels in America" are always tied to the real world of the mid-1980s by Kushner's principal characters, who include two young couples: a pair of gay lovers, and a politically ambitious, rectitudinously Mormon lawyer and his wife. (*Chicago Tribune,* March 6, 1992, Rich)

Almost anything can happen as history cracks open in "Angels in America." A Valium-addicted Washington housewife, accompanied by an imaginary travel agent resembling a jazz musician, visits a hole in the ozone layer above Antarctica. An angel crashes with an apocalyptic roar through the ceiling of a Manhattan apartment to embrace a dwindling, Christ-like man spotted with Kaposi's sarcoma. A museum diorama illustrating the frontier history of the Mormons comes to contentious life. (*The New York Times,* November 10, 1992, Rich)

In his sweeping panorama of American life in Ronald Reagan's America of 1986, playwright Tony Kushner escorts us from the hypocritical centers of power to the dark recesses of a loveless marriage, from the gallows humor of an AIDS patient to the smoldering confusion of a taciturn Mormon. (*The San Francisco Chronicle,* May 27, 1991, Winn)

As if writing in his own fever dream, Mr. Kushner brings into dramatic conjunction the America of the Reagan-Bush years, a dying Roy Cohn, some extraordinary Mormons, the ghost of Ethel Rosenberg, tales of loathsome duplicity in positions of public trust, memories of the Old Left and of the immigrant experience, with everything viewed through the prism of

Prior Walter's tangled relations with his gay friends and ex-lovers. Hovering over it all are God's angels, who have become more insistently meddling since God's recent, somewhat hasty disappearance from heaven. (*The New York Times,* January 30, 1994, Canby)

# Negative Images of Mormons

Most of the critics' negative images were directly or indirectly related to Mormons' roles as emblematic of negative aspects of conservatism. In some cases, this is directly tied to political conservatism and the Reagan 1980s. In other cases, Mormons seem to be chosen to represent religious social conservatives. One critic describes how "The Mormon couple emerge from the wreckage of their false Donna Reed life to go their separate, risky ways."

## Mormons as Politically Conservative

The Mormon character, Joe, in particular seems to the critics to embody conservative contradictions (along with the Roy Cohn character, to which he is linked). He is usually characterized as Reaganite, Republican, and conservative. In Kushner's context, the critics see those characterizations as essentially negative.

Part of what makes the role of Joe Pitt negative for critics is his Republicanism, which they see Kushner as clearly critiquing. Another negative is the conflict of his conservatism with his homosexuality. Another is the negative effect on his wife, Harper, who is seen as neurotic and distressed.

[A] Reaganite Mormon lawyer (*The Toronto Star,* November 27, 1993, VanWagner)

Alternating the real and irreal, which is Kushner's basic scheme, Part Two then moves on to the interlocked narrative. Louis Ironson, who lived with Prior for three years then abandoned him when he got AIDS, continues his affair with Joe Pitt, a button-down Mormon Republican lawyer who has abandoned his wife, Harper. Harper, agoraphobic and delusional, is more or less looked after by her widowed mother-in-law, Hannah, who has moved to Manhattan from Salt Lake City. (*The Boston Globe,* November 24, 1993, Kelly)

There is Harper, the depressed agoraphobic Mormon wife with a Valium addiction, and Joe, her straight-arrow Republican lawyer husband, trying to deny his homosexuality. (*Los Angeles Times,* May 5, 1993, Winer)

Joe Pitt (Jeffrey King) is a young lawyer, a conservative Republican, a Mormon, an idealist and a closet homosexual. The growing emotional distance between him and his wife Harper (Cynthia Mace) has driven the fragile, agoraphobic woman to Valium-induced distraction. (*Daily Variety,* November 10, 1992, Evans)

## Mormons as Straight-Laced, Moralistic, and Conservative

Mormonism is clearly perceived by critics (and Kushner) as a conservative religion. Straight-laced, straight-arrow, button-down, and strict are terms used by critics to evoke the "conservative" image of Mormons. These uses seem to be critical and negative. Such terms come up frequently in descriptions of the characters Joe and Harper.

Part of the problem for Joe and Harper, according to critics, is their link to a moralizing religion that contradicts their own personal crises. They are both implicit and explicit images of falseness and hypocrisy; one critic talks of "their false Donna Reed life."

Joe Pitt, a strait-laced Mormon court clerk, questions his own sexual identity while his Valium-addicted wife, Harper, drifts into hallucinations. (*The Houston Chronicle,* March 26, 1995, Evans)

Meanwhile, the tightly wound Republican Mormon attorney Joe Pitt. (*The San Francisco Chronicle,* October 14, 1994, Winn)

Angels was not only the first gay-centered play to win the Pulitzer Prize for drama, it came to the fore just as the argument about gays in the military was putting the gay cause at center stage for the first time in U.S. history. With its aggressive scorn for Ronald Reagan and Republicanism; for Mormons and moralizing; and its demonic view of lawyer-dealmaker Roy Cohn, a gay-bashing closet gay and a top-level G.O.P. influence peddler for more than three decades, Angels disproved truisms about the unmarketability of political drama. Instead it compellingly reasserted the theater's place in public debate. Hearteningly to theater partisans, Angels generated excitement about a drama comparable to the biggest buzz about musicals. (*Time,* December 6, 1993, Henry III)

Kushner's brilliance is in painting a canvas of epic strokes while hugging close to the intimate lives of his characters. Their interwoven stories revolve around the theme of awakening from denial—awakening from the '80s. The Mormon couple emerge from the wreckage of their false Donna Reed life to go their separate, risky ways. (*The Atlanta Journal and Constitution,* December 5, 1993, Hulbert)

Showy as these performances are, they are not as effective as the solid, less flamboyant work of Jeffrey King, as the tightly wound, sexually confused Mormon attorney Joseph Pitt, and Kathleen Chalfant, whose mournful voice and slight frame are ideally suited for her dual roles as Pitt's steely mother and the implacable ghost of Ethel Rosenberg. (*Chicago Tribune,* November 13, 1992, Christiansen)

Also on stage are Belize (portrayed by K. Todd Freeman, who took the title role last season in Steppenwolf Theatre's "The Song of Jacob Zulu"), a gay black man who becomes Cohn's private nurse in the lawyer's final agonizing days, and a parade of male and female supporting characters portrayed by two actresses—a doctor, a rabbi, an angel messenger, Pitt's strict Mormon mother, a real estate saleswoman and, in one of the play's most telling touches of fantasy, the ghost of Ethel Rosenberg, who was executed as a Russian spy in 1953 and has now come back to haunt Cohn. (*Chicago Tribune,* November 13, 1992, Christiansen)

Joe Pitt (Jeffrey King), an ambitious Republican lawyer clerking in Federal court, deserts his loyal but long-suffering wife, Harper (Cynthia Mace), once his homosexual longings overpower his rectitudinous Mormon credo. (*The New York Times,* November 10, 1992, Rich)

## Mormons as Conflicted, Neurotic

The Mormon couple, Joe and Harper, also seem to represent what critics and Kushner see as a neurotic American society. The characterization of Harper by critics, in particular, dwells on words like pill-popping, Valium-addicted, neurotic, agoraphobic, and depressed. Although this is linked by some critics to her Mormon religion and Joe's conservatism, others see Harper as a broader representative of stressed women in American society.

Harper Pitt (Marcia Gay Harden), pill-popping housewife and devout Mormon, has recurrent nightmares that a man with a knife is out to kill her; she also has real reason to fear that the man is her husband, Joe (David Marshall Grant), an ambitious young lawyer with a dark secret and aspirations to rise high in Ed Meese's Justice Department. (*The New York Times,* May 5, 1993, Rich)

Ms. Harden's shattered, sleepwalking housewife is pure pathos, a figure of slurred thought, voice and emotions, while Mr. Grant fully conveys the internal warfare of her husband, torn between Mormon rectitude and uncontrollable sexual heat. (*The New York Times,* May 5, 1993, Rich)

There is Harper, the depressed agoraphobic Mormon wife with a Valium addiction, and Joe, her straight-arrow Republican lawyer husband, trying to deny his homosexuality. (*Newsday,* May 5, 1993, Winer)

The theme of '80s denial is hammered in further as we learn that Joe, the well-scrubbed married Mormon, is in fact secretly homosexual. (Gannett News Service, May 4, 1993, Le Sourd)

The other pair contains Joseph Pitt, an earnest Mormon attorney and Cohn protégé whose straight arrow exterior conceals repressed homosexuality, and Pitt's wife Harper, a Valium-popping, desperately unhappy woman who fantasizes that she is under the protection of a kind of travel agent angel who will transport her away from her troubled marriage into a clean, clear world. (*Chicago Tribune,* November 13, 1992, Christiansen)

Joe Pitt (Jeffrey King) is a young lawyer, a conservative Republican, a Mormon, an idealist and a closet homosexual. The growing emotional distance between him and his wife Harper (Cynthia Mace) has driven the fragile, agoraphobic woman to Valium-induced distraction. (*Daily Variety,* November 10, 1992, Evans)

He ends up crowing about his part in the destruction of the Rosenbergs, fighting a fraud rap in Washington, and, for reasons never satisfactorily explained, persuading a Mormon law-clerk to join him. Here is the play's second strand, and it, too, has its peppy moments. Nick Reding's uptight Utah boy is, it turns out, desperately struggling to keep himself safely shut in the sexual closet: which helps explain the woozy, half-tranquillised hysteria of his wife, Felicity Montagu. (*The Times,* January 25, 1992, Nightingale)

## Making Fun of Mormons and Overt Anti-Mormonism?

Mormons clearly provide much of the comic relief in the plays. Some of the laugh lines are meant to be at least somewhat negative, reflecting negative associations like homophobia, such as when Harper says, "My church doesn't believe in homosexuals," and Prior retorts, "My church doesn't believe in Mormons." Only one critic observed that the play made fun of Mormons, particularly of the visitors' centers. "The anti-Mormonism is an easy shot," he said.

In Cohn, we get self-loathing, self-righteous confusion, repressed homophobia mixed with mad middle-class moralizing that's a plague of its own. Only a few caveats: Kushner doesn't quite fuse the forces set loose in Act I; his gays seem either victims or heroes; the anti-Mormonism is an easy shot; and, finally, I've no idea why two actresses play men's roles. (*The San Francisco Chronicle,* June 23, 1991, Nachman)

Most critics noted the humor but didn't particularly note it as negative and did not cite the most negative examples, unless one considers the comic use of the "Diorama Room" at the New York Visitors' Center as negative.

Along the way is some devastatingly pointed hilarity in the face of disease and betrayal, much of it at the expense of the Mormons. This includes a couple of priceless scenes involving a diorama at the Visitor's Center displaying the Mormon hegira to Utah, and the depiction of heaven as a place of beauty much like San Francisco. (*Daily Variety,* November 24, 1993, Gerard)

Another depicts Prior and Harper visiting the Diorama Room of the Mormon Visitors' Center in New York, where they envision the dummy of a Mormon pioneer coming to life as Joe—who is then romanced by Louis. In its way, the hilarious scene also conveys the second sight of Prior and Harper in intuiting what has happened to their ex-partners. (*The New York Times,* March 27, 1994)

There are plenty of flashy and cheeky stage effects in "Perestroika," including Prior's fog-swirled climb to heaven on a neon ladder, an amusing
bit of trompe l'oeil that blends live actors with stuffed dummies in a Mormon diorama and Jules Fisher's hellfire-and-brimstone lighting effects.
(*The San Francisco Chronicle,* November 24, 1993, Winn)

Designer Robin Wagner has managed to keep the dozens of scenes flowing, with special effects that are spectacular, yet with a sweetly homemade
look, especially a Mormon diorama that comes hilariously to life. (*Newsday,* November 24, 1993, Winer)

## Mormons as Homophobic

Critics noticed Mormons being used as examples of institutional-
ized homophobia, including Kushner's comments to that effect in interviews. In a play whose sympathy is clearly with the plight of gay
AIDS victims, the use of Mormons as the representatives of homophobia is worrisome for the creation of images about Mormons. It is noted
that Joe's mother, Hannah, has an initial negative reaction to his homosexuality, although she is seen as a character who develops strong
empathy later, particularly for Prior, the AIDS victim.

What would happen to Joe's old-fashioned Mormon mother, Hannah, who
sold her Salt Lake City home and traveled to New York to "rescue" her son
from his newly revealed sexual identity? (*The Houston Chronicle,* April 21,
1995, Evans)

The Church of Jesus Christ of Latter-Day Saints is notoriously homophobic, as bad in that regard as the Roman Catholic Church. But I do find other
aspects of Mormon theology appealing. You're judged by your deeds rather
than by your intentions. That's something Mormonism and Judaism share:
you have to do good to be good. (*The New York Times,* March 27, 1994)

## Mormons as Innocent, Confused

At least one critic sees Mormons as innocent and confused, which
has both positive and negative connotations.

Nor is Joe Pitt the innocent, confused Mormon who must come to grips
with his homosexuality portrayed condescendingly. (*The Times,* May 6,
1993, James)

## Mormons as Ambitious

Similarly, several critics implicitly or explicitly see Joe as representing 1980s-style ambition. While that is not necessarily a negative
image to many people, the perceived consequences in this play seem
negative.

> Ambitious Mormon lawyer Joseph Pitt (Michael Scott Ryan) and his
> Valium-addicted wife Harper (Anne Darragh) are the unhappy couple
> seeking their destiny along separate paths. (*The San Francisco Chronicle*,
> May 27, 1991, Winn)

# Positive Images of Mormons

## Mormons as Conservative but Admirable, Transformed

Not all images of Mormons as conservative are negative. In particular, Hannah, Joe's mother, is shown conservatively and negatively
at first but develops into one of the more admirable people in the
play.

> Whatever one thinks of his artistry or his politics, Kushner is a great en-
> tertainer. The one-liners are hilarious. Hannah, the prim, severely-coiffed
> Mormon elder, who emerges as one of the play's most admirable people,
> asks Prior Walter, the AIDS-stricken unwilling prophet first if he is a ho-
> mosexual and then if he is a hairdresser. "Well it would be your lucky day
> if I was." (*The Boston Globe*, March 16, 1995, Siegel)

The Mormon characters seem to show a positively perceived capac-
ity for growth. The clearest example perceived by the critics is the
transformation of Hannah into a very sympathetic and empathetic
character. But Joe and Harper are also shown as growing out of crises,
although perhaps not in ways that most Mormons would find admirable: Joe acknowledges and acts out his homosexuality, while
Harper decides to leave him and make her own way.

> The other revelatory performance in "Perestroika" comes from Kathleen
> Chalfant, whose playing of multiple roles, including a brief turn as Cohn's

doctor, gives the play some of its most memorable moments. Her transformation as the Mormon mother Hannah Pitt proves one of the most humanizing touches in the play. (*The Hartford Courant*, November 28, 1993)

Chalfant opens "Perestroika" as an elderly male Bolshevik passionately denouncing the worldwide collapse of idealism, then portrays a grim Mormon matriarch who blossoms as an AIDS caregiver. (*The Atlanta Journal and Constitution*, November 17, 1993, Hulbert)

"Anyone who goes to the play with an open mind," Kushner said, "will see that the subject of Mormonism is treated with respect and dignity—that the Mormon characters are not in any way made fun of and the religion is not treated with a lack of respect. I would hope people would go and give themselves a chance to enjoy it." (*The Salt Lake Tribune*, November 26, 1995, Melich)

Kushner said he has boxes full of letters from practicing Mormons and former Mormons, people with connections to the LDS Church. Most of the letters have concerned Joe. "Many are from Mormon men," Kushner said, "who discovered their homosexuality and either left the church or left their marriage or went through an experience similar to Joe's." With the exception of one letter from a woman in Idaho, all have been positive. And the one negative letter turned into a positive experience. "I ended up having a very nice exchange of letter with her," Kushner said, "We're still in touch. She is a practicing Mormon and her concern was more with the sexual explicitness of some of the material." (*The Salt Lake Tribune*, November 26, 1995, Melich)

In this same article, Kushner discusses his first "encounter" with a Mormon named Mary, then a teenager. He describes her as "a great kid, incredibly energetic, straightforward, sincere, intelligent—characteristics I associate with Mormons." He also remembers her LDS parents as "decent people who nevertheless opposed what I consider to be a generally progressive agenda." (*The Salt Lake Tribune*, November 26, 1995, Melich)

## Mormons as Idealistic

Some of the critics perceive Kushner as portraying Mormons, particularly Joe, as idealistic.

At the center is an idealistic young Mormon man, seduced into the dangerous orbit of 1980s power-broker Roy Cohn (the volcanic Ron Leibman), a
demonic gay-baiter who in the Decade of Denial denies he has AIDS. (*The
Atlanta Journal-Constitution,* September 19, 1993, Hulbert)

At the same time, Joe Pitt (David Marshall Grant), a promising lawyer and
devout Mormon, is trying desperately to hold his marriage together. (*The
New York Times,* May 16, 1993, Richards)

## Peaceful Coexistence of Mormons, Jews, Others

Critics perceive the play as showing a final resolution and coexistence of very diverse characters, presumably reflecting the ending of
Part Two, where Hannah sits with Prior, Louis, and Belize. That seems
to reflect a view that Mormons have a peaceful, useful role to play in
America, which "is a land in the midst of social tinkering and tolerance, where the old Mormon world and the, truth to tell, just as old
urban Jewish gay world may not often intersect but can comfortably
coexist."

Consisting of a half-dozen plots that run simultaneously, the play encompasses the AIDS death of superlawyer Roy Cohn, bossy angels, a Valium-
crazed woman who chews down a tree like a beaver and the breaking up
and coming together of gays, Mormons, families and friends. (*USA Today,*
November 24, 1993, Stearns)

He derides individualism as outmoded and urges an ill-defined group responsibility. But one can challenge his easy assumption that Reagan and all
his works have been discredited; his implicit parallel with the Soviet Union
is absurd. Russia may be a land in tumult. America is a land in the midst
of social tinkering and tolerance, where the old Mormon world and the,
truth to tell, just as old urban Jewish gay world may not often intersect but
can comfortably coexist. (*Time,* December 6, 1993, Henry III)

# Misunderstanding Symbols?

One final point to remember is that those outside Mormon culture,
including the critics who are interpreting the play for a larger audience,
do not necessarily understand the symbols in the same way Mormons

do. One telling example concerns the onstage use of temple garments, which many Mormons find offensive. The only one to mention the garments simply cites that the "Mormon's white nightgown" echoes Prior's bed sheet, which the critic sees as "one of many exquisite touches."

> Here Wolfe lets us see and sense the connections—Prior's bedsheet tellingly echoed by a Mormon's white nightgown in one of many exquisite touches—as Kushner twines his two stories together. (*The San Francisco Chronicle*, May 5, 1993, Winn)

## Conclusion

The most striking conclusion is that theater critics do indeed act as gatekeepers between Tony Kushner and the reading public. Despite the visibility of Mormon themes and characters in the plays, only 68 of 370 national reviews mention Mormons. Since one of our main concerns was the degree to which mass communication processes may affect the assimilation of Mormons into American culture, this omission by the gatekeepers is significant.

It would be interesting for further research to uncover why critics make such choices in gatekeeping selections. We can speculate that the choice not to discuss Mormons may have resulted from personal ideology or worldview, lack of background on Mormons (particularly compared with Jews and gays), focus on current issues (particularly AIDS, gays, conservative politics), and a lack of salience of Mormon history and culture for many reviewers. We do know from earlier studies that reporters and editors tend to focus on stories that have immediacy, that are sensational to readers, that touch on issues and themes familiar to readers, that deal with cultures that are familiar to both media professionals and readers, and that are linked to famous personalities (Galtung and Ruge, 1965).

On the other hand, a number of critics did include coverage of Mormons in their reviews. For them, the play incorporates and assimilates Mormon history and symbols into American culture. A number of critics (10) noted that Mormon symbols and mythology were important to the play and to America. One saw the play "embracing such diverse and compelling native legends as the Army-McCarthy hearings, the Mormon iconography of Joseph Smith and the MGM film version of

'The Wizard of Oz'." In this context, six of the critics mentioned the Mormon migration west, and three mentioned the Joseph Smith story. Several of the critics (5) noted that Kushner had singled out Mormons and Jews to focus on in his discussion of the relevance of theology at the turn of the millenium. Two of the critics, including one in an interview with Kushner, noted Mormons as the "home-grown" American religion. These mentions were all essentially positive, although some Mormons may not want to think of their religion and history compared with *The Wizard of Oz*.

Other themes in the reviews were more critical. These largely came as critics focused more on Kushner's use of Mormons as a key part of the 1980s' Reagan era. Some of the reviews that tied Mormons to the 1980s were neutral, such as the critic who noted the "dramatic conjunction of the America of the Reagan-Bush years, a dying Roy Cohn, some extraordinary Mormons, the ghost of Ethel Rosenberg, tales of loathsome duplicity in positions of public trust, memories of the Old Left and of the immigrant experience." However, most mentions of Mormons tied to the Reagan era focus were negative.

While most of the positive mentions were linked to major themes involving Mormonism, most of the negative mentions of Mormons were linked with description of specific characters. Joe Pitt was characterized by 11 reviews as Reaganite, conservative, Republican, well-scrubbed, tightly wound, taciturn, straight-arrow, sexually confused, closet homosexual, innocent, confused, idealistic, ambitious, and a lawyer. Harper was characterized by 10 reviewers as a fragile, woozy, depressed, Valium-addicted, pill-popping, agoraphobic, devout Mormon, shattered, sleepwalking, and desperately unhappy. Hannah is shown by four reviewers in both negative and positive ways, as grim, prim, severely coiffed, and old-fashioned but also as a "Mormon matriarch who blossoms as an AIDs caregiver."

Overall, we find a rough balance between positive and negative mentions of Mormonism by the theater critics who reviewed *Angels*. So while Mormon critics such as Abbott (1992) have some cause to be concerned over the impression that *Angels* gives of Mormons, the play does show an essentially positive acceptance of a great deal of Mormon history and imagery into the American canon of popular culture and history. The diversity of reviewers' themes and images of Mormons cited from *Angels* shows us that we cannot assume just from our own reading of a text like *Angels* what the media professionals' or public's discourse about Mormons will be.

# References

Abbott, S. (1992). One Lord, one faith, two universities: Tensions between "religion" and "thought" at BYU. *Sunstone* (Sept.), pp. 15–23.

Blumler, J. and Katz, E. (1974). *Sage Annual Review of Communication Research.* Beverly Hills, CA: Sage.

Evenden, M. (1994). Angels in a Mormon gaze or utopia, rage communitas, dream dialogue, and funhouse mirror aesthetics. *Sunstone* (Sept.), pp. 55–63.

Fiske, J. (1987). *Television Culture.* New York: Methuen.

Fore, W.F. (1987). *Television and Religion: The Shaping of Faith, Values, and Culture.* Minneapolis, MN: Augsburg.

Galtung, J. and Ruge, M.H. (1965). The structure of foreign news. *Journal of Peace Research* 2, 64–69.

Goodman, K.L. and Heaton, T.B. (1986). LDS church members in the U.S. and Canada. *ANCAP Journal* 12(1), 88–107.

Heaton, T.B. (1992). Vital statistics. In D.H. Ludlow (Ed.), *Encyclopedia of Mormonism.* New York: Macmillan, 4:1518–37.

Heaton, T.B., Goodman, K.L., and Holman, T.B. (1994). In search of a peculiar people: Are Mormon families really different? In M. Cornwall, T.B. Heaton, and L.A. Young (Eds.), *Contemporary Mormonism: Social Science Perspectives.* Urbana and Chicago: University of Illinois Press, pp. 87–117.

Henry, W.A. (1993) Angels of no mercy. *Time,* (Dec. 6) 142(23), 75-76.

Katz, E. and Lazarsfeld, P. (1956). *Personal Influence: The Part Played by People in the Flow of Mass Communication.* New York: Free Press.

Lewin, K. (1947). Channels of group life. *Human Relations* (1), pp. 143–53.

Lewis, G. (1977). *Telegarbage: What You Can Do about Sex and Violence on TV.* Nashville, TN: Thomas Nelson Publishers.

Medved, M. (1992). *Hollywood vs. America: Popular Culture and the War on Traditional Values.* New York: Harper Collins.

Mauss, A. (1994). Refuge and retrenchment: The Mormon quest for identity. In M. Cornwall, T.B. Heaton, and L.A. Young (Eds.), *Contemporary Mormonism: Social Science Perspectives.* Urbana and Chicago: University of Illinois Press, pp. 24–42.

McQuail, D. (1994). *Mass Communication Theory: An Introduction.* London: Sage.

Morley, D. (1980). *The Nationwide Audience: Structure and Decoding.* London: British Film Institute.

Robbins, T. (1988). *Cults, Converts and Charisma: The Sociology of Religious Movements.* Newbury Park, CA: Sage.

Roof, W.C. (1993). Toward the year 2000: Reconstructions of religious space. *Annals of the American Academy of Social and Political Science* 527, 155–70.

Shields, V.R., and Dervin, B. (1993). Sense-making in feminist social science research: A call to enlarge the methodological options of feminist studies. *Women's Studies International Forum* 16(1), 65–81.

Stark, R. (1987). How new religions succeed: A theoretical model. In D.G. Bromley and R.E. Hammond (Eds.), *The Future of New Religious Movements*. Macon, GA: Mercer University Press, pp. 11–29.

Stark, R. (1994). Modernization and Mormon growth: The secularization thesis revisited. In M. Cornwall, T.B. Heaton, and L.A. Young (Eds.), *Contemporary Mormonism: Social Science Perspectives*. Urbana and Chicago: University of Illinois Press, pp. 13–23.

Stout, D.A. (1994). Resolving conflicts of worldviews: LDS women and television. *AMCAP Journal* 20(1), 61–79.

Valenti, J. and Stout, D.A. (1996). Diversity from within: An analysis of the impact of religious culture on media use and effective communication to women. In D.A. Stout and J.M. Buddenbaum (Eds.), *Religion and Mass Media: Audiences and Adaptations*. Thousand Oaks, CA: Sage, pp. 183–96.

Young, L.A. (1994). Confronting turbulent environments: Issues in the organizational growth and globalization of Mormonism. In M. Cornwall, T.B. Heaton, and L.A. Young (Eds.), *Contemporary Mormonism: Social Science Perspectives*. Urbana and Chicago: University of Illinois Press, pp. 43–63.

# Newspaper Articles*

*The Atlanta Journal-Constitution,* September 19, 1993, "Autumn in New York Broadway handicapping the season," Dan Hulbert, Sec. K., p. 1.

*The Atlanta Journal-Constitution,* November 17, 1993, "Broadway drama left to 'Angels' while Gurney revisits WASP angst," Dan Hulbert, Sec. B, p. 11.

*The Atlanta Journal-Constitution,* December 5, 1993, Dan Hulbert, Sec. 5, p. 1.

*The Boston Globe,* November 24, 1993, Wednesday, City Edition, Kevin Kelly, *Living,* p. 37.

*The Boston Globe,* March 16, 1995, Thursday, City Edition, Ed Siegel, *Living,* p. 53.

*Chicago Tribune,* March 6, 1992, Friday, Chicagoland North Edition, "'Angels in America' truly astounding in London," Frank Rich.

*Chicago Tribune,* November 13, 1992, Friday, North Sports Final Edition, "'Angels' treads on '80s sensibilities," Richard Christiansen, chief critic, Sec. 5, p. 1.

*Chicago Tribune,* April 25, 1993, Sunday, Final Edition, "A gay epic, Tony Kushner's play offers a unique view of America," Hilary de Vries, Sec. 13, p.6.

*Chicago Tribune,* May 5, 1993, Wednesday, North Sports Final Edition, "'Millennium' fits times: Drama treats AIDS, homosexuality with sensibility," Richard Christiansen, chief critic, Sec. 1, p. 30.

*Daily Variety,* November 10, 1992, Tuesday, "Angels in America: A gay fantasia on national themes," Greg Evans.

*Daily Variety,* November 24, 1993, Wednesday, Jeremy Gerard.

Gannett News Service, May 4, 1993, Tuesday, "Too much hype, too little substance," Jacques Le Sourd.

*The Hartford Courant,* November 28, 1993, A Edition, Malcolm Johnson, P, G1.

*The Houston Chronicle,* March 26, 1995, Sunday, 2 Star Edition, Everett Evans, *Zest,* 8.

*The Houston Chronicle,* April 21, 1995, Friday, 2 Star Edition, Everett Evans, *Houston,* p. 1.

*Los Angeles Times,* May 5, 1993, Wednesday, Home Edition, "'Angels' on Broadway: Good trip from L.A.; Tony Kushner's play lives up to the hype," Linda Winer, Sec. F., p. 1.

*Newsday,* May 5, 1993, Wednesday, Nassau and Suffolk Edition, "Pulitzer-winning 'Angels' emerges from the wings," Linda Winer, p. 63.

*Newsday,* November 24, 1993, Wednesday, Nassau and City Edition, Linda Winer, p. 60.

*The New York Times,* September 13, 1992, Sunday, Late Edition—Final, "The new season/theater; An angel sat down at his table," Susan Cheever, Sec. 2, p. 7.

*The New York Times,* November 10, 1992, Tuesday, Late Edition—Final, "Marching out of the closet, into history," Frank Rich, Sec. C, p. 15.

*The New York Times,* May 5, 1993, Wednesday, Late Edition—Final, "Angels in America; Millennium approaches; Embracing all possibilities in art and life," Frank Rich, Sec. C, p. 15.

*The New York Times,* May 16, 1993, Sunday, Late Edition—Final, "Visions of heaven—and of hell; Angels in America—An epic, all right, but it's the details and future that count," David Richards, Sec. 2, p. 1.

*The New York Times,* November 24, 1993, Wednesday, Late Edition—Final, Frank Rich, Sec. C, p. 11.

*The New York Times,* January 30, 1994, Sunday, Late Edition—Final, Vincent Canby, Sec. 2, p. 57.

*The New York Times,* March 27, 1994, Sunday, Late Edition—Final, interview with Kushner, Sec. 2, p. 5.

*The Salt Lake Tribune,* November 26, 1995, Sunday, "A look at the characters and themes of 'Angels'," Nancy Melich, Sec. E, p. 3.

*The San Francisco Chronicle,* May 27, 1991, Monday, Final Edition, "Marvelous 'Millennium' first part of Kushner opus strives for connections in an alienating era," Steven Winn, Chronicle Staff Critic, p. E1.

*The San Francisco Chronicle,* June 23, 1991, Sunday, "On the state of charm, doom and Portermania," Gerald Nachman, Sun. Datebook, p. 17.

*The San Francisco Chronicle,* May 5, 1993, Wednesday, Final Edition, "'Angels' gets even better, Broadway production benefits from restaging, recasting," Steven Winn, p. D1.

*The San Francisco Chronicle,* November 24, 1993, Wednesday, Final Edition, Steven Winn, Daily Datebook, p. 19.

*The San Francisco Chronicle,* October 14, 1994, Steven Winn, p. C1.

*Time,* December 6, 1993, U.S. Edition, William A. Henry III.

*The Times,* January 25, 1992, Saturday, "Aids stretched to its limit," Benedict Nightingale.

*The Times,* May 6, 1993, Thursday, "Flying still higher," Jamie James.

*The Times,* November 22, 1993, Monday, "Angels lose their direction," Benedict Nightingale.

*The Toronto Star,* November 27, 1993, Saturday, Final Edition, Vit VanWagner, Arts, p. J3.

*USA Today,* November 12, 1992, Thursday, Final Edition, "Daffy and absolutely divine," David Patrick Stearns, Life, p. 13D.

*USA Today,* November 24, 1993, Wednesday, Final Edition, "Spirit of 'Angels' lifts 'Perestroika'," David Patrick Stearns, p. 1D.

*The Washington Times,* May 8, 1995, Nelson Pressley, Sec. D., p. 1.

------

*Please note that newspaper articles are cited from Lexis-Nexus and therefore page numbers are not always available and publication titles may be abbreviated.

# CHAPTER 13

# Coming out of Abstinence: A Root-Metaphor Study of Nazarenes' Relation to Movies and Media

JOHN DOUGLAS LEPTER
THOMAS R. LINDLOF

The cultural geography of America has always been populated with groups that oppose or resist aspects of popular media. Resistance strategies have been studied on the cultural and political left, but media researchers tend to ignore groups that embrace conservative tenets. Basing their worldviews on traditional sources of moral authority, religious institutions are often on the leading edge of conservative criticism of the media. The views of these institutions can be learned from their publications and pronouncements; however, much less is known about the meanings held by their members, who must decide on a daily basis how to engage with the surrounding culture. This chapter explores the interface between the secular media culture and a conservative, Protestant community—the Nazarene cultural membership—where the historical response has been one of abstinence.

Abstinence (or withdrawal) is not a unique response to the question of media engagement. Many people withdraw from certain types of media for reasons that range from simply wanting to use their time better to motives linked to taste, class, and morality. Christian fundamentalist groups have sometimes responded to the secular world around them by seeking separation. For example, Romanowski's (1995) study of the Christian Reformed Church's policy on movie attendance reveals a posture closely parallel to that of the Nazarenes, with total abstinence serving as the behavioral norm. Umble's (1990) study among the Mennonites found that moviegoing was restricted alongside the traditional prohibitions against smoking, alcohol consumption, social dancing, gambling, and political participation.

Perhaps the more socially cohesive and self-reliant a group is, the more reasonable the decision to withdraw may appear. In any case, conformity of lifestyle to the teachings of faith—i.e., a politics of purity—is seen as critical to the way one must live if one is to be a fully accepted member of these communities. However, with the advent of new media technologies and more diverse ways of using content, strict conformity becomes harder to sustain. The issue of abstinence becomes reframed as the relationship between the institution and the divergent discourses of its membership. This chapter studies a qualitative snapshot of a group coming out of abstinence and entering a more uncertain world of individual decision making.

## Analytic Framework

We conceive of religious community identity in modern life as one of many identities that arise from social interaction. Giddens (1991) observes that change in cross-generational identity was slow in traditional cultures, and changes in life span identity were clearly delineated by rites of passage. Modernity transformed identity into a project where "the altered self has to be explored and constructed as part of a reflexive process of connecting personal and social change" (p. 33). To speak of a biographical identity does presume continuity across time and space but also involves reflexive interpretation of and by the self in a variety of contexts.

These contexts include "reference groups" that influence an individual in the process of self-interpretation (e.g., Merton, 1965). The concept of the reference group ties in with more recent discussions of "interpretive communities" that share a commonality of experience, discourse, and interpretive frameworks (Fish, 1980). With respect to media culture (Lindlof, 1988; Radway, 1984), such communities usually develop around a set of texts whose symbolic potency is either well-known and easily decoded (as in the case of large audiences) or closely bounded and enigmatic to outsiders (as in subcultures).

However, an interpretive community can also develop around an interest in avoiding certain kinds of media altogether. That is, the members of a social collective may construct a body of discourse focusing on the meanings of the excluded media, their sites and messages, and their impacts on the world around them. The role of institutional policy may be to generally set the collective's orientation of avoidance (or withdrawal). This is not to suggest a uniformity of interpretation, nor that the institution will always be successful in this effort of control. As long as they have contact with groups and systems of meaning outside the community, the members will be able to conceive, and act upon, variant viewpoints.

Understanding how a religious interpretive community experiences change depends in part on understanding how power and control in the social collective tend to retard change. As Dennis Mumby (1993) observes, "organizations are not simply neutral sites of meaning formation; rather, they are produced and reproduced in the context of struggles between competing interest groups and systems of representation" (p. 21). Discourse is the principal means by which institutional organizing takes place. Discourse that centers on what is real, normal, and acceptable can be a powerful means of maintaining the positions, privileges, and perspectives of ruling groups. It provides a sense of institutional stability, but in some instances it also "deludes those groups that do not rule about their situation, their possibilities, their real interests" (Berger, 1995, p. 59). Effective ideological strategies avoid the use of theoretical language in favor of practical, unifying, and legitimating themes. A dominant group or class will use available resources, forums, technologies, and roles to articulate meaning in action-oriented terms that are naturally and reasonably supportive of the status quo (Eagleton, 1991).

Foucault's (1978) insights complement this discussion with his view of power as an integral part of the construction of meaning. Power is exercised in promoting certain versions of knowledge and truth that, in turn, are concretely realized through discursive practices. Foucault's (1972) "archaeology" of knowledge examines the historical role of discourse in objectifying, acknowledging, defining, and validating different perspectives and interests within the social formation. Obviously, those who are in a position to articulate dominant discourses can label some perspectives as false, anomalous, or destructive, or they may simply ignore them, thus placing these perspectives beyond the boundaries of "legitimate" discourse.

Mumby (1988) noted that dominant ideologies are often expressed symbolically through the categories of verbal, action, and material symbols. These types of symbols are used for description, energy control (motivation), and system maintenance. Language, and specifically metaphors, establishes and helps to reinforce the commonsense logic of ideological social structures. The social actor is linguistically positioned to respond to a widely accepted worldview; however, the actor may also encounter contradictions between ideology and social and material conditions. That is, the legitimacy of messages may be questioned if there is too wide a gap between ideological strategies and the press of personal experience.

This chapter explores the tensions manifested in discourse sampled from Church of the Nazarene members. Within this religious interpretive community, laity often talk about media attendance—and, specifically, movie viewing—in relation to their life worlds and church teachings. Discursive metaphoric frames are used to identify and interpret the internal tensions that may exist between their lived experiences and codified denominational positions. To the extent that the church's discursive strategies regarding media and popular culture may be said to have an ideological purpose, this chapter seeks to understand ways in which lay members negotiate the sense and effects of these strategies. Two questions guide the analysis: What root metaphors underlie contemporary Nazarene worldviews in relation to media attendance and denominational policy? How does the emphasis of some root metaphors over others serve the ideological interests of different groups? The next section provides an overview of the ethos of the Church of the Nazarene and the development of its media policy, which lays a context for the metaphoric analysis later in this chapter.

## The Ethos of an Organization

A conservative, evangelical, Protestant denomination located within the Wesleyan holiness tradition, the Church of the Nazarene has grown to a reported world membership of over 1.2 million (The Church at Work, 1999, p. 32). An early and consistent theological focus has been the doctrine of entire sanctification: the restoration of sinful people to holiness, or a spiritual purification of heart (the center of one's spiritual being) and life (outward conduct and manifested character). This interest in conduct and character gave rise to the articulation of behavioral norms associated with Nazarene membership.

"Liberty easily becomes license. Better by far the rigid principles of Puritanism than the loose morals which are undermining the present structure of society" (Corlett, 1934, p. 4). Published 65 years ago, this editorial statement still stands as a guide for most Nazarenes. Framing holiness, in part, as separation from a sinful world motivated Nazarene leaders to designate those behaviors considered to be "worldly" for each generation and cultural period. In its moral sense, "worldliness" is viewed as a poor stewardship of life itself, a misdirected investment of resources, time, and energy in evil indulgences. The perennial task for Nazarenes is one of defining the specifics of worldliness in secular cultural activity.

The term "standards" has been the euphemism across the decades for the official written statements of lifestyle requirements in the quadrennial editions of the *Manual of the Church of the Nazarene.* These standards for normative behavior—officially, the General and Special Rules section of the *Manual,* including the Appendix—continue to be seen by many in the membership as the church's "do's and don'ts." For example, the 1898 *Manual* called for the avoidance of "songs, literature, and amusements that are not to the glory of God" (pp. 28–30). Theaters were originally understood as venues for live performance and therefore were sites of defilement. The emergence of motion pictures soon broadened this category and generated discussion in the decades to follow about how to respond to this medium. Commentary on lifestyle issues also often appears in the *Herald of Holiness,* the denomination's official periodical, and has often centered across the decades on media concerns. The *Manual* and the *Herald* are key references for understanding church policy in all matters; importantly, the *Manual* is a resource used by clergy in socializing new members to the norms of the church.

Throughout the century, the growing denomination admonished against moviegoing in these publications. For example, one prominent Nazarene pastor wrote in the *Herald* that "reel life" is far different from "real life" (Reed, 1941, p. 9), citing five reasons for abstinence:

denominational disloyalty, distortion of reality, irreligious content, unwholesome lifestyles, and excessive sensory stimulation. Similar concerns were expressed about radio listening and television viewing. Television, in particular, was seen as a "Trojan horse," since "the very hallowedness of home may cast a false aura of sanctity about the thing which is eating away at the vitals of . . . Christian sensitiveness to sin" (Smith, 1951, p. 6). While radio and television were occasionally given some positive value, the movie industry occupied a distinctly deplorable status for Nazarenes.

Ensuring the fidelity of the next generation to doctrinal and lifestyle positions was an ongoing subject of polemics by church leaders and writers through the 1970s. Nazarenes continued to be warned that darkening the door of a movie theater would amount to an association with evil and unwitting support of a corrupt industry. Responding to the idea of individual "discernment" as a strategy, *Herald* writer Wesley Tracy wrote that "the only safe position is that position which the Church of the Nazarene has always maintained—total abstinence! May God deliver us from ever holding any other view" (Tracy, 1961, p. 5).

By the 1980s, abstinence versus discernment became the key debate, highlighted by "the apparent lack of discrimination in home television, resulting in an inconsistency in regard to our official stand on the movie theater" (*Manual,* 1980, p. 344). Nazarenes were now contending with new media that multiplied the influences alleged to exist in broadcasting and motion pictures. Viewing discernment with regard to VCRs, cable, and satellite programming, anchored in conservative Christian principles, was emphasized by many at the local and national levels of the church. The idea seemed to be that a good Nazarene could discern the valuable and wholesome aspects of a movie, no matter where it was shown. Blanket condemnation of a medium or venue would not be necessary, or desirable, if one could discern well. However, abstinence from "the motion picture theater (cinema) except films produced by Christian organizations" endured as *Manual* policy, despite several General Assembly resolutions to have the words deleted in favor of a policy of careful discernment.

Finally, the 1997 Nazarene General Assembly approved resolutions that advised avoidance of "all types of entertainment ventures and media productions that produce, promote, or feature the violent, the sensual, the pornographic, the profane, or the occultic, or that feature or glamorize the world's philosophy of secularism, sensualism, and materialism, and undermine God's standard of holiness of heart and life"

(*Manual,* 1997, p. 46). In other words, church leaders and pastors were now allowed to talk about "fundamental truths [which] will develop the principle of discrimination between the evil and good to be found in these media" (*Manual,* 1997, p. 46). Although some in the church hierarchy still declare that "what we need in our church in this age of high-tech sin is a principled people who resist and avoid sub-Christian . . . entertainment in any medium" (Tracy, 1997, p. 35), the laity now have a policy which allows them to "discern" the values of each media text they might encounter.

## Method and Data Analysis

Kentucky and Tennessee were selected as the primary sites for this research, based partly on these states' location in the Bible Belt of the United States. Historically, southern Nazarene congregations have been theologically and culturally conservative, slow to change, and supportive of denominational policies. Any evidence of resistance to, and reform of, policy regarding movies would stand out in stark relief against the dominant tenor of this region.

A purposive sampling design was utilized to provide the widest range of responses within a concentrated context. Anonymous written surveys were administered in 1996 to laity at three churches in Tennessee, three churches in Kentucky, and one church in Ohio. Targeted churches represented congregation sizes ranging from under a hundred to several hundreds of parishioners in average attendance. One pastor of a large church declined for fear of stirring up a controversy, and another large church pastor suggested avoidance of a Sunday school class of older, conservative adults for the same reason. Surveys were also given to students from two communication courses at Trevecca Nazarene University in Nashville, a liberal arts institution serving the Church of the Nazarene, to ensure that the sample included 18- to 29-year-old members. The total laity surveys collected and used in this study numbered 126, which provided a sufficient body of text for analysis.

Narrative data were generated through questions used to get the participants "talking" about media issues. (Oral interviews were eschewed in order to encourage more candid responses. Previous experience by the first author indicated that lay members would be more willing to disclose their stances on controversial issues "privately" in writing.)

The first set of three questions called for short essays inquiring about attitudes, beliefs, and feelings concerning movies at the theater, through premium cable channels, and by the rental of movies on video. The next set of questions asked respondents to write their perceptions of the church position and teachings about movie attendance, what they had heard their pastors say about the subject, how consistent their pastors' views were with those of the denomination, and how differences of behavior or viewpoint were handled by the respondents. The last section elicited data involving gender, age, membership status, and media involvement.

The questions guiding this study centered on the identification of metaphors within laity discourse. Root metaphors are instrumental in the expression of social realities (Montagne, 1988) and may be understood as parsimonious, symbolic constructions of worldviews. Barrett and Cooperrider (1990) note that metaphors facilitate the learning of new knowledge, provide a steering function for perceptions and future actions, and transform worldviews by combining two separate realms of experience. Examples of previous research of the relationship of root metaphors to personal and organizational perceptions of social issues include Smith and Eisenberg's (1987) study of labor and management conflict at Disneyland and Montagne's (1988) study of the metaphorical roots of discourse about drugs and drug consumption.

Root metaphors serve as frameworks of grounded belief that may give rise to multiple narrative expressions. Multiple root metaphors may even compete in a given context. It was thought that different kinds of metaphoric language would abound in Nazarene discourse, due to the conflicted nature of the religion-media issues. Identification of metaphorical constructs and the context of their application can lend insight into the positions of groups as well as the points of conflict surrounding this social and media policy issue.

Acknowledging the claim by Lakoff and Johnson (1980) that metaphors are ubiquitous in all linguistic utterances, we selected a basic criterion for recognizing metaphors. They were viewed as instances within a text where two dissimilar concepts were connected, with one being spoken of in terms of the other—for instance, when a respondent speaks of a "media diet." The narratives were read and reread with identified metaphors highlighted in the process. To ensure greater depth in interpretation of the use and meaning of the expressions, notations were made about who wrote them and in what context. The next stage involved examining the metaphoric units for connectedness of meanings. This process of "categorizing" (Lincoln and Guba, 1985) or "semantic sorting" (Smith and Eisenberg, 1987; Koch and Deetz, 1981) was kept flexible. While construction of clusters of metaphors with related patterns of meaning was the analytic goal, it was important to not move toward closure too soon.

In the end stage of analysis, repeated comparisons were made between each metaphoric unit and the developing typology of root metaphors. We also looked at between-category comparisons to make sure the patterns were distinct. Once all units had been placed in a category and no new metaphoric categories could be found, the analysis was complete.

## Nazarene Movie and Media Usage Profile

Of the 126 respondents, 63 of the 79 females indicated that they were members of the Church of the Nazarene as did 38 of the 47 males in the sample. The age profile of the sample corresponded roughly with the overall Nazarene membership: 46 respondents were 18–29 years old; 48 were in the 30–49 year group; 28 were in the 50–69 year group; and four were 70 or older.

Analysis of the media ownership and usage variables revealed a wide range of involvement with media technologies and content. Nearly two-thirds of the sample ($N = 70$) reported "never" or "hardly ever" going to movies at theaters, with most public moviegoing occurring between once every two weeks and once every two months ($N = 44$). Movie viewing on television was a regular activity for most of the sample; however, 30 respondents said they "never" or "hardly ever" watch movies on television. An overwhelming majority had VCRs in their homes, with 116 reporting that they own at least one. Despite this high level of ownership, 48 respondents said that they "never/hardly ever" rent a movie; the other responses were evenly spread across the categories of "once a month" (23), "twice a month" (26), and "once a week" (22). Only two rented movies more than once a week. (Five respondents did not answer this item.)

Only 16 persons said that they subscribe to premium cable channels such as HBO, Cinemax, and Showtime. In open-ended comments, many respondents cited some form of unacceptable content as the deciding factor, along with the perception that movies with unacceptable content dominate these channels. Several written responses commented on the cost of premium channels as a reason for not subscribing. Rental tapes, in contrast, were perceived as allowing a greater range for content discernment.

Results from the three media usage questions were cross-tabulated with gender, age, and church membership and did not generally reveal any unusual relationships. However, theater attendance and video movie rentals were cited much more often by younger respondents. This may simply reflect a normal pattern in which youth are more frequent consumers of these media, or it may indicate that older Nazarenes are more closely tied to denominational standards.

Selected comments on the denomination's stance on movie theater attendance more fully illuminate some of these data. A 31-year-old female noted that "we don't attend movies because of the *Manual* prohibition." She went on to add that "the denomination needs to do something about the plain discrepancy in not allowing movies, [since] most Nazarenes are viewing those same movies after their release as video tapes." A 63-year-old female wrote that she saw "nothing inherently wrong with viewing a movie at a theater. But as long as the church continues with its ban, I would feel uncomfortable attending a movie in a theater." Finally, a 35-year-old female observed that "the doctrine says not to watch movies—one reason why I am not a member. I can't reconcile my limited viewing."

## Laity Narratives

Nazarene discourse about media attendance can be represented by the following five root metaphors: contest, purity, journey, accounting, and color (Lepter, 1996). The first two dominated the discourse, are arguably the most important for the present discussion, and are developed in this chapter. The latter three root metaphors added a richness to the analysis, even if they appeared less often in the discourse. To summarize these metaphors, some members were concerned about their journeys (legitimate lifestyle paths; directional influences upon others), an appropriate accounting of their lives (good stewardship of time and resources; a sense of responsibility toward God and others), and color (black and white as clear vision and oppositional distinctions; gray as symbolic of compromise or indecision).

We should also point out that no metaphor cluster can be identified with either a positive or negative stance on movie attendance, although a predominant valence was observed within some. In other words, terms isolated from their context cannot predict a respondent's position on media issues. While the root metaphors apply differentially to the respondents' media usage situations, there does appear to be a common metaphorical pool from which they draw.

## Who's Winning? Contest as a Root Metaphor

Active participation within contested life experiences is a dominant theme in Nazarene discourse and is represented clearly in laity narratives about media attendance. Three main arenas for contests were suggested by the metaphorical patterns: the battlefield, the courtroom, and the athletic game field.

*The Battlefield.*    The battlefield carries connotations of military struggle and warfare, complete with a sense of imminent danger that was present within the laity narratives. A young adult declared that she would not subscribe to premium cable channels "because whether you watch or not, you are paying for very dangerous and harmful material" (F, 26). She added that VCR rental movies "are not harmless just because they are at your home where no one else knows you are watching them." Another who had "no problem going to a theater to see a movie," because "after all, it's just a building," did recall the pastor admonishing them "to be aware of the snares of sin and to live above sin" (F, 60). Another participant remembered his pastor providing the advice "to be careful and guard our minds from cultural corruption" (M, 39). This spiritual sentry duty relating to movies not only encompassed watchfulness against Satan's influence without, and individual moral and value corruption within, but also included relationships with others in that "it is our influence we have to guard" (F, 54). The majority of instances in which battlefield imagery was employed demonstrated a negative stance against movies. The discourse ranged from calls for theater avoidance to a significant number addressing the perceived ills of premium cable channel movies and video rentals.

One interesting caveat within the battlefield contest metaphor was the idea of the "rebel" as a sense of self. In an interesting generational contrast, an older respondent professed that "I guess some in the Nazarene church might think I am a rebel, but if there is such a thing as a movie that a Christian can go to, I see nothing wrong with it" (M, 60). A young man wrote that "as a proclaiming member of the Church of the Nazarene, I feel the need to live a life in keeping with the church's position on matters so as to not appear as a 'rebel'" (M, 19). Both narratives capture the general idea of nonconformity, with the strong implication that being viewed as disloyal to the mission of the church is the risk one takes as a more independent (or "discerning") media consumer.

Ideologically, the battlefield metaphor was used both by those seeking to preserve the church stand against theater attendance (especially by portraying the denomination in a state of moral retreat) and by those advocating a more liberal policy as traitors to the holiness cause. However, it appeared that the real issue for most respondents centered on content rather than place of viewing. For many, it seemed that inappropriate media content was slipping into Nazarene homes in the form of the "Trojan horses" of VCR rentals, cable channel offerings, and the generally deteriorating morality of programming.

*The Courtroom.*   A second metaphorical framework for expressing the idea of contest can be described as a courtroom setting with ensuing tensions surrounding laws, rules, judgments, and justifications. Again, the contested issue is movie attendance as it relates to the policy of the church and the practice of its parishioners.

The majority of those whose narratives employed a legal motif adopted a position generally supportive of a more liberal approach to movie attendance. Discretion, described by one woman (F, 67) as the new "loophole" in the church's policy, was advocated by several respondents. One argued that "where you view a movie is not a concern for me. What the movie is about and what it portrays is what the movie is judged on" (M, 45). He added that "my being a Christian is not based on 'guidelines' set up by the Church. They are arbitrary, not absolute!"

Fidelity to the perceived rules or laws of the church appeared to be an issue within this area of narrative expression. "I don't get caught up in the legalism of our church," noted one individual, who later commented that movies are "a personal choice. One rule cannot be made for a whole group or all people" (F, 25).

The courtroom metaphor offered many respondents an opportunity to defend a more liberal position. They claimed an ultimate court of appeal to God in light of accusations by their peers or self-condemnation as they perceived denominational standards. In spite of references to a higher power, however, some laity struggled with feelings of apparent guilt.

*The Athletic Game Field.*    While not as profuse as the other two contest themes, there were instances where the language utilized to talk about the media centered on athletic game field contests. Often the athletic contest is seen as more than competition with others on a game field, but actually as competition with oneself to maintain discipline and endurance. Nazarenes have often equated certain behavioral activities such as movie attendance as detriments to spiritual progress and hindrances to successful completion of the contested sites of spiritual struggle. Here, as in some of the other metaphoric roots, we find a connection with scripture references that are important to the theological and doctrinal Nazarene teachings. In this case, a key reference would include Hebrews 12:1b (New International Version): "[L]et us throw off everything that hinders and the sin that so easily entangles, and let us run with perseverance the race marked out for us." The scripture text can be seen as an institutional "prooftexting" of specific behavioral admonitions, where the connection between the scriptural principle and the behavior is often presented as commonsense.

An ideological shift is evident in the application of this metaphor cluster to the movie issue. Historically, the denomination stressed throwing off all hindrances to spiritual progress, such as the movie theater, if a Christian was to successfully complete life's race and win the prize of eternal life. Some of the respondents questioned these "rules of the game" and suggested that the denomination was too strictly calling "foul" in the individual media decisions of members.

## Clean Hands and a Pure Heart: Purity as a Root Metaphor

A second major root metaphor is the idea of purity. The biblical concept of holiness as emphasized by Nazarenes was mentioned earlier in the chapter. Purity relates centrally to that theological emphasis and, in this context, metaphorically addresses the "internal" and "external" issues of an individual's motives and behavior. Purity, and its contrastive concept of pollution (or dirt), figure prominently in discourses throughout history, including the religious (Douglas, 1966/1984) and political (Alexander and Smith, 1993) arenas, as paradigmatic signs for the sacred and the profane, respectively, and thus are potent means for regulating ritual behavior. The analysis revealed two subclusters within the root metaphor, one pertaining to hygiene and the other to diet.

*The Outward Issues of Hygiene.*   Regardless of the medium of delivery for movies, exposure to the refuse of this world was the evident concept of many respondents, who frequently utilized the language of "trash," "garbage," "filth," and "dirty movies." This concern for purity as it related to media is represented in the expression of this 68-year-old male: "We must be very selective in the rental and viewing [of] movies at home where children and young people watch. Again, even renting movies supports the filth of Hollywood. We must be careful as to what enters our minds. We need to stand firm for what is clean and pure."

The metaphorical call to good media content hygiene actually provided some incentive to theater attendance. One woman admitted enjoying G-rated movies at a theater on rare occasions with her family and suggested that her "intake of violence and filth is less through this media than TV" [*sic*] (F, 35). Another noted that VCR tape rentals provide the "freedom to choose healthy family-related viewing" and a premium cable offering "like the Disney Channel seems to be wholesome" (F, 21). These comments overlap with the second cluster in the purity root metaphor: the "internal" issue of media "consumption."

*The Inward Issues of Diet.*   Purity applies to the spiritual wholesomeness of the media menu from which selections are made, and consequences of choice are experienced in areas of spiritual health and growth. Many Nazarenes attribute a deleterious influence of movies on the spiritual and emotional states of individuals, which in turn affects behavioral patterns. "Some movies I feel are certainly not good for our spirits. Many only serve to feed our flesh and our worldly desires" (F, 21). This concern appeared even in the comments of one who took a more relaxed stance in regard to theater attendance. "My first concern is how I think God would feel about it, not necessarily the Church of the Nazarene. Everything in the secular world is not bad. I am very careful about what I feed my soul" (F, 26).

Expressions in the form of admonitions abound in this metaphorical framework. "Movies that are of poor taste should be avoided" (M, 42). One should teach children to be "wise consumers of videos" (F, 45). "What you put in your mind is put there to stay" (M, 36). One woman cautioned against movie influences found both in home and theater. She wrote of the difficulty that videos create in "controlling the movie diet in the home," but also wrote that the theater's "large screen draws you into the fantasy realm and can be addictive in its very nature" (F, 42).

With relatively few exceptions, the root metaphor of purity expressed in both hygiene and dietary terms was applied to issues of appropriate movie content discernment, rather than a blanket prohibition of all media involvement. As such, this construct is ideologically situated to preserve the Nazarene holiness theology, while inclusively realizing commitment from a large segment of the laity to discernment as a media policy.

## Conclusion

Nazarenes are not the only religious group with a separatist past, now standing at the intersection of their beliefs and the secular media environment. As mentioned in the first part of this chapter, Calvinists (Romanowski, 1995) and Mennonites (Umble, 1990) have also tried to keep the world at a distance and created elaborate institutional discourses and policies to justify their norms of withdrawal. Stout's (1996) study of Mormon teachings about mass media reveals a policy in transition. While expressing concerns about being "at war" with mass media that are "unclean" and of "the world"—imagery that closely resembles Nazarene rhetoric—recent Mormon teachings have focused on differentiating between types of media content and media effects. For many conservative Christians, much of what is popular in the media poses a danger to the welfare of their children, families, and values. As Ammerman (1987) notes, in her study of a fundamentalist Christian congregation, "Saying 'no' to television is another of the ways believers discipline their own lives and distinguish themselves from the indulgent world around them" (p. 88). Abstinence may now be less of a viable option, but members often find ample support for their own modes of refusal of commercial culture.

The response of the Nazarene church and other institutions to movies and media attendance can be situated within a larger context of social policy debates, often called the "culture wars" (Hunter, 1991). According to this thesis, intrafaith debates have historically centered on theological issues, but the recent rise of contentious issues in the public sphere have brought about interfaith alliances, sometimes involving coalitions and cooperative ties among Protestants, Catholics, and Jews. Advocacy positions have shifted to categories that Hunter (1991, p. 44) characterizes as orthodox and progressivist. Both lay claims to moral authority, but each defines its assumptions differently.

Adherents to orthodoxy are committed to an "external, definable, and transcendent authority," whereas progressivism tends to emphasize rationalism, subjectivism, and truth as a process in which "reality . . . is ever unfolding" (p. 44). Redal (1995, p. 1) describes the objectives of these philosophical positions in similar ways: "[O]n the one hand, the maintenance of a stable social order established upon a system of absolute values and moral principles; on the other, the ability to live freely in a 'tolerant' and pluralistic society built upon a panoply of sometimes competing but mutually legitimate value systems, none of which takes any social precedence or authority over another."

While open conflict with the progressivist agenda has not occurred among Nazarenes to the extent that it has in other conservative religious communities, some features of progessivism have subtly influenced the thinking of some lay members and church leaders. For earlier generations, denominational loyalty was highly significant, and the church could more easily control the behavior of its members by decree. While most of the respondents in this study continue to support the Church of the Nazarene, there were also unmistakable signs of the limits to their allegiance and the erosion of a previous era's strong self-identity. These changes may be due to the pluralistic contexts in which many of them live, work, and socialize, with the church and its pronouncements on social issues now becoming one voice among many. Accordingly, the power of those with institutional resources to determine the range of acceptable lifestyle choices of the laity has diminished. The comments of one 47-year-old male, with regard to the media policy of abstinence, represent this more outward-looking view: "[I]s it like birth control to the Catholics? The church doctrine is against it, but almost everyone ignores it and views it as outdated and provincial."

The new media technologies have made access to movies and other entertainment content ubiquitous and thrust the Church of the Nazarene into a position of articulating a broader ethical response to the media. However, even as Nazarenes attempt to identify their place in a world where media are a pervasive experience, they still draw from a distinct symbolic environment to map out their worldviews. The growth of interpretive positions within the Nazarene community is still bounded by and expressed through metaphorical language forms, some of which are identified in this study. The meanings that media have for Nazarenes are the products of this common rhetorical inventory that is deeply embedded in their culture and theological ethos. While a few respondents argued that the movies are a "dead issue," most of the discourse examined for this study suggests otherwise. Rather, the focus of talk about movies is shifting away from the theater itself to a vigorous conversation about appropriate media content. As empowered as many of them now feel about discussing these issues, Nazarenes still face difficult decisions about how far to engage the "world."

# References

Alexander, J.C. and Smith, P. (1993). The discourse of American civil society: A new proposal for cultural studies. Theory and Society, 22, 151–207.

Ammerman, N.T. (1987). Bible believers: Fundamentalists in the modern world. New Brunswick, NJ: Rutgers University Press.

Barrett, F.J. and Cooperrider, D.L. (1990). Generative metaphor intervention: A new approach for working with systems divided by conflict and caught in defensive perception. The Journal of Applied Behavioral Science, 26 (2), 219–239.

Berger, A.A. (1995). Cultural criticism: A primer of key concepts. Thousand Oaks, CA: Sage.

The church at work. (1998, April). Herald of Holiness, pp. 32–33.

Corlett, D.S. (1934, July 18). Our position on movies. Herald of Holiness, p. 4.

Douglas, M. (1966/1984). Purity and danger. London: Routledge.

Eagleton, T. (1991). Ideology: An introduction. New York: Verso.

Fish, S. (1980). Is there a text in this class? Cambridge, MA: Harvard University Press.

Foucault, M. (1972). The archaeology of knowledge and the discourse on language (A.M. Sheridan Smith, Trans.). New York: Pantheon.

Foucault, M. (1978). The history of sexuality, Volume I: An introduction. New York: Random House.

Giddens, A. (1991). Modernity and self-identity. Stanford, CA: Stanford University Press.

Hunter, J.D. (1991). Culture wars. New York: Basic Books.

Koch, S. and Deetz, S. (1981). Metaphor analysis of social reality in organizations. Journal of Communication Research, 9 (1), 1–15.

Lakoff, G. and Johnson, M. (1980). Metaphors we live by. Chicago: University of Chicago Press.

Lepter, J. (1996). A root metaphor analysis of Nazarene discourse regarding media attendance. Unpublished doctoral dissertation, University of Kentucky. Lexington, KY.

Lincoln, Y.S. and Guba, E.G. (1985). Naturalistic inquiry. Beverly Hills, CA: Sage.

Lindlof, T.R. (1988). Media audiences as interpretive communities. In J.A. Anderson (Ed.), Communication yearbook (pp. 81–107). Newbury Park, CA: Sage.

Manual of the Church of the Nazarene. (1898). Los Angeles: Church of the Nazarene.

Manual of the Church of the Nazarene. (1980). Kansas City, MO: Nazarene Publishing House.

Manual of the Church of the Nazarene. (1997). Kansas City, MO: Nazarene Publishing House.

Merton, R.K. (1965). Social theory and social structure. New York: Free Press.

Montagne, M. (1988). The metaphorical nature of drugs and drug taking. Social Science and Medicine, 26, 417–424.

Mumby, D.K. (1988). Communication and power in organizations: Discourse, ideology, and domination. Norwood, NJ: Ablex.

Mumby, D.K. (1993). Narrative and social control: Critical perspectives. Newbury Park, CA: Sage.

Radway, J. (1984). Reading the romance: Women, patriarchy and popular literature. Chapel Hill: University of North Carolina Press.

Redal, W.W. (1995, May). Waging the culture war: Media strategies of the Christian right. Paper presented at the annual meeting of the International Communication Association, Albuquerque, NM.

Reed, L.A. (1941, March 22). Why I do not patronize the theater. Herald of Holiness, pp. 9–10.

Romanowski, W.D. (1995). John Calvin meets the creature from the Black Lagoon: The Dutch Reformed Church and the movies, 1928–1966. Christian Scholar's Review, 25 (1), 47–62.

Smith, R.C. and Eisenberg, E.M. (1987). Conflict at Disneyland: A root-metaphor analysis. Communication Monographs, 54, 367–379.

Smith, T.L. (1951, May 7). On turning off the television. Herald of Holiness, p. 6.

Stout, D.A. (1996). Protecting the family: Mormon teachings about mass media. In D.A. Stout and J.M. Buddenbaum (Eds.), Religion and mass media: Audiences and adaptations (pp. 85–99). Thousand Oaks, CA: Sage.

Tracy, W.D. (1961, January 25). Reconsidering our stand against the movies. Herald of Holiness, pp. 4–5.

Tracy, W.D. (1997, October). The question box. Herald of Holiness, pp. 34–35.

Umble, D.Z. (1990). Mennonites and television: Applications of cultivation analysis to a religious subculture. In N. Signorielli and M. Morgan (Eds.), Cultivation analysis: New directions in media effects research (pp. 141–155). Newbury Park, CA: Sage, 141–155.

# CHAPTER 14

# Church Ties and Use of Radio News Genres for Political Information

## JUDITH M. BUDDENBAUM

Researchers working in the community ties tradition (Park, 1929; Merton, 1950; Janowitz, 1952) have generally assumed that those who attend church are more likely than nonattenders to use local news media because they are better integrated into their communities and, therefore, have a greater need to know about it. However, that relationship may not hold true for all religions.

My studies of religion and media use in Middletown (Muncie, Indiana) (Buddenbaum, 1996) confirmed earlier work by Stamm and Weis (1986), which found that Catholics who felt close to their church, attended regularly, read a diocesan newspaper, and were active on behalf of political issues important to the church were more likely to subscribe to the local general circulation newspaper and be involved in other community activities than were less active Catholics. In Middletown, the same pattern held true for Mainline Protestants; however, among more conservative Protestants, those who were more tightly tied to their churches through worship attendance and shared beliefs were least likely to trust, subscribe to, or use daily newspapers for political information.

Those findings are most likely related to religious beliefs and to church teachings about the media. Historically, conservative Protestantism has tended to foster a more dualistic worldview that encourages withdrawal from the world and its temptations (Driedger, Currie, and Linden, 1983). Because their leaders have repeatedly linked mass media to a secular humanist plot to destroy religion (Hunter, 1991; Fackler, 1990), my finding that conservative Protestants tended to avoid using the daily newspaper was not unexpected. However, it does raise the question of where, in light of their recent political activism (Fowler, Hertzke, and Olson, 1999, pp. 97–103, 137–156.), they are getting the information they use for political decision making.

Here, one possibility is radio.

But whether people acquire the same information from radio as they do from other media is questionable. To reach the largest possible audience, television stations and daily newspapers provide a wide array of news and views. However, most radio stations now cater to narrowly segmented target audiences.

Content analyses indicate that talk radio presents a generally conservative slant on public issues; listening to it is associated with distrust of all public institutions, including the media (Hibbing and Theiss-Morse, 1998; Pfau et al., 1999; Hollander, 1996). The same slant can also be found on many Christian radio stations (Hilliard and Keith, 1999). In contrast, National Public Radio appears more liberal, making it a frequent target for religio-political conservatives (Engelman, 1996).

This tailoring of programming to attract a particular audience may make radio the ideal mass medium for conservative Protestants who prefer to expose themselves selectively to information that supports their own worldview (Buddenbaum, 1997; McFarland, 1996). Indeed, many of the religious conservatives interviewed as part of my Middletown studies explicitly said they used Christian radio because, in contrast to newspapers and television, which they described as "biased," Christian news sources "tell it like it is." That finding is consistent with earlier work by Wright and Hosman (1986) that found that the importance people attach to radio as a news source is positively correlated with listening to religious music.

Although some studies have noted a link between community integration and radio listening (Neuwirth, Salmon, and Neff, 1989; Finnegan and Viswanath, 1988; Hofstetter and Gianos, 1997) and others have noted the connection between political conservatism, alienation and use of talk radio (Hibbing and Thiess-Morse, 1998; Pfau et al., 1999; Hollander, 1996), none has looked at the role religion may play in use of the various news genres available on radio. Therefore, this study was designed to explore whether there is a relationship between people's ideological and behavioral ties to a religious community and their use of talk radio, National Public Radio, and Christian radio for political information. It also examines how radio use may fit with use of other media and, ultimately, with political involvement.

Data come from a telephone survey of a random sample of 397 Middletown (Muncie, Indiana) residents conducted in the two weeks before the 1996 presidential election.[1] Muncie was selected for this work because of its history as a site for community studies dating back to the Middletown studies conducted by the Lynds (1929, 1937).

As in my previous Middletown studies (Buddenbaum, 1996), Smith's (1990) classification scheme was used as a guide to place the 391 respondents who identified themselves as Christian into one of five traditions: Pentecostal, other Fundamentalist, Evangelical, Mainline Protestant, and Roman Catholic. Because of demographic differences in media use and church membership, I used partial correlations to control for age, education, and income within and across Christian traditions.

## Radio Listening in Middletown

In the weeks leading up to the 1996 presidential election, National Public Radio attracted the largest number of regular listeners; Christian radio attracted the fewest. At the same time, slightly more respondents reported never listening to NPR than was true for talk radio, which attracted the largest audience when occasional listeners are also included in the number.

Just over half of all survey respondents said they never turned to NPR; 12 percent reported listening to it "a lot" for political information. Only half as many reported listening to Christian radio "a lot"; three-fourths said they never listened. For talk radio, just under half said they never listened; 8 percent said they turned to it "a lot" for political information.

If the three genres could not claim a large audience, neither could they claim an exclusive one. Just under half of all respondents said they listened to both talk radio and Christian radio at least occasionally for political information; one-third reported listening to both talk radio and NPR; one-fifth listened to both NPR and Christian radio.

Consistent with findings from other studies, talk radio appealed to the broadest audience (Hollander, 1996; Stempel and Hargrove, 1996; Hofstetter and Gianos, 1997). NPR attracted an up-scale audience (Ohmann, 1997). As tends to be true for religious television (Hoover et al., 1986; Buddenbaum, 1981), Christian radio appealed to those with lower socioeconomic status.

NPR listeners were older, more educated, and significantly more likely to enjoy a higher income; listeners to Christian radio were significantly more likely to be younger, be less educated, and also have a lower household income. Those who listened to talk radio and to Christian radio were significantly more likely to be conservative in their politics and religion. For the population as a whole, politics and religion were not related to listening to NPR. However, differences emerge when the audiences are examined within and across religious traditions.

## Talk Radio

Overall, using talk radio as a source of political information was highest among Pentecostals and lowest among Roman Catholics. Whereas two-thirds of all Pentecostals in the sample said they listened at least occasionally, only about half of the Roman Catholics said they ever listen. Still 10 percent of the Catholics counted themselves as heavy listeners, as did 13 percent of the Pentecostals. Heavy listening was lowest among Evangelicals, only 3 percent of whom said they listened "a lot."

Although differences in the amount of listening were not statistically significant with this size sample, differences did emerge in the kinds of people within each tradition who used talk radio as a source of political information. In general, the patterns were similar to the ones found for newspaper subscribing and use in Middletown (Buddenbaum, 1996). (See Table 14.1.)

Conservative Protestant listeners tended to be the least tightly tied to their religious traditions through shared belief and religious activity. Pentecostal listeners described themselves as religiously conservative, but not particularly orthodox in their beliefs. Neither were they born again or charismatic. Evangelical listeners did consider themselves born again, but they described themselves as liberal in their beliefs and

TABLE 14.1.    USE OF TALK RADIO FOR POLITICAL INFORMATION IN FIVE
CHRISTIAN TRADITIONS—PARTIAL CORRELATIONS, CONTROLLING FOR AGE,
EDUCATION, AND HOUSEHOLD INCOME

| | Pentecostal (n = 32) | Other Fundamentalists (n = 202) | Evangelical (n = 34) | Mainline Protestant (n = 92) | Roman Catholic (n = 31) |
|---|---|---|---|---|---|
| | | Religious correlates | | | |
| Salience | −.035 | .013 | −.123 | .136 | .172 |
| Beliefs | | | | | |
| Religious conservatism | .417 | .181 | −.344 | .299 | .249 |
| Orthodoxy | .012 | −.012 | −.303 | .154 | −.266 |
| Born Again | .017 | .078 | .198 | .163 | −.421 |
| Charismatic | −.414 | −.271 | −.270 | .125 | none are |
| Behavior | | | | | |
| Attendance | −.364 | .261 | −.522* | .037 | .357 |
| Leadership | −.229 | .168 | −.263 | .212 | .535** |
| Friends | −.042 | .088 | −.068 | .015 | .081 |
| | | Media correlates | | | |
| Use | | | | | |
| Attention | .100 | −.119 | −.366 | .399**** | .009 |
| Effort | .733**** | .105 | .134 | .506**** | −.133 |
| NPR | .006 | .379 | .056 | .197 | .351 |
| Christian radio | −.256 | .299 | .493* | .188 | —a |
| Motives | | | | | |
| Surveillance | .126 | .127 | −.089 | .266* | .003 |
| Learning | .246 | .123 | −.150 | .411**** | −.248 |
| Talk | −.099 | .053 | −.082 | .134 | −.306 |
| Excitement | −.287 | .186 | .382 | .202 | −.058 |
| | | Political correlates | | | |
| Salience | | | | | |
| Election interest | .339 | −.004 | −.209 | .398**** | −.173 |
| Election importance | .147 | .001 | −.138 | .175 | .343 |
| Beliefs | | | | | |
| Political conservatism | .360 | .367** | .256 | .277 | .434 |
| Party (Republican) | .325 | −.128 | −.021 | .210 | .031 |
| Activity | .476* | .151 | −.286 | .214 | .146 |

aBecause only two Catholics reported listening to Christian radio, no figures are reported.
*p < .1, **p < .05, ***p < .01, ****p < .001

scored low on the orthodoxy scale. Neither Pentecostal nor Evangelical listeners to talk radio reported worshipping regularly or being otherwise active in their churches.

Although the other Fundamentalists tended to consider their religion
important and to describe themselves as conservative and born again
but not charismatic, they also tended to rank low on the orthodoxy
scale. At the same time, they worshipped rather regularly and tended to
take an active part in church life. Like the Fundamentalists, Mainline
Protestant listeners tended to take their religion seriously, worship

regularly, and participate in church activities. However, they held religious beliefs that were more conservative than those taught by their religious tradition. Only the Catholic listeners were tightly tied to their church through shared beliefs. They also worshipped regularly and were significantly more likely than nonlisteners to hold leadership positions.

Somewhat isolated from their religious community, Pentecostal listeners to talk radio tended to be quite attentive to the media as a source of political information. They were, in fact, significantly more likely than nonlisteners to say they put a great deal of effort into finding political information from mass media sources although that effort did not translate into heavy use of NPR or Christian radio. Describing themselves as politically conservative and Republican, they were somewhat more likely than nonlisteners to be interested in the presidential election and consider its outcome important to them personally. Therefore, they tended to use the media to find out what was going on and to learn about candidates and issues. They also were significantly more likely than nonlisteners to be politically active.

While the other Fundamentalists did not report paying much attention to political information available through mass media, they were somewhat more inclined than nonlisteners to report putting some effort into getting political information. There was, for example, a tendency for those who listened to talk radio also to use NPR and, to a slightly lesser extent, Christian radio. Significantly more likely than nonlisteners to consider themselves politically conservative but also somewhat more likely to be Democrats, they also tended to be more politically active than Fundamentalist nonlisteners.

Evangelical listeners were significantly more likely than nonlisteners to report relatively heavy use of Christian radio. But with that exception, they seemed as disconnected from the media and from politics as they were from their religious tradition. While they tended to be conservative Democrats, they were significantly less likely than nonlisteners to be active in politics. To the extent they used the mass media, they did so primarily to get into the excitement of the presidential race even though they were not particularly interested in the election and did not consider its outcome important.

Just as they were more connected to their churches through behavioral ties than were their counterparts in more conservative Protestant traditions, the Mainline Protestants who listened to talk radio were significantly more inclined toward mass media use, particularly for surveillance and learning purposes. Like the Fundamentalists, they also tended to listen both to NPR and Christian radio. On matters of politics, however, the Mainline Protestant listeners to talk radio had more in common with Pentecostals than with the other Fundamentalists or Evangelicals. Like the Pentecostals, they described themselves as politically conservative Republicans. They also were significantly more likely to be interested in the presidential race and somewhat more likely than nonlisteners to be active in politics.

Although they were not particularly inclined toward mass media use, Catholic listeners to talk radio were as likely as Fundamentalist and Mainline Protestant listeners to say they listened to NPR. As politically active conservative Republicans, they considered the outcome of the presidential election important.

## National Public Radio

About three-fourths of the Pentecostals and Mainline Protestants said they listened to National Public Radio at least occasionally as did about half of the other Fundamentalists, Evangelicals, and Roman Catholics. Heavy listening ranged from a low of about 10 percent for the Pentecostals to a high of 16 percent of all Catholics in the sample. Again, differences in amount of listening were not statistically significant, but there were differences among traditions in the kinds of church members who listened to National Public Radio. (See Table 14.2.)

As with talk radio, the Pentecostals who listened to NPR tended to be alienated from their religious tradition. They were significantly more likely than nonlisteners to say they don't attach much importance to their religion and to describe themselves as neither born again nor charismatic. Although they were as likely as not to report attending worship services, they tended not to be otherwise active or to have church friends.

Although the other Fundamentalists who listened to NPR were significantly more likely than nonlisteners to have friends at church and somewhat more likely to be active in their church, they tended to be almost as out of step with church teachings as the Pentecostals. These other Fundamentalist listeners did not consider their religion particularly important. They described themselves as religiously liberal and not particularly orthodox, charismatic but not born again.

In contrast to those Evangelicals who tuned to talk radio, the Evangelicals who listened to NPR were very much a part of their church

TABLE 14.2.   USE OF NATIONAL PUBLIC RADIO FOR POLITICAL
INFORMATION IN FIVE CHRISTIAN  TRADITIONS—PARTIAL CORRELATIONS,
CONTROLLING FOR AGE, EDUCATION, AND HOUSEHOLD INCOME

|  | Pentecostal ($n = 32$) | Other Fundamentalists ($n = 202$) | Evangelical ($n = 34$) | Mainline Protestant ($n = 92$) | Roman Catholic ($n = 31$) |
|---|---|---|---|---|---|
| Religious correlates | | | | | |
| Salience | −.502* | −.233 | −.196 | .106 | .350 |
| Beliefs | | | | | |
| Religious conservatism | −.157 | −.241 | −.159 | .079 | .049 |
| Orthodoxy | −.435 | −.061 | .135 | .041 | .014 |
| Born Again | −.602** | −.105 | .037 | .025 | .092 |
| Charismatic | −.475* | .022 | −.415 | −.072 | none are |
| Behavior | | | | | |
| Attendance | .056 | −.080 | .340 | −.009 | .369 |
| Leadership | −.357 | .178 | .650** | .398**** | −.145 |
| Friends | −.310 | .520**** | .211 | .104 | .429 |
| Media correlates | | | | | |
| Use | | | | | |
| Attention | −.545* | −.168 | .596** | .197 | .390 |
| Effort | .146 | .199 | .388 | .203 | .294 |
| Talk radio | .006 | .379** | .056 | .197 | .351 |
| Christian radio | .031 | .054 | .146 | .148 | —a |
| Motives | | | | | |
| Surveillance | .315 | .315* | .121 | −.110 | .505* |
| Learning | .560** | −.071 | .154 | .264* | .361 |
| Talk | −.298 | .456** | −.125 | .082 | −.179 |
| Excitement | −.239 | .250 | .222 | .138 | −.232 |
| Political correlates | | | | | |
| Salience | | | | | |
| Election interest | .072 | .087 | .225 | .223 | −.225 |
| Election importance | −.192 | .330* | −.053 | .165 | .165 |
| Beliefs | | | | | |
| Political conservatism | −.396 | .222 | −.322 | .122 | .130 |
| Party (Republican) | .219 | −.333* | −.249 | .167 | −.351 |
| Activity | −.163 | −.221 | .087 | .207 | −.195 |

aBecause only two Catholics reported listening to Christian radio, no figures are reported.
*$p < .1$    **$p < .05$    ***$p < .01$    **** $p < .001$

even though they tended to describe themselves as religiously liberal
and to say religion was not very important to them. They reported going to church rather regularly and having church friends. They were
significantly more likely than nonlisteners to describe themselves as
church leaders.

Like the Evangelicals, Mainline Protestant and Catholic listeners
seemed very much a part of their churches. They considered their religion important and reported beliefs that closely matched those of their
religious traditions. Although Mainline Protestant listeners tended not to

worship regularly, they described themselves as church leaders. Catholic listeners were less likely than nonlisteners to count themselves among the leaders, but they worshipped regularly and had church friends.

Whereas those Pentecostals who listened to talk radio tended to pay attention to the media and were significantly more likely than nonlisteners to put a lot of effort into getting political information, listeners to NPR were only slightly more inclined than nonlisteners to put effort into getting political information from the mass media. They were, however, significantly more likely to report using the mass media to learn about candidates and issues. At the same time, they were significantly less likely to report paying attention to whatever political information they happened to come across. In contrast to the politically active conservative Republican Pentecostals who listened to talk radio, NPR listeners tended to be politically inactive liberal Republicans who found the presidential election campaign neither very interesting nor important.

Media use by other Fundamentalists appeared to be more focused than that of the Pentecostals, perhaps because they were significantly more likely than nonlisteners to say the outcome of the election was important to them. Politically, these Fundamentalist listeners considered themselves conservative Democrats. Although they tended not to pay much attention to news about politics or to be politically active, they did put some effort into finding political information from the mass media. They were, for example, more likely than nonlisteners to tune in to talk radio and to use mass media to find out what was going on. At the same time, they were significantly more likely than nonlisteners to say they used the mass media to find things to talk about and somewhat more inclined than nonlisteners to use the media for excitement rather than for learning.

Evangelical listeners were significantly more likely than nonlisteners to pay attention to political information. While they tended to put some effort into getting that information and using Christian radio, they were more likely to use media to get into the excitement of the election than for surveillance or learning. They tended to be inactive, liberal Democrats for whom the election was interesting but not important.

Among Mainline Protestants, NPR listeners were somewhat less active in their media use than were talk radio listeners. However, they, too, were significantly more likely than nonlisteners to turn to the media to learn about candidates and issues and somewhat less likely to use

the media for surveillance purposes. Conservative in their political beliefs, these Mainline listeners were more inclined than nonlisteners to
tune in to talk radio and Christian radio. They also tended to be politically active and to consider the election interesting and important.

Catholic NPR listeners were significantly more likely than nonlisteners to use the media for surveillance purposes. They also tended to
use the media to learn about candidates and issues. As part of that use,
they also listened to talk radio. Politically, however, Catholic listeners
to NPR had much in common with conservative Protestant listeners.
Like the Pentecostals and Evangelicals, they tended to be inactive, conservative Democrats. But whereas those Protestants found the election
interesting but unimportant, Catholic listeners to NPR tended to find it
uninteresting but to say its outcome mattered.

## Christian Radio

In Middletown, use of Christian radio as a source of political information was confined almost exclusively to Protestants. Only two Roman Catholics in the sample reported any listening; both listened only
occasionally. Among Protestants, conservatives were significantly
more likely to report heavy listening than were liberals.

Almost half of the Pentecostals said they listened at least occasionally, and 16 percent reported listening "a lot." Only about one-fourth of
the other Fundamentalists or Mainline Protestants and only about one-
third of the Evangelicals reported any listening; fewer than 6 percent
from those traditions said they used Christian radio "a lot" for political
information.

In contrast to the users of talk radio and of NPR, those Protestants
who turned to Christian radio as a news source took their religion seriously and shared the beliefs of their religious traditions. Only the
Mainline Protestants held beliefs that were different from those taught
by their churches; they were significantly more likely than nonlisteners to consider themselves religiously conservative, to hold orthodox
beliefs, and to be both born again and charismatic. (See Table 14.3.)

Only the Evangelicals tended not to worship regularly; only the
Fundamentalists tended not to be active in their church. Like the Pentecostals, the other Fundamentalist listeners were significantly more
likely than nonlisteners to attend church regularly. Both Pentecostal
and Mainline Protestant listeners were significantly more likely than
nonlisteners to count themselves among the church leaders. Listeners

TABLE 14.3.    USE OF CHRISTIAN RADIO FOR POLITICAL INFORMATION IN
FOUR CHRISTIAN TRADITIONS—PARTIAL CORRELATIONS, CONTROLLING FOR
AGE, EDUCATION, AND HOUSEHOLD INCOME

| | Pentecostal (n = 32) | Other Fundamentalist (n = 202) | Evangelical (n = 34) | Mainline Protestant (n = 92) |
|---|---|---|---|---|
| | | Religious correlates | | |
| Salience | .284 | .553**** | .240 | .350** |
| Beliefs | | | | |
|   Religious conservatism | .130 | .382** | .073 | .302** |
|   Orthodoxy | .530 | .284 | .225 | .362** |
|   Born Again | .099 | .499**** | .364 | .470**** |
|   Charismatic | .429 | −.202 | −.073 | .364** |
| Behavior | | | | |
|   Attendance | .538* | .450** | −.015 | .195 |
|   Leadership | .515* | −.055 | .204 | .293** |
|   Friends | .332 | .520**** | .255 | .228 |
| | | Media correlates | | |
| Use | | | | |
|   Attention | −.590** | .413** | .130 | .178 |
|   Effort | −.178 | .384** | .485* | .135 |
|   Talk radio | −.256 | .299 | .493* | .188 |
|   NPR | .031 | .054 | .146 | .148 |
| Motives | | | | |
|   Surveillance | −.367 | .053 | .173 | .123 |
|   Learning | −.319 | −.007 | −.242 | .291** |
|   Talk | −.394 | .186 | .022 | .082 |
|   Excitement | −.162 | .163 | .059 | −.111 |
| | | Political correlates | | |
| Salience | | | | |
|   Election interest | .124 | .055 | .285 | .350* |
|   Election importance | .359 | .023 | .409 | .290** |
| Beliefs | | | | |
|   Political conservatism | −.353 | .437** | .471* | .432**** |
|   Party (Republican) | .020 | .172 | .018 | .201 |
| Activity | −.015 | .170 | −.125 | .368*** |

*Note:* The Catholic tradition has been omitted from this table because only two Catholics in the sample reported any use of Christian radio.
$*p < .1, **p < .05, ***p < .01, ****p < .001$

from all traditions were also more likely than nonlisteners to have church friends.

If the Protestant users of Christian radio were quite similar in their religious beliefs, they differed rather substantially in their use of other media. Pentecostals, in particular, seemed to shun mass media. Only in that tradition was listening to Christian radio negatively associated with attention to or effort in getting information from mass media and with listening to talk radio, as well as with all of the motives for mass media use.

In contrast to the Pentecostals, other Fundamentalist users of Christian radio were significantly more likely than nonlisteners to say they put a lot of effort into getting political information and also to pay attention to that information. They also tended to listen to talk radio; however, their media use was more likely to be for having something to talk about or for excitement rather than for surveillance or learning.

Like the other Fundamentalists, Evangelical listeners to Christian radio put effort into getting information from the mass media. They were also significantly more likely than nonlisteners to listen to talk radio. At the same time, they were disinclined to use the mass media for learning about candidates and issues; among listeners to Christian radio, only Mainline listeners were significantly more likely than nonlisteners to use the media for that purpose.

Across all Protestant traditions, listeners from conservative Protestant traditions considered themselves Republican; only the Pentecostals tended to see themselves as politically liberal. With the exception of the Pentecostals, listeners to Christian radio were generally attentive to news about the political campaign. However, media use translated into political involvement only for the Mainline Protestants. In that tradition, listeners were significantly more likely than nonlisteners to say they were interested in the presidential election, to consider its outcome important, and also to be politically active.

## Conclusion

In contrast to the early work in the community ties tradition, the results of this study support my earlier work indicating that media use varies by religion. At the same time, findings from this study indicate that the links between religion and radio use are much more complex than those for religion and newspapers.

The Catholics who used National Public Radio and talk radio were most tightly tied to their church through shared beliefs and church activity. Unlike the conservative Protestant listeners who were generally more liberal than their tradition and the Mainline Protestants who were more conservative, the Catholics gave responses to the belief questions in line with church teachings. The Catholic listeners also were more regular in worship attendance.

In Pentecostal and Evangelical traditions, those who used National Public Radio and talk radio were, for the most part, somewhat isolated from their religious tradition. The same may also be true for talk show listeners from Mainline churches. However, Mainline listeners to National Public Radio generally gave answers in tune with church teachings on core beliefs; they also tended to be active in their church.

As was true for newspapers, this study found some evidence that conservative Christians whose churches caution against mass media use may engage in selective exposure, shunning media that could threaten their worldview in favor of more supportive information sources. Members of conservative Protestant churches who were tightly tied to their religious tradition through ideological and behavioral ties gravitated toward the ideologically more conservative Christian radio and talk radio. So did Mainline Protestants who were religiously more conservative than their churches.

Although Catholics who were tightly tied to their churches did not shun secular media, they did shun the overwhelmingly conservative Protestant Christian radio stations.

Whatever functions these three radio genres may serve for the individuals who listen to them, the listening patterns suggest there may be real implications at the institutional and societal levels. Within the conservative churches, listening to either talk radio or Christian radio undoubtedly re-enforces the conservative religio-political messages disseminated in individual churches. At the same time, their generally conservative message may be one source of the divisions and diminished loyalty so often noted in Mainline churches, particularly because regular listeners tend to be very conservative, active church leaders.

While the same threat may occur within Catholic churches, it may not be as severe both because members tend not to listen to both conservative talk radio and conservative Christian radio and because those who do listen to talk radio generally hold certain core beliefs that are consistent with church teachings.

But if talk radio and Christian radio may pose some threat to Mainline and Catholic churches, the same thing may be said of National Public Radio and the more conservative churches. Listening may further solidify the more liberal worldview of Pentecostals who listen. Although most of those Pentecostals are so inactive in their church that they are unlikely to bring any divergent viewpoints into the congregation, the Evangelical listeners are in leadership positions; they also tend to worship regularly, have church friends, and use the media for excitement. Although they may not worship as regularly or be in equally high leadership roles within their churches, the other Fundamentalists do have many church friends; they also use the media for surveillance purposes and to have something to talk about, thus making it likely they, too, will share whatever they learn.

If listening to these radio genres has implications for the institutional church, both Christian radio and talk radio would seem to have at least as much power to promote the conservative agenda as does religious television. The links between listening to the more conservative talk and Christian radio genres and political conservatism and activism are much stronger than they are for National Public Radio. In the case of NPR, links between listening and political interest and involvement are positive only for Mainline Protestants.

Talk radio may have its greatest effect on marginal members of the Pentecostal tradition, but it is associated with political inactivity only for Evangelical listeners. Christian radio seems to have its greatest political effect on religiously and politically conservative Mainline listeners. Therefore, conservative radio genres, and Christian radio in particular, may support and magnify conservatism even in otherwise liberal communities.

## Note

1. This study was funded by the Center for Middletown Studies, Ball State University, Muncie, Indiana.

## References

Buddenbaum, J.M. (1981). Characteristics and media related needs of the audience for religious television. *Journalism Quarterly, 51,* 266–272.

Buddenbaum, J.M. (1996). The role of religion in newspaper trust, subscribing and use. In D.A. Stout and J.M. Buddenbaum (Eds.). *Religion and mass media: Audiences and adaptations* (pp. 123–134). Thousand Oaks, CA: Sage.

Buddenbaum, J.M. (1997). Reflections on culture wars; Churches, communication content, and consequences. In M. Suman (Ed.). *Religion and prime time television* (pp. 47–60). Westport, CT: Praeger.

Driedger, L., Currie, R., and Linden, R. (1983). Dualistic and wholistic views of God: Consequences for social action. *Review of Religious Research, 24,* 225–245.

Engelman, R. (1996). *Public radio and television in America.* Thousand Oaks, CA: Sage.

Fackler, M. (1990). Religious watchdog groups and prime-time programming. In J.P. Ferré (Ed.). *Channels of belief: Religion and American commercial television* (pp. 99–116). Ames: Iowa State University Press.

Finnegan, J.R., Jr., and Viswanath, K. (1988). Community ties and use of cable TV and newspapers in a Midwest suburb. *Journalism Quarterly, 65,* 456–463, 473.

Fowler, R.B., Hertzke, A.D., and Olson, R. (1999). *Religion and politics in America: Faith, culture, and strategic choices.* 2nd Ed. Boulder, CO: Westview Press.

Hibbing, J.R. and Theiss-Morse, E. (1998). The media's role in public negativity toward Congress: Distinguishing emotional reactions and cognitive evaluations. *American Journal of Political Science, 42,* 475–498.

Hilliard, R.L. and Keith, M.C. (1999). Waves of rancor: Tuning in the radical right. Armonk, NY: M.E. Sharpe.

Hofstetter, C.R. and Gianos, C.L. (1997) Political talk radio: Actions speak louder than words. *Journal of Broadcasting and Electronic Media, 41,* 501–515.

Hollander, B.A. (1996). Talk radio: Predictors of use and effects on attitudes about government. *Journalism and Mass Communication Quarterly, 73,* 102–113.

Hoover, S.M., Gerbner, G., Gross, L., Morgan, M., and Signorielli, N. (1986). The size of the electronic church: An analysis of data on cable television. Unpublished paper, The Annenberg School of Communications, University of Pennsylvania. Philadelphia.

Hunter, J.D. (1991). *Culture wars: The struggle to define America.* New York: Basic Books.

Janowitz, M. (1952). *The community press in an urban setting.* Glencoe, IL: Free Press.

Lynd, R.S. and Lynd, H.M. (1929). *Middletown: A study in modern American culture.* New York: Harcourt Brace Jovanovich.

Lynd, R.S. and Lynd, H.M. (1937). *Middletown in transition: A study in cultural conflicts.* New York: Harcourt Brace Jovanovich.

McFarland, S.G. (1996). Keeping the faith: The roles of selective exposure and avoidance in maintaining religious beliefs. In D.A. Stout and J.M. Buddenbaum (Eds.). *Religion and mass media: Audiences and adaptations* (pp. 173–182). Thousand Oaks, CA: Sage.

Merton, R. (1950). Patterns of influence: A study of interpersonal influences and of communications behavior in a local community. In P. Lazarsfeld and F. Stanton (Eds.). *Communications research, 1948–49* (pp. 180–219). New York: Harper and Row.

Neuwirth, K., Salmon, C.T., and Neff, M. (1989). Community orientation and media use. *Journalism Quarterly, 66,* 31–39.

Ohmann, R. (1997, November 17). Public radio: A cultural medium for the professional-managerial class. *Chronicle of Higher Education, 44,* 12.

Park, R.P. (1929). Urbanization as measured by newspaper circulation. *American Journal of Sociology. 34,* 60–79.

Pfau, M., Moy, P., Holbert, R.L., Szabo, E.A., Lin, W-K, and Zhang, W. (1999). The influence of political talk radio on confidence in democratic institutions. *Journalism and Mass Communication Quarterly, 75,* 730–745.

Smith, T.W. (1990). Classifying Protestant denominations. *Review of Religious Research, 31,* 225–245.

Stamm, K.R. and Weis, R. (1986). The newspaper and community integration: A study of ties to a local church community. *Communication Research, 13,* 125–137.

Stempel, G.H., III, and Hargrove, T. (1996). Mass media audiences in a changing media environment. *Journalism and Mass Communication Quarterly, 73,* 549–558.

Wright, J.W., II, and Hosman, L.A. (1986). Listener perceptions of radio news. *Journalism Quarterly, 63,* 802–808, 814.

CHAPTER 15

# Testifications: Fan Response to a Contemporary Christian Music Artist's Death

STEPHEN D. PERRY
ARNOLD S. WOLFE

Americans invest more than five hours per week with recorded music in addition to the average 2.9 hours spent using radio ("Abstract," 1997). Also around $9 billion per year is spent on recordings (Black, Bryant, and Thompson, 1997). The Christian music segment of that industry now accounts for three percent of all album sales (Turow, 1999). In fact, according to the Record Industry Association of America's annual consumer profile report, contemporary Christian music (CCM), the most popular genre of Christian music, "ranks sixth in popularity behind rock, country, urban contemporary, pop, and rap" in the area of recording sales (Price, 1997, p. 45). *Variety* magazine reported that Christian music sold nearly 44 million albums in 1997 with an average growth of 22 percent each year in the 1990s. The CCM radio format was also credited with more than 20 million weekly listeners. Furthermore, Christian music attracted $1.3 billion in revenues in 1997 record sales and concert tickets (Sandler, 1998).

The audience for Christian music content in general and CCM in particular is substantial. It can also be said that some members of the CCM audience are committed listeners. Eidenmuller (1998) examined the CCM audience and found that those who listen to this format report higher attendance to the lyrics than fans of any other genre of non-religious music. The CCM audience was also more likely to agree that the words in the music were accurate and truthful and that they advocated societal change. Thus, it seems clear that the CCM audience derives meanings from this music. The question is, what meanings do audience members make of the music they hear? Underlying the question of meanings are issues of how the music facilitates social cohesion, identity, and subculture membership among listeners.

Carroll et al. (1993) studied the "meanings" factor in radio. Their quantitative survey analysis showed a combination of radio uses and impacts. Both the popular and scholarly press contain numerous references to these "uses" and "impacts." While we look at "meanings" qualitatively in this chapter, it is useful to examine what a more quantitatively oriented analysis reveals about musical media.

DeFleur and Dennis (1996) make specific reference to music as a force that may influence thoughts, attitudes, and behaviors, noting that some believe it influences drug use, sexual activity, and satanic worship (see also Larson, 1996) among youngsters. The popular press suggests that racial polarization could be an equally important effect of popular music (Leland, 1992; Painton, 1992; Pareles, 1991). Johnson, Jackson, and Gatto (1995) found a more positive attitude toward violent acts and a reportedly higher likelihood of participating in violence after exposure to violent rap music videos. They also report that African-American youths tended toward materialistic identification and away from a desire to succeed in education after such exposure. Zillmann et al. (1995) on the other hand found no negative effects on African-American high school students after exposure to "gangsta rap." They did, however, find prosocial effects among white students who were more likely to support racial harmony efforts after viewing videos of this genre. Hansen (1995) says these responses are actually similar in cause. She cites primed schema as the causal link that ties these two articles and other experiments together. Both attitudes toward violence and toward racial harmony may reside in complex cognitive structures, or schema, within individuals primed for triggering by external stimuli. Music videos with antisocial themes or those that debunk traditional sex roles have been found to lead to similar attitudes in audience members for at least the short term.

While some scholars see the media as influential, others see social movements and popular culture (including music) as "reciprocal and mutually reinforcing" (Eyerman and Jamison, 1995, p. 464). Instead of seeing the societal and musical developments as different modes of activity, some see them as interactive. This interactivity "contribute(s) to wide-ranging and long-term processes of cultural transformation" (p. 464). Wolfe's (1995) inquiry into the lasting popularity of the Beatles' song-recording "All You Need Is Love" (AYN) documents the "reciprocal and mutually reinforcing" (Eyerman and Jamison, 1995, p. 464) interchange between a subculture (here, Beatles fans or those youthful enough during the 1960s to identify with the subcultural category of "youth") and that subculture's mass media expressions. Wolfe (1995) studied two distinct types of data, namely, books, scholarly articles, and articles from popular sources about the Beatles, AYN, and popular musical communication in general (p. 73). He and his associates then interviewed adults who were college age when AYN was first released and executives at radio stations that still aired the song in the early 1990s. By means of qualitatively analyzing both data sets, Wolfe (1995) found that culture had an impact on the creation and dissemination of the specific musical text. He also discusses its enduring popularity and found that, at least in part, AYN remains popular due to the meanings ascribed to it by listeners. The enduring popularity of certain songs is part of what keeps some social movements alive (Eyerman and Jamison, 1995).

Zillmann and Bhattia (1989) suggest that use of particular genres of media-disseminated music is related to belonging to an "imagined subculture" (p. 265). The use of such music promotes social cohesion and identity among subculture members, which in turn "foster[s] feelings of social power" (Zillmann et al., 1995, p. 5; see also Carroll et al., 1993). Grossberg (1986) echoes this idea in his critical cultural study of rock music when he writes, "Rock and roll is always located within a seemingly random collection of events that interpenetrate and even constitute the specific rock and roll culture, including styles of dance, dress and interaction, images of the band and its fans, etc." (p. 54). The music may promote identification with and imitation of the artist who sings it (Dotter, 1987).

Beyond the Eidenmuller (1998) study, researchers have largely neglected CCM, a contemporary popular music subculture in which music promotes social cohesion and identity among its members. Perry (1993) and Perry and Carroll (1995) examine CCM by focusing on formats used on religious radio stations, but they do not address questions of culture and social cohesion.

One CCM station in the Chattanooga market called itself "Positive Hits 107." Some stations use the term "family country" for country-style pop with mostly religious lyrics. Others dub their CCM format "positive country" (Hawkins, 1996). Early descriptions of CCM even called it "positive pop" (Eberly, 1982).[1] The term "positive" is vague, plausibly a strategic ambiguity (see Eisenberg, 1984). What some see as positive, others see as negative. Promoting specific religious beliefs in pop songs is surely considered positive by those who hold the same religious beliefs professed in the song. However, believing such promotion as at best misguided, an atheist listener, however, might change the station.

Arguments abound on the issue of the fitness of either "positive" or "pop" as veridical descriptors of CCM. This research, however, files these arguments away for another time and focuses on the meanings CCM fans make of this music. Pauly (1991) insists that "for the qualitative researcher, knowledge exists only within the framework of some discourse that names the situation in which such knowledge works" (p. 7). Researchers, he writes, "cannot simply replace or supersede the terms by which groups understand themselves" (p. 6) and the life worlds they construct. Therefore, this chapter calls "positive" that which CCM listeners call positive.

Many musical genres may have songs that promote values fans call positive. The Beatles' "All You Need is Love" exemplifies a song used to promote love during a time of world strife (Wolfe, 1995). Nevertheless, only in CCM are the beneficial claims of those who make and air the music so overt.

## The Research Question

This chapter examines the impact and uses (i.e., the "meanings" in Carroll et al.'s [1993] term) of CCM in the lives of its fans. These meanings are categorized as either spiritual or nonspiritual, and the claimed depth or importance of such meanings for fans is reported and analyzed. Succinctly stated, the research question is:

What meanings do CCM fans make of the life and music of one CCM recording artist as revealed by a record of fan responses inscribed in the wake of the announcement of his unexpected death?

## The Sample for Analysis

While there are many artists and groups performing music in the CCM genre, an unexpected tragedy led many fans to voice their experiences with the music of one particular artist, Rich Mullins. Mullins, 42, was killed in a traffic accident near Peoria, Illinois, on September 19, 1997. He was en route to play a concert in Wichita, Kansas (Rockafellow, 1997). Over the next week, a CCM radio station in the Peoria market dedicated a tribute line for callers to leave a 60-second message about what Rich Mullins' music had meant to them. Those calls were aired with only minor editing for clarity and playability one week after the accident (phone interview with Chuck Pryor, program director, September 25, 1997). The resulting tributes were one part of the data analyzed.

An additional, and much lengthier, source of data was identified on an Internet site for fans of the late artist. Upon hearing of Mullins' death, a college student fan created a new page on his Rich Mullins fan site specifically for the posting of e-mailed tributes. The page's text stated, "I am in the process of compiling [tributes] and I hope to print them out and bind it in a book form to send to his mother" (Williams, 1997). He acknowledged the "thousands" of people who had e-mailed him with their "sorrow and grief, as well as their expressions of thanksgiving and joy at the miracle of Rich's ministry." He then indicated that he would post all e-mails received so that "with the words of support from each other, we can together praise God for a life well lived while dealing with our own sorrow at his passing." Since the e-mailed postings received by September 26, one week after Mullins' passing, took up 100 printed pages in small type font, and since this date coincided with the date of the radio tribute, that date was used as a cut off for tributes from this source.

A third, smaller, sample of tributes was gathered from another Internet site that was found a few days later. *CCM Magazine*'s web site was also found to have a tribute page. However, the magazine's online staff had only selectively posted e-mails on its site. Nevertheless, these were included because they were quality narratives that revealed meanings attributed to CCM by fans ("Rich Mullins Tribute," 1997).

# A Case for Representativeness

A fundamental assumption guiding this study is that the fan response to Mullins' death signifies meanings assigned not only to his music but to CCM as a genre. Our assumption is rooted in the following considerations: (1) since Mullins was both a singer and songwriter, we considered which musical artists had recorded his songs, (2) we examined and analyzed what had been written about him in the industry's premier magazine, *CCM Magazine,* and (3) we looked for evidence that his songs had received high enough sales and airplay to be accorded "hit" status. Below we argue that Mullins was a mainstream CCM artist.

## Mullins' Songs Recorded by Others

By 1986, Amy Grant, widely regarded as the queen of CCM, had recorded three of his songs. Her version of his "Sing Your Praise to the Lord" was considered to be a megahit (Granger, 1990; Lessner, 1997). Grant also recorded Mullins' "Doubly Good to You" and "Love of Another Kind." She included the latter on her *Unguarded* recording project, which was successful not only among CCM fans but also in the mainstream market. Mullins also wrote songs with titles that remind one of public domain songs. Two were "The Battle Hymn of the Republic," recorded by CCM artist Benny Hester, and "O Come All Ye Faithful," recorded by successful pop and CCM crossover artist Debby Boone (Scruggs, 1986). These recordings were released as CCM titles.

## Mullins' Work Lauded by *CCM Magazine*

Before his death, *CCM Magazine* published five stories featuring Mullins. These spanned the period from January 1986 (Scruggs, 1986) to November 1995 (Long, 1995). The articles reported news about then-new recording projects released by Mullins' label (Halverson, 1993; Newcomb, 1992), profiled Mullins' personality (Long, 1995; Scruggs, 1986), and talked about his concert style (Granger, 1990).

## Mullins' Succeeded within the CCM Genre

In a monthly survey of its readers' listening preferences, *Christian Music Review* magazine listed his album *Never Picture Perfect* (1990) as one of the top 50 most listened to albums for 5 months ("Top 50," 1991). Mullins also recorded more than 50 hit songs in his career (Lessner, 1997). His "My One Thing" went to number one on the pop Christian charts (Newcomb, 1992), a measure of airplay and album purchase, while "Awesome God" was listed one of the top three most popular songs of the 1980s decade by Christian Research Report (Rockafellow, 1997). "Awesome God" also received a Dove Award nomination, the Christian music equivalent of the Grammy Awards, for Song of the Year in 1989, one of 10 songs nominated in that category (Granger, 1990). He was nominated for 12 other Dove Awards during his life and received some posthumously. He was named Artist of the Year for 1997 ("1998 Dove Awards," 1998). He then won the Song-writer of the Year, Hard Music Song of the Year, and Song of the Year awards at the 1999 ceremony, a feat made possible because many of the songs he had written were recorded or rerecorded by other artists after his death ("The Gospel Music," 1999).

One final indication of Mullins' popularity is revealed by increases in "hits," or requests for access to web sites, that covered news of his death. Christian radio station KTLI, Wichita, Kansas, reported more than a fourfold increase in monthly hits to its web pages: The station's web site receives on average 25,000 visits a month. Within one week of Mullins' death, however, the station experienced 93,000 hits to its web site and received 9,000 e-mails (Kennedy, 1997). *The Wichita Eagle*'s coverage triggered six times more hits than coverage of any other story the paper published in the 10 months since it had gone online (Kennedy, 1997).

Other evaluations of his music are less measurable but at least as revealing. Granger (1990) credited him with "turning out some of the most creative and thought-provoking songs in contemporary Christian music." The *Wichita Eagle Online* called him a "core artist in contemporary Christian radio, someone whose songs become the pillars around which other artists' songs are programmed" (Lessner, 1997, paragraph 14). Pop Christian star Michael W. Smith said, "Rich Mullins' life and music has impacted me more than anyone I know. He had the ability to take the mundane and make it majestic. Nobody on this planet wrote songs like he did[,] and I feel we've lost one of the only true poets in our industry" ("Christian Music," 1997, paragraph 15).

Among the responses collected for this study, fans who paid tribute to Mullins likened him most frequently to the late Keith Green, who, like Mullins, was more known for his songwriting than for his singing quality ("Keith Green," 1982). Green, too, died an untimely death, but in the early 1980s.[2] One respondent imagined Mullins in heaven playing the dulcimer (an instrument he often played) with Green accompanying him on piano. Mullins was also compared with Mark Heard, another Christian musician who died an untimely death, as well as CCM artists David Meece and Michael Card, both of whom have recorded numerous albums and write much of their own music and lyrics.

In short, the aforementioned indicators categorize Mullins as a mainstream CCM recording artist. We are consciously attempting to make sense of fan response to his death within the horizon of what we call "the CCM discursive system." In her examination of mass media audiences, Morgenstern (1992) reminds us that every text is made intelligible with respect to a particular (discursive) system (p. 301).

## Analysis of the Tributes

### Identification

Many respondents indicated a deep level of identification with the artist. One radio tribute said, "Rich wouldn't have recognized my name or face, but he knew me. . . . better than anybody next to God. . . . He poured out his soul, and I found a friend in a complete stranger."

Fans indicated that they were praying for Mullins' family or e-mailed a prayer. One fan wrote, "Father, we pray that you will give peace and comfort to the family of Rich Mullins at this time. . . . Let them know that they will see him again in Paradise. . . . In His Name." Responses such as "May our prayers be with his family" and "Remember to pray for all whom Rich's life touched" were typical.

Other fans showed their depth of connection with Mullins by their tears. One web user wrote, "Why does my heart ache for someone that I have never met. I rarely ever cry, but I can hardly stop." Another wrote, "I didn't cry for [Princess] Diana. I didn't cry for Mother Teresa. But when I lost Rich Mullins, it was more than I could stand." Still another, stirred to the point that he said the football game had faded into a buzz in the background and the phone was on the floor in a heap, wrote, "What is it to love a man who has brought you out of darkness, drawn a tear from the hardest of rock, broken the greatest . . . fortress of a man's soul. . . . What is it then that lets us love this man that we have never known."

Many fans remarked on Mullins' musical ability. They ranged from straightforward comments such as "Mullins has stood out as one of the greatest inspirational songwriters of our time," "The way he played the Hammer Dulcimer . . . it was like he was the dulcimers' creator," and "Mullins . . . the world's finest musician" to more poetic responses. "His songs gave me hope when I was hopeless, strength when I was weak, and joy when I was sorrowful," wrote one. Another respondent wrote, "I paid a very small fee to see him [in concert], I received more than money could buy." One radio tribute wove pieces of lyrics from his music into a poetic ensemble:

> Over the last decade, you have carried us through "God's reckless, raging, furious love." You've shown us "The Color Green" more vivid and beautiful than we have ever seen it. . . . we have "heard the prairies calling out your name." We've sat in a temple of "silence and stars," crying out the name of the one who loves us. And we've watched God put "leanings on our silent hearts." We've sat back and watched you wrestle with our God, asking him the questions that we were afraid to, and then found our answers in your songs. . . . You have the ability to say what our hearts were full of, the stuff that we really felt but couldn't put into words of our own. Yet [your words] became our own. Our praise was made beautiful with your lyrics.

The most frequently mentioned lyric was from his song "Elijah," which recounts the passing of the prophet Elijah, who, in the biblical account, was taken to heaven without dying. The lyrics of the chorus say:

> When I leave I want to go out like Elijah,
> With a whirlwind to fuel my chariot of fire.
> And when I look back on the stars,
> It'll be like a candlelight in Central Park,
> And it won't break my heart to say goodbye.

One web tribute took the lyrics to that song, including the verses, and rewrote them in the past tense in an attempt to convey the thought that, like the prophet, Mullins had been transported to paradise. Another fan did the same with Mullins' song "The World as Best as I Remember It," renaming it "As Best as I'll Remember Him."

These examples of how Mullins' fans prayed, encouraged prayer, and wept in response to news of his death, and those responses that applauded Mullins' musicianship or that poetized or used his lyrics, signify strong bonding with Mullins. Following Wolfe (1995) and Wolfe and Haefner (1996), it is our contention that a useful point of departure in any attempt to account for the bonds fans formed with Mullins lies in the musical texts he produced rather than, for instance, in his rather unextraordinary physical appearance. The meanings Mullins' music made in the lives of its listeners are examined next.

## Spiritual Meanings

Some fans credited Mullins' music for their conversion to Christianity. One wrote, "[I] just found Christ this year, and it was thanx to Rich and his music that I did." Another indicated that Mullins' "songs led me into Christianity." A third distinguished between knowledge about Christianity and deciding to change one's life because of Mullins' music. Still another said, "I made my first *real commitment* to the Lord Jesus Christ through Rich's music" (emphasis mine).

At least two fans mentioned one specific Mullins song, "Hold Me Jesus," as key to their conversions. One said, "I had trouble finding Christ, but then one day I heard Rich sing 'Hold Me Jesus.' Hearing this song was [as] if Christ had spoken to me, and I too learned to stop beating my head against those walls and found peace in the arms of my personal Savior." Another fan credited the song "Creed" for starting a conversion process that eventually ended with the listener adopting the Catholic faith.

For others, Mullins' music supported or reinforced their faith. One fan's radio tribute said, Mullins "uplifted me many times with his music . . . throughout my different high points and low points with the Lord." For some, Mullins' encouragement came on the heels of a spiritual conversion. "When I became a Christian, someone gave me one of his tapes[,] and I've been inspired and ministered to ever since." Still another said, "His songs . . . lifted me up when I was down, brought me back to earth when I was getting too stuck on myself." Typical of a faith-reinforcing comment was "During the mountaintops of my relationship with God, Rich's music pointed me to paths of [even] higher worship."

In addition to those whose faith it reinforced, Mullins' music encouraged some fans to renew or re-establish their faith. One radio listener "had [not] been . . . really walking with the Lord like I should have been." He attended a Mullins concert, and it "just turned my life around. . . . [Mullins] turned around some things in my life that needed to be turned around." An e-mailer wrote, "Even when I fell away, I couldn't stop listening to his music, and gently, patiently, God used that to bring me back." Mullins "challenged, inspired, and pushed me upwards in my walk with God," another fan wrote. A third said, "Something about Rich's music brought . . . us to a 'greater intimacy with God.'" An e-mailed tribute posted by *CCM Magazine* stated, "He made a lot of us uncomfortable in our downy faith nests." One fan even reported he "had a flash of the Holy Spirit and it seemed in a way as though I had been looking at the cross."

Others have been influenced to take a career path toward Christian ministry. One listener wrote that Mullins is "the single biggest reason that I am going into the ministry." He described Mullins as "the mentor that I needed as I searched for the Lord's will for my life and career." Still others already in the ministry also reported being nourished by Mullins' music. One minister said that Mullins' song "Creed" inspired a sermon he later preached. Another reported using Mullins' "Prince of Peace" as the theme for a parish renewal weekend. A fan who also works as a Christian musician said, "as I was forming what and who I am today as a musician, Rich's music directed my course."

## Social-Spiritual Meanings

Mullins' life and death also had a bonding effect within families in both social and spiritual ways. One parent said, "As I drove my son to school this morning, we cried all the way and sang 'Hold Me Jesus' (my son's favorite song)." Another said, "We used to sing 'Awesome God' as a family[,] and it really blessed us. . . . Those were some of the most memorable times I can think of." A mother's tribute written in thanks to Mullins stated, "Thanks not only for me but for my 5-year-old son. 'Cause now he sees me crying, not only for losing you, but for losing his daddy in an accident just like you[rs]. . . . Your music is helping me raise my son to know a God who loves him passionately." Perhaps the words of a child demonstrate how Mullins' music, and his death, helped create a family-bonding experience. Using his own grammar and spelling, the child wrote, "Dear Rich; you were my favorite singer in the whole world. This morning when I found out you had been killed in a car accident I cried and cried, my mom told me don't cry you'll see him in heaven someday. I hope you are having a good time in heaven right now!"

Besides catalyzing family bonding between parent and child, Mullins' music in at least one case resulted in marriage. The couple's tribute said that the album *A Liturgy, a Legacy, and a Ragamuffin Band* "mirrored perfectly many of our concerns spiritually and the fear of the awesome steps we were both taking, getting married and I moving from my home country of Ireland. . . . God used that album to hold us together in a way which transcended love on a human plane."

## Social Meanings

Another theme evident in the responses was voiced by fellow musicians or other persons with creative aspirations. One "songwriter" noted, "I had hoped to attain the level of spiritual depth and maturity that Rich so fluently expressed." Another amateur musician wrote, "I will continue to sing his songs in church." A six-year-old was also inspired, though with guidance, according to a parent who wrote, "My daughter . . . has learned hand motions to 'Awesome God' at the Catholic school she attends." Another communicator noted how a "class of 4th, 5th, and 6th graders . . . [was trying to learn] 'Awesome God' in their music lessons."

A parent credited Mullins' music with motivating her daughter to sponsor a needy child through Compassion International, a group for which Mullins performed benefits. Many other fans mentioned participating in such sponsorships. This same daughter was also considering teaching on a Native American reservation. Mullins had taught on such a reservation ("Christian Music," 1997).

## Psychological Meanings

Many listeners expressed how Mullins' music gave them comfort or strength when they were disturbed or weak. One listener reported how listening helped him grieve the death of a friend. Mullins' "Awesome God" was used in the funeral ceremony. Mullins' music gave another fan courage to undergo cancer surgery. "Unable to sleep the night before her trip to the hospital[,] we prayed and sang together, and every song was written by Rich. . . . Throughout her stay in the hospital her Walkman was playing Rich Mullins albums." Similarly, a woman diagnosed with inoperable cancer listened to Mullins' music "over and over again" for comfort while dealing with her disease.

Mullins' music helped a college student through her freshman year, when she was "almost suicidal." Another fan noted that it was Mullins' music that "welcomed (him) to America in 1993." A 16-year-old recalled how, when younger, she used to sing "Awesome God" or listen to Mullins' recordings whenever she had a bad dream or had trouble sleeping. One fan claimed in a tribute sent to *CCM* that an infant son, born with complications and confined to the hospital, "ALWAYS responded to Rich's songs" (emphasis in original) when his mom sang or played them for him. Similarly, a father reported how his infant son's tears stopped flowing when he heard a Mullins' song. "Now everytime he gets a little fussy, all we have to do is play Rich's music[,] and he cheers up." A mother noted how she played Mullins' recordings during her labor and delivery. Our daughter "came into the world hearing the songs," the woman noted. "She'll be hearing his music for some time to come."

## Conclusion

In this chapter we demonstrate how fans responded to Mullins' death. In a study of CBS network news coverage of John Lennon's death, Wolfe (1988) found that the coverage echoed "significant characteristics of Lennon's music" (p. v). Similarly, the responses of Mullins fans echoed the "positive," pro-Christian aspects of Mullins' music and of the genre in which he worked. Beyond identifying Mullins as a "friend" and reporting feelings of loss over his death, fans shared their conversion to Christianity and views consistent with those Mullins and other musicians in his discourse community advocated. CCM fans linked his music with support for their previously held religious beliefs and with renewal of those beliefs. Cultural meanings between Mullins and his fans seem to have been shared and mutually reinforced (Eyerman and Jamison, 1995). Other fans told of the influence of Mullins' CCM on their career path in ministry. Christian ministers also reported how Mullins' CCM aided their spiritual undertakings.

Not patently religious, some responses asserted that Mullins' work encouraged them to either become or to remain CCM musicians and to either help or continue to help the less fortunate. These responses show a level of fan identification within the CCM world that at least equals what Dotter (1987) observed in other, more popular musical discourse communities.

Fans also claim Mullins' CCM gave them comfort and strength in times of physical disease and distress and catalyzed bonding among family members and between romantic couples. Claims were also recorded of CCM's positive impact on infants.

## Future Research

Clarification of the points presented here could be achieved through interviews or focus groups. But the data gathered for this chapter were almost entirely anonymous. Therefore, contacting these same individuals for such an effort would be difficult. Still, comments such as "this prophet poet knew how to write songs that broke into my world, that broke my heart, and helped me to see the boy and man God wanted me to be" are rich as they stand. Even more, and despite their anonymity, we insist that they are worthy of scholars' attention.

Seeking responses on a wider range of the CCM genres' music would also be helpful. Does the music of Amy Grant or Michael W. Smith, artists who have achieved "secular" success, have the same meaning to CCM fans as Mullins' music? There is some evidence that the CCM responses analyzed are generalizable to the CCM community. Listener letters to the CCM-formatted WNAZ-FM in Nashville said, "just a note to thank you all again for your beautiful music. I am a cancer patient and your music helps so much. I use it to worship and to praise my Father and my Savior" ("Dear WNAZ-FM," 1997, p. 2), and "It helps with tolerating rush hour traffic and those 'bad' days!" ("Thank you," 1997, p. 2). Another said, "The music would lull me to sleep, calming my spirit from the cares and concerns of the day" ("I had formed," 1998).

Other research might choose to use the experimental techniques employed by Zillmann et al. (1995). Specific social and psychological effects or meanings of CCM may well emerge through such research, even if Christian or other spiritual effects or meanings may not. Finally, scholars with diachronic knowledge of the history of Christian message production and consumption might find in these data themes and expressions—such as "brought [me] out of darkness"—that owe their origin to earlier theological, if not specifically Christian, discourse.

## Notes

1. See Schultz (1988) and Perry (1993) for histories of evangelical radio and CCM, respectively.

2. Another similarity between the artists is their work with the less fortunate. Green ran a shelter for the homeless in California, while Mullins lived with Navajo Indian children and taught them music, a subject not available in their schools.

# References

"1998 Dove Awards." (1998, April 23). *CCM Magazine* [online], 45 pages. Available: www.ccmcom.com/doves/ [June 10, 1998].

"'Abstract' takes measure of America." (1997, December 4). *USA Today* [online], 16 paragraphs. Available: www.usatoday.com/life/lds011.htm [December 4, 1997].

Black, J., Bryant, J., and Thompson, S. (1997). *Introduction to Media Communication* (5th ed.). Boston: McGraw Hill.

Carroll, R.L., Silbergleid, M.I., Beachum, C.M., Perry, S.D., Pluscht, P.J., and Pescatori, M.J. (1993). Meanings of radio to teenagers in a niche-programming era. *Journal of Broadcasting and Electronic Media, 37(2)*, 159–176.

"Christian Music Industry Remembers Rich Mullins." (1997, September 29). *CCM Update* [Online], 16 paragraphs. Available: www.ccmcom.com/ ccmupdate/ 97-09-29/news.html [October 8, 1997].

"Dear WNAZ-FM" [Letter to the editor]. (1997, October). *WNRZ, WNAZ, WENO Newsletter.* p. 2.

DeFleur, M.L., and Dennis, E.E. (1996). *Understanding Mass Communication: A Liberal Arts Perspective* (updated 1996 ed.). Boston: Houghton Mifflin.

Dotter, D. (1987). Growing up is hard to do: Rock and roll performers as cultural heroes. *Sociological Spectrum, 7(1)*, 25–44.

Eberly, P.K. (1982). *Music in the Air: America's Changing Tastes in Popular Music, 1920–1980.* New York: Hastings House.

Eidenmuller, M.E. (1998). Contemporary religious music preference and audience orientation: Do the lyrics really matter? *The Journal of Communication and Religion,* 37–45.

Eisenberg, E.M. (1984). Ambiguity as strategy in organizational communication. *Communication Monographs, 51,* 227–242.

Eyerman, R., and Jamison, A. (1995). Social movements and cultural transformation: Popular music in the 1960s. *Media, Culture and Society, 17,* 449–468.

"The Gospel Music Association announces the winners for the 30th annual Dove Awards." (1999). GMA Community: Dove Awards [online], 41 paragraphs. Available: www.doveawards.com [April 7, 1999].

Granger, T. (1990, May). Hope to carry on. *CCM Magazine* [Online], 5 pages. Available: www.wsu.edu/~williamb/release/ccmmay90.html [October 1, 1997].

Grossberg, L. (1986). Is the rock after punk? *Critical Studies in Mass Com-munication, 3,* 50–74.

Halverson, H. (1993, December). A ragamuffin's Oz. *CCM Magazine* [On-line], 4 pages. Available: www.wsu.edu/~williamb/release/ccmdec93. html [October 2, 1997].

Hansen, C.H. (1995). Predicting cognitive and behavioral effects of gangsta rap. *Basic and Applied Social Psychology, 16(1 and 2),* 43–52.

Hawkins, K.M. (ed.) (1996). *1996 Directory of Religious Media.* Manassas, VA: National Religious Broadcasters.

"I had formed a habit" [Letter to the editor]. (1998, June). *Zfm Spectrum,* p. 2.

Johnson, J.D., Jackson, L.A., and Gatto, L. (1995). Violent attitudes and de-ferred academic aspirations: Deleterious effects of exposure to rap mu-sic. *Basic and Applied Social Psychology, 16(1 and 2),* 27–41.

"Keith Green, 11 others, killed in plane crash: The singer's evangelism and publishing ministries will continue, his wife says." (1982, September 3). *Christianity Today,* v. 26, pp. 47, 50–51.

Kennedy, E. (1997, September 27). Mullins fans gather here tonight to grieve. *The Wichita Eagle* [Online], 2 pages. Available: www.wichitaeagle. com/news/religion/grieve0927.htm [September 29, 1997].

Larson, B. (1996). *In the Name of Satan.* Nashville: Thomas Nelson.

Leland, J. (1992, June 29). Rap and race. *Newsweek,* pp. 46–52.

Lessner, L. (1997, September 27). "It feels like I lost a brother." *The Wichita Eagle* [Online], 14 paragraphs. Available: www.wichitaeagle.com/ news/religion /mullins-service0927.htm [September 29, 1997].

Long, J. (1995, November). O, to be rich. *CCM Magazine* [Online], 4 pages. Available: www.ccmcom.com/ccmmag/95nov/1195mullins.html [Octo-ber 1, 1997].

Morgenstern, S. (1992). The epistemic autonomy of mass media audiences. *Critical Studies in Mass Communication, 9,* 293–310.

Newcomb, B.Q. (1992, June). Step by step: A conversation with Rich Mullins. *CCM Magazine* [Online], 6 pages. Available: www.wsu.edu/~williamb/ release/ ccmjun92.html [October 1, 1997].

Painton, P. (1992, March 30). Country rocks the boomers. *Time,* pp. 62–66.

Pareles, J. (1991, December 8). Should Ice Cube's voice be chilled? *The New York Times,* p. H30.

Pauly, J.J. (1991). A beginner's guide to doing qualitative research in mass communication. *Journalism Monographs, 125,* 1–32.

Perry, S.D. (1993). *Niches within the Niche: Music Intensive Religious For-mats and the Stations That Air Them.* Unpublished master's thesis, Uni-versity of Alabama, Tuscaloosa.

Perry, S.D., and Carroll, R.L. (1995). Subgenre radio formats: The case of music-intensive religious stations. *Journal of Radio Studies, 3,* 41–58.

Price, Deborah Evans. (1997). A field in flux. *Billboard, 109,* 45–47.

"Rich Mullins tribute in the works." (1997). *CCM Update* [Online], 7 pages. Available: www.ccmcom.com/mullins.html [October 1, 1997].

Rockafellow, L. (1997, September 22). Contemporary Christian music veteran killed in automobile accident. Myrrh Records press release [Online]. Available: www.myrrh.com/mullins/release.htm [October 2, 1997].

Sandler, Adam. (1998). Christian music: The word is out. *Variety, 370,* pp. 32–34.

Schultze, Q.J. (1988). Evangelical radio and the rise of the electronic church, 1921–1948. *Journal of Broadcasting and Electronic Media, 32,* 289–306.

Scruggs, M. (1986). Rich Mullins: Songs of another kind. *CCM Magazine* [Online], 2 pages. Available: www.wsu.edu/~williamb/release/ccm-jan86.html [October 1, 1997].

"Thank you, WNAZ staff" [Letter to the editor]. (1998, February). *WNRZ, WNAZ, WENO newsletter,* p. 2.

"Top 50 album list." (1991, April). *Christian Music Review,* p. 47.

Turow, J. (1999). *Media Today: An Introduction to Mass Communication.* Boston: Houghton Mifflin.

Williams, B. (1997). Richard Wayne Mullins: October 21, 1955–September 19, 1997 [Online]. Available: www.wsu.edu/mullins.html [September 26, 1997].

Wolfe, A.S. (1988). *Irony, Ambiguity, and Meaning in CBS Television Network News Coverage of the Death of John Lennon.* Unpublished doctoral dissertation, Northwestern University, Evanston, IL.

Wolfe, A.S. (1995). Song of the '60s: Toward a cultural history of a mass media text. *Journal of the Northwest Communication Association, 23,* 70–90.

Wolfe, A.S., and Haefner, M. (1996). Taste cultures, culture classes, affective alliances, and popular music reception: Theory, methodology and an application to a Beatles' song. *Popular Music and Society, 20,* 127–155.

Zillmann, D., and Bhattia, A. (1989). Effects of associating with musical genres on heterosexual attraction. *Communication Research, 16,* 263–288.

Zillmann, D., Aust, C.F., Hoffman, K.D., Love, C.C., Ordman, V.L., Pope, J.T., Seigler, P.D., and Gibson, R.J. (1995). Radical rap: Does it further ethnic division? *Basic and Applied Social Psychology, 16 (1 and 2),* 1–25.

# CHAPTER 16

# Branding Religion: Christian Consumers' Understandings of Christian Products

ERIC HALEY
CANDACE WHITE
ANNE CUNNINGHAM

Recent years have witnessed a boom in Christian marketing, both the marketing of Christian products and the use of "Christian-owned" as a loyalty-building tool for businesses. Rather than resisting the merging of marketing and Christian values, some Christians have embraced marketing as a tool to make Christian values more appealing to American youth. And it seems to be working.

Despite the enormous growth in Christian retailing, researchers have paid little attention to the phenomenon. "Religion, especially contemporary religion, is among the most understudied topics in American Studies, compared to its weight in the larger culture" (Hulsether, 1995, p. 127). This chapter offers an entrée into the subject by focusing on one of the central targets for the marketing of religion, young adult Christian consumers. Specifically, this research examines how self-described Evangelical Christians, who are the primary consumers of Christian products, make sense of their purchases and use of Christian products. This study is important in that it examines a growing multibillion-dollar-per-year product category, one of a few consumer-oriented categories that are identified with strong ideological values. Therefore, the study extends our understanding of branding from the context of product and service marketing to the marketing of ideology.

## The Christian Products Market

Recent figures from the Christian Booksellers Association (CBA) put sales in the Christian retail industry, which includes Christian books, music, gifts, clothing, and jewelry, above $3 billion in 1996, up approximately 9 percent from 1995 (Lee, 1997). The CBA also estimates that up to 3,500 specialty Christian retailers now exist nationwide (Dressler, 1996, p. 5). Even mainstream retailers such as Wal-Mart are devoting more shelf space to religious products ("Christian Retailing," 1998, p. 63). As Richard Heaton, marketing director for Christian apparel manufacturer Exodus, explains, "It's the Kmartization of Christian retailing." (Dressler, 1996, p. 5).

While the CBA says that the average Christian shopper is a well-educated caucasian, age 30 to 49, with a net income of more than $40,000 ("Christian Retailing," 1998, p. 63), one of the newest Christian crazes, "What would Jesus do?" apparel and jewelry, particularly targets teens and young adults. As reported in *The Seattle Times,* "The latest in 'witness wear' for Christian teens is a bracelet inscribed 'W.W.J.D.?' If you ask what the letters stand for, the wearer might just whip it off and give it to you, along with the answer—'What would Jesus do?'" ("Christian Jewelry," 1997, p. B7). W.W.J.D. can now be found on everything from jewelry to bumper stickers to clothing. Sales of W.W.J.D. items for one manufacturer topped $9 million last year (George, 1998, p. 4).

## Literature Review

Given that little attention has gone to Christian marketing in the academic literature, the researchers prepared for the investigation by consulting the literature on symbolic communication, clothing and communication, and religious symbols in clothing. The purpose of the review was to sensitize the researchers to issues and themes that may emerge from the qualitative investigation. As is standard in emergent qualitative investigations, additional literature was consulted after the data were analyzed. This literature is presented in the discussion of the findings section of this chapter.

## Marketing Religion

Moore (1994) offers one of the few examinations of contemporary religion, particularly as it relates to American consumerism. In tracing the history of American religion, Moore argues against the popular belief that religion has become secularized in the past century. "The argument is not that religion has only recently found it necessary to embrace techniques of commercial expansion to get ahead. Commercial aspects of religion are traceable in any century" (p. 7). Even so, since the 1950s, religion has seeped further into the mainstream.

> For many Americans, the spiritual help available in churches or in movie houses or on television or in a best-selling book or at a businessman's prayer breakfast tended to become equivalent. Organized religion had not made full peace with popular culture, and some small denominations remained at war with it. From one perspective, however, it was becoming hard to view religion as something distinct from popular culture. (p. 241)

Moore concludes with an important question about the impact of religious commercialization on American society. "Having issued . . . tardy reminders about the charitable activities and spiritual life of American churches, we must still wonder whether they have been rendered less effective by the processes of commercialization that support them. Is religion somehow not religion in the way that it was" (p. 273)? Moore suggests no answer to this question but leaves the reader to decide.

## Communicating with Symbols

Since the beginning of organized Christian faith, symbols have been used to communicate religious ideas, whether through objects, art, or rituals. One perspective that gives insight into how people make meaning of the world through such symbols is symbolic interactionism.

"Symbolic interactionism," a term coined by Herbert Blumer and developed as a theory by George Herbert Mead, refers to the symbols used to create and express experiences and understandings (Baran and Davis, 1995). Objects, gestures, logos, and even brands can symbolize ideas and beliefs. McCracken (1988a) notes that the meaning of objects first travels from the culture to the object and then from the object to the individual who uses the object. In many cases, advertisers and marketers attempt to control this process to create desire for objects.

The transfer of meaning to the object defines the object so that it symbolizes, and therefore can communicate, a complex idea, belief, or ideal. For instance, the American flag as an object is pieces of red, white, and blue cloth sewn together. However, the flag as a symbol represents a nation; displaying the flag communicates ideas such as patriotism and pride in the nation. Sewing an American flag to the seat of one's pants, on the other hand, communicates other sentiments. Communication through symbols relies on shared meaning; those who share the meaning can read the symbols just as we can read and understand language (Cunningham and Lab, 1991).

## Clothing as Symbols

While the Christian products category consists of books, music, and many other products, Christian clothing is perhaps one of the most visible products in this category. Most social scientists take for granted that an individual's clothing expresses meaning (Rubinstein, 1995). Clothing can communicate personal worth, values, religious beliefs, and group association. In all cultures through the ages, people have decorated their bodies to signify status or beliefs. Hood (1984) notes that the character of an individual is often the symbolic interpretation of physical appearance and dress. Consciously or unconsciously, an individual chooses clothing with a particular meaning. Most people dress according to their tastes and pocketbooks without deliberate concern for what their clothing communicates, while others intentionally make a "statement" with their attire as is apparent in the dress of status and brand conscious consumers, rebellious teenagers, and nuns and monks of certain religious orders.

The language of clothing is symbolic. Clothing, more than any other artifact, symbolizes the relationship between people and their sociocultural environment (Cordwell and Schwarz, 1979). Symbols, however, are not as exact in meaning as language and are only recognizable to those who share their meaning. Therefore, clothing can be worn to communicate to a subgroup (Cunningham and Lab, 1991). Examples are Masonic symbols and the attire of gang members. The valid interpretation of these symbols requires understanding the sociocultural context within which the image appears (Cunningham and Lab, 1991).

Sociologist Erving Goffman (1959) posited that tie-signs and tie-symbols in clothing are used to define individuality, create associations, reflect group affiliations, and reflect our beliefs. Tie-signs in clothing provide information about a desired or existing social identity such as group identity, social status, or occupational role (Cunningham and Lab, 1991). Examples are the readily identifiable clothing of the Hell's Angels, the wearing of expensive brand labels, and military uniforms. Clothing tie-symbols are expressions of support or association with a particular idea or cause (Goffman, 1959). Examples today would be the X on Spike Lee's cap, which serves to associate him with Malcolm X, or exhibiting red AIDS or pink Breast Cancer Awareness ribbons on one's lapel.

Symbols and their adoption as a means of self-association and self-expression are personal choices. In a social context, clothing can serve to connect people to a reference group using symbols that are recognized by others with shared values (Rubinstein, 1995). Clothing symbols can also be used to validate the personal identity of a person or to promote an internal sense of belonging or well-being (Cunningham and Lab, 1991).

## Religious Symbols in Clothing and Other Products

Literature about the history of fashion and clothing and costumes is prolific. Much has been written about the use of clothing to symbolize religious beliefs. However, much of this body of work looks at ecclesiastical dress and liturgical vestments, primarily worn by religious leaders or members of religious orders (Mayo, 1984; Littrell and Evers, 1985). Studies about clothing worn by lay persons to convey religious meaning focus on "costumes" such as baptismal and wedding gowns, communion dress, or modes of dress such as that adopted by the Amish and Mennonites (Rubinstein, 1995).

In his work on conversion rituals, Hood (1981; 1986) suggests that gestures, acts, and signs such as clothing may be used to mark the transformation of a religious convert. "[C]onversion rituals have emerged in America as a means of giving evidence that an internal change has occurred within the individual" (1981, p. 1). As this relates to clothing and jewelry, Hood (1986) writes:

> William James introduced the concept of the "material me" into thought about representations of the self. . . . Christians accumulate tokens of the conversion experience. In denominations a common practice is to issue a certificate of Christian baptism. Some persons choose to witness to their faith through wearing a necklace with a cross pendant or a lapel pin. (p. 7)

These acts are to be seen by others as an expression and validation of the wearer's Christian faith.

In the sociology of religion literature, one study was found that looked at the wearing and displaying of clothing and items such as bumper stickers, T-shirts, and jewelry, that depict religious symbols— items that might be called "witness wear" by marketers today. Wicklund and Gollwitzer (1982), in a study designed to explore the concept of symbolic self-completion, asked subjects from varied religious backgrounds how often they wore or displayed clothing or items that could be considered symbolic of their religious beliefs and where and how often they used such items. The study found that subjects from homogeneous religious backgrounds (both parents and family members of the same religion) were more likely to wear clothing or display items with religious symbolism. The researchers concluded that those with social and familial networks of similar and strong religious convictions were more comfortable and complete in their religious convictions.

In general, the literature supports the idea that products such as clothing can function symbolically to communicate personal identity, affiliation with groups, and even personal beliefs. The Wicklund and Gollwitzer (1982) study was the only study found that directly addressed the use of Christian products. The study precedes the recent growth of the Christian product and sheds little light on the meaning of Christian products to users, which is the purpose of the present investigation.

## Method

This study of the meanings of Christian products to consumers is based in a constructivist research paradigm (Guba, 1990). Constructivism is a set of assumptions that holds realities to be multiple and socially constructed. Reality is not inherent in objects, rather it is created in the interaction between the object and the interpreter of that object, that is, the individual (Taylor and Haley, 1994). As such, it can be expected that there will not be a singular meaning of the products. Constructivists also believe that the nature of knowledge is subjective. That is, all knowledge is the product of human constructions; therefore, absolute objectivity is impossible. As such, abstraction of the phenomenon into supposedly objective measures does not serve the purpose of the research. Finally, the object of a constructivist inquiry is phenomenological understanding of how the subjects of interest construct or make sense of the phenomenon of study. In this case, how do Evangelical Christians make sense of Christian products?

## Why Study Evangelical Young Adults?

In determining the best sample for this study, eight interviews with owners and managers of Christian retail stores were conducted. These managers suggested that, while the average store shopper was an upper-middle-class female in her 30s or 40s, the most "influential" market segment was the younger demographic, primarily 16–25. Store owners and managers also identified the primary user of Christian products as Evangelical. When asked to define "Evangelical," there was little consensus about which religious denominations were considered Evangelical. Interviewees revealed that while most Baptists may consider themselves Evangelical, not all would define themselves as such. Similarly, some concluded that while most Presbyterians would consider themselves Protestant rather than Evangelical, some would describe themselves as Evangelical. Given this, we defined our population of interest as Christian young adults who describe themselves as Evangelical. Because of difficulties in securing parental consent for interviewing minors, all participants were over 17.

## What Tool to Use to Study the Phenomenon?

To accomplish the study's mission, the long-interview method was employed. The long interview has been described as one of the most powerful tools in the qualitative toolbox (McCracken, 1988b). The interview can take you into the mind of the participant and glimpse the logical categories through which that person creates the world. The long interview is a semistructured interview in which the interviewer is free to follow the respondent's train of thought. We developed a discussion guide based on a review of relevant literature and anticipation of how a conversation about the topic of interest might proceed. However, the interviewers maintained freedom to modify the guide and incorporate unanticipated subjects, discard questions that proved to be unimportant to the subjects, and change the order of questions in order to capture the way in which each individual makes sense of the topic of interest.

Respondents were recruited through known members of Evangelical churches in a midsized, conservative southeastern U.S. city. These church members were asked to recommend young adults whom they felt would be willing to talk to the research team about Christian products. Each interviewee was asked two screening questions: age and church affiliation. When asking about church affiliation, potential interviewees were asked to categorize the church to which they belonged as Catholic, Protestant, Evangelical, or other. Only those who classified their church as Evangelical were asked to participate.

Interviews were conducted until a point of information redundancy was reached. McCracken (1988b) suggests that redundancy may be achieved with as few as eight interviews depending on the homogeneity of the population. In this study, information redundancy was defined as the point at which no new unique understandings of Christian products emerged from the interviews. Redundancy was apparent after eight interviews, but interviews were conducted past the point of redundancy to ensure that information saturation had been reached. In total, the results of this study are based on 15 one- to two-hour interviews with self-described Evangelical Christian young adults between the ages of 18 and 36.

To ensure that the research was as accurate a representation of the respondents' views as possible, two trustworthiness measures were incorporated into the research design: transcription verification and a member check (Lincoln and Guba, 1985). The transcripts were verified against the tape-recorded interviews to make sure that the respondents' words were correctly recorded when converting the data from oral to written form. The member check involved sharing the transcripts with the research participants to make sure the interview accurately reflected the participants' views. Participants were interviewed after they reviewed their own transcription and given a chance to make additional comments or clarify statements. These additional interviews were recorded and transcribed and became part of the data set as well. Only in one case did an interviewee wish to modify earlier statements.

The data were analyzed using analytic induction. Analytic induction involves line-by-line reading of transcripts to develop themes and categories that emerge among interviews. These categories were expanded, contracted, or merged as additional transcripts were read. Negative cases that contradict the categories were sought within the transcripts in order to expand the analysis (Corbin and Strauss, 1990). The final analysis is a composite representation of the divergent meanings of Christian products to self-described Evangelical Christians.

# Results

So what do Christian products mean to self-described Evangelical Christian young adults? Christian products such as witness wear and music hold varied meanings for these Christians. First of all, it is important to note that while the predominant user of this product category is Evangelical, not all self-described Evangelicals buy or use products from the category. In order to understand the varied meanings, the understandings of both users and nonusers of these products will be examined.

## Nonusers

In the study seven of the 15 participants said that they personally did not buy or use Christian products. Among these seven participants were self-described fundamentalists, moderates, and liberals. Within this group of divergent people, a dominant theme emerges. That is, this group could not cognitively reconcile perceived conflicts between Christian ideology and marketing.

### Jesus Wouldn't Buy the T-shirt

> Products are not the way I choose to express my spirituality. I do have difficulty reconciling marketing with spirituality. When religion becomes a marketing campaign I get a little turned off. For centuries, many churches have profited by the sweat and suffering of many. I do not condemn all organized religion. Mother Teresa was truly an angel. Jim Baker on the other hand. . . . Be it T-shirts or condominiums, these things are incongruent with the teaching I believe in.

The above comments from a married, 31-year-old businesswoman, wife, and mother for whom church is not among the most important events in her week were echoed by a young man in his 20s who described himself as a "strict fundamentalist" who is at church "every time the door is open and sometimes even when it's not."

> Treasures in heaven, not treasures on earth. That's what we're supposed to strive for. Jesus destroyed the temple when it was used for selling stuff. The bible, the unadulterated word of God, that's all we need. Not T-shirts, or bracelets or CDs, or none of that stuff. It's profiting from the blood of Jesus, and that isn't right.

The perceived contradictions between Christian ideas and marketing are only an example of a larger issue, according to the following male college student:

> What I get so burnt on is that we're taught through advertising and everything else that the only way to show somebody you love them is to buy them something. The more expensive the item, the more you love them. Now, it's like that with faith. It's like they're telling you that you don't have strong faith if you don't buy or use these T-shirts or buy these records or whatever.

Similarly, other nonusers objected to the equation of things with faith, as the following single, young woman stated:

> There are so many ways to show a person's faith: kindness, love, compassion, patience, a pat on the back, a smile, a kind word. Nothing that you can buy can replace these real expressions of faith.

Another male nonuser noted:

> Actions, not symbols, are true reflections of somebody's beliefs. I hope that I don't need a T-shirt for people to know that I'm a Christian.

A married, professional female nonuser had strong words to say about users of the products:

> I think they are hypocrites. I think a true believer would wear a $10.99 T-shirt from a discount store to keep their body covered, warm and pro-

tected, and use the other $9.01 they would have spent on the W.W.J.D. T-shirt in the collection plate on Sunday, or better yet, spend that money on food for the local pantry. I don't proclaim to be a saint myself, and I certainly understand the dynamics of American society today. It is the hypocrisy that offends me. If you ask me 'what would Jesus do?' I don't think he'd buy the shirt.

In summary, these nonusers cite conflicts with teachings and the value of things as expressions of beliefs as the primary reasons for not using Christian products. Despite their different backgrounds and the differing role of religion in their daily lives, these Evangelical Christian nonusers hold a common meaning of Christian products as inappropriate expressions of Christian beliefs.

## Users

Now that the understandings of nonusers have been explored, what do users of these products believe? The dominant reasons for buying or using Christian products for those Evangelical Christians who did so related to affect. That is, buying and using Christian products meant feeling good. Feeling good through the purchase and use of Christian products was expressed in three main ways: feeling good by belonging, doing the right thing, and expressing pride in being a Christian.

*I'm on the Winning Team: Belonging.*   Christian products like T-shirts, bracelets, and music are symbols of affiliation for many users:

> I love wearing my Jesus T-shirt. It says "hey, I am supporting the winning team."

With affiliation comes comfort for some wearers:

> It's a great feeling to see someone I don't know wearing a T-shirt or W.W.J.D. bracelet because I know that I'm with a brother or sister.

> It's a good feeling to know someone is a Christian and that they are proud of it. It's so comforting for believers to know that they are among believers.

> I think that these bracelets and things are great for teenagers especially, it helps them know that it's ok to be a Christian.

The W.W.J.D. bracelets are great because they can be a catalyst for bringing people closer together.

Sometimes you feel the world is against you and then you see somebody being proud about their faith and that helps you know that you're not alone.

It's such a great feeling when you're wearing something like the bracelet when you realize that wow, you're part of something greater than anything of this world.

Looking down and seeing my bracelet on my arm makes me feel better because it reminds me that Jesus is with me.

In addition to affiliation, buyers and users of the product category say that they feel good because the products help them to do the right thing. For users of Christian products in this study, feeling good equaled "doing the right thing."

*Spreading the Word: Doing the Right Thing.*    "If you're doing good, it is only going to make you feel better."

For users, "doing good" was equated with "spreading the word of God" and "doing what Jesus would do." Christian products were assigned the function of helping spread the word.

You need to witness to other people and it's just a way of witnessing really. By wearing shirts like that, you bring attention to other people that you're a Christian.

It's a great feeling to see people reading your shirt. You know that you're doing good.

Some users say that they are often uncomfortable in fulfilling the mandate to witness and cite Christian products as making up for their inadequacies thereby helping them feel good about "doing the right thing."

I'm really not all that comfortable telling people about my beliefs and I know that I should be so that makes me feel bad. But the great thing about the T-shirt and stuff like that is that it's an easy way for me to spread the word and that makes me feel good.

I love it when somebody asks me about my W.W.J.D. bracelet. I'm not good at going up to people and just talking about Jesus. It makes me feel good to tell them that it means "what would Jesus do." I don't ever say much more than that, but still, it makes me feel good to know that I'm doing what I should do.

Similarly, other users say that using devotional calendars and bracelets for personal guidance throughout the day makes them feel good in doing the right thing:

My favorite thing is seeing my little table-top devotional calendar every morning. I just start the day in a good mood and I'll think back on it all day long and that helps keep me in a good mood. I look forward to it every morning.

I like wearing my W.W.J.D. bracelet. It keeps me from temptation. Without it, I might not be as strong. You know, I can feel good about myself knowing that I'm not straying.

*Wooed by the Spirit: Excitement about One's Beliefs.*    The users of Christian products also explain feeling good as showing pride and getting excited about being a Christian through use of the products:

The great thing about Christian music is that it gets you excited about being a Christian.

Christian music lifts me up. It's edifying, it fills your soul. Secular music drags you down.

Christian products are good because they show your spirit and how proud you are to be a Christian. I think it's a wonderful thing.

As discussed above, the dominant theme in the discussions with users about Christian products is the affective dimension of "feeling good." Cognitive factors did emerge at times but usually in response to a question by the interviewer that addressed more of a cognitive issue. For example, given that in some interviews with nonusers the criticism of profit and worldliness was dominant, the interviewers were curious to see how the devout users of Christian products make sense of the criticisms. These criticisms were addressed only after the interviewees had exhausted what they felt were the important aspects of buying and using Christian products.

When asked about who profits from Christian products, the devout users who have been represented thus far in the section labeled "users" responded in the following ways:

> If the makers were not doing a good thing, God wouldn't let them be profitable and continue in His name.

> You know, if they weren't fulfilling a need, then they wouldn't be making money. And they have to make money to fulfill their ministry, so the fact that people are making money is necessary and probably good. I'm sure they are donating some of that money to the Church or something.

> I wish I had thought of it. I'd be rich by now.

> I suppose it could be bad if they were only doing it for profit, but I know that there is divine inspiration in there. I can feel it. Those who don't have divine inspiration don't talk to people in ways that people will respond to, so they won't stay in business long.

In the above quotes, it is apparent that the users who had an opinion regarding profit did not see a conflict between marketing and Christianity as did the nonusers. When asked about the people who criticize Christian products, the devout users responded:

> There are right and wrong reasons for using these things. The wrong reasons are if they are just a fad or fashion or something. I'm critical of those people because they aren't living up to what they are advertising. If you're going to advertise Jesus, your actions had better be worthy. I would guess that the people who are critical are just seeing those people who are giving religion and Jesus a bad name by claiming they are Christian but then not acting like it.

> The people who make fun of W.W.J.D. and say it means "we want Jack Daniel's" and stuff like that, they are just weak in the faith. Their faith is not as strong as it should be.

Not all users of Christian products were without reservations about the products. Among users, there was a group of "lighter users" who were not as devout about the role and function of Christian products. These buyers or users may have received a Christian product as a gift or purchased something for their children but do not report wearing and using Christian products frequently. The less devout users cite their primary concerns as not wanting to be pushy with their faith and sending incorrect messages.

> Some of the T-shirts are ok, but I really have a problem with some of them and a lot of the bumper stickers. Some are really mean-spirited and too pushy. There are too many people trying to wage religious war through bumper stickers. And I don't like when religious stickers are criticizing politicians. Jesus was about making peace, not war.

> I think many people just use these things to look the part so they don't have to act the part (of being a Christian). Our culture worships people with strong convictions, so people want to look like they have strong convictions even when they don't. So it can be good and bad and I'm not really sure which it is.

> It's important to express your beliefs, but you can't step on the toes of others. I guess the T-shirts and things are less pushy than leaving leaflets or bible verses in your work space. We have a guy at work that does that and it really bothers us.

> I don't think that the bracelets are harming anybody. My children have them, mainly because the other kids have them. But before I'd buy them, I'd made the kids learn what the W.W.J.D. meant and that they would be expected to act accordingly if they were going to wear them. I guess they learned the lesson. The other day my youngest one got into trouble and I asked him what he was thinking. He looked up at me with tears in his eyes and said, "but I wasn't wearing my 'what would Jesus do' bracelet." I don't want to send the wrong message by letting my kids use those things without understanding them.

In summary, the primary difference between nonusers and users of Christian products is in the dominant way the two groups think about the products. The nonusers think of the category primarily in cognitive terms and are unable to resolve the intellectual inconsistencies they perceive between marketing and Christian teachings. For these Evangelical Christians, the products are an inappropriate expression of values and beliefs. The devout users, on the other hand, think of the category primarily in affective terms, responding to the feelings generated by the products. For users, using Christian products means feeling good about themselves. Among the less devout users, the affective evaluations of the category are somewhat tempered by cognitive considerations.

## Discussion

When looking at the diverse types of products that make up the Christian products category (e.g., books, music, giftware, jewelry, and clothing), the unifying element is the fact that these products are identified as "Christian." For devout users, the meaning of the product is derived from the product's identification as "Christian" more than from the significance of the product alone (i.e., a CD or a T-shirt). Similarly, the nonusers do not object to CDs or T-shirts, rather to the labeling of those items as "Christian." In this sense, the issue seems to stem from the use of "Christian" as a brand for products.

The functions ascribed to Christian products by devout users are similar to the various functions of brands in general. Can "Christian" be seen as a brand? In many respects, yes. From the branding literature, we know that brands are composed of both cognitive and affective components, and the concept of brand involves any aspect of importance that the consumer attributes to it. The importance of a brand is defined within the consumer's mind (Farquhar, 1989). From the words of the consumers in the present study, "Christian" when associated with products does carry both cognitive and affective significance. However, the cognitive and affective dimensions have different meanings for the users and nonusers in this study, such that they form different attitudes about using the products.

According to Park et al. (1986), brands can be viewed by consumers as functional, symbolic, and experiential. Clearly, the users of Christian products in this study attribute all three functions to the "Christian" brand. In terms of functionality, users of Christian brand products see the functionality as, for example, gifts or protective clothing. However, in support of Holbrook's (1994) contention that the functionality of a product may be separated from the consequences of the brand, some users of Christian products in this study were able to separate the functionality of the product (e.g., a T-shirt as something to cover your body) and the consequences of the brand (e.g., a Christian T-shirt as a way to feel good about yourself). In fact, with Christian products the practical functionality of the product changed when it was branded "Christian." Once a bracelet was branded "Christian," its function grew from one of adornment and self-pleasure to one of fulfilling a religious mandate. The bracelet is now a teaching tool, not just a piece of jewelry. This ideological aspect of the Christian brand may differentiate it from other brands like Polo or Marlboro in that the brand actually changes the practical functionality of the product, not just the affective consequences of the purchase.

Users of Christian brand products often speak of what Park et al. (1986) label the symbolic function of brands. According to Park et al. (1986), Biel (1993), and Aaker (1996), brands act to symbolically link users with a group or emphasize the brand's relationship with self. In the case of the Christian products, the users talk at length about how Christian brand products make them feel a part of a larger group. This parallels the function that Rubinstein (1995) assigns to clothing in general. In keeping with Park et al.'s (1986) contention that brands can define the user's relationship with self, users of Christian products in this study talk about the role of Christian products in helping them to see that they are not alone in their beliefs and helping them to feel more confident in their own personal beliefs. Again, in the clothing literature, Cunningham and Lab (1991) suggest that clothing can provide validation of personal identity.

Brands may also have experiential function (Park et al., 1986). The experiential aspect of the Christian brand was the overarching function that consumers attributed to the use of Christian merchandise, that is, feeling good. This ultimate function of "feeling good" incorporated getting excited, showing spirit, and doing the right thing, and it was also closely related to the comfort found in the symbolic function described above.

In summary, it can be concluded from this study that users of Christian products do view "Christian" as a brand and ascribe meanings to the Christian brand that parallel the general meanings of brands, in general. However, as noted above, the use of "Christian" as a brand may be somewhat different than other types of brands. Specifically, the Christian brand is an outgrowth of an ideological system, whereas other brands are created to give meaning to products. The brand Coke was built to differentiate one carbonated beverage from another. As a strong brand, it is a complex system of associated meanings, but the sole intent of creating those meanings is to make the product more significant to the consumer. The brand Christian is also a complex system of associated meanings ascribed to products in order to market them. However, the brand is also an extension of a larger pre-existing belief system.

## Future Research

This study is among the first in the marketing and consumer behavior literature to examine consumers in the fast-growing Christian products category. The category is one of a few consumer-oriented categories that is identified with strong ideological values. Some categories may appeal to ideological values like environmentalism, but the Christian products category is unique in that it is purportedly driven by a specific belief system. Numerous other products not touched on by this study, such as tours, financial planning, and self-help seminars, appeal to the Christian consumer and, therefore, warrant examination as to how consumers make sense of these products in light of the ideological context of the religion. Is a "Christian brand" financial planner understood in the same manner as a Christian brand T-shirt? Is a claim that a business is "Christian owned and operated" interpreted in the same fashion as a Christian brand bracelet? Clearly the functionality of the financial planning service may be very different than that of a T-shirt, but do the affective consequences of the Christian brand (i.e., feeling good) transcend product categories? Or is the blending of the witnessing mandate, the functionality of the product category, and the affective consequence unique to products like T-shirts, bracelets, and music? Future research can further explore these questions.

This study is also interesting in that it represents the blending of two institutions and two ideologies: a system of market and a system of religion. Hamilton (1932) claims that we live in a web of institutions. Changes in one institution will inevitably bring changes in others (Carey, 1960). Future studies from a critical perspective could examine more fully the effects that the marketing and religious institutions have on one another.

Parallels could also be drawn between this study and the function of products (clothing, music, etc.) in other social movements like gay rights, other social groups like gangs, or other contexts like political contests or sporting events. For instance, showing spirit, pride, and comfort through affiliation, which users ascribed as functions or meanings of Christian products, may be applicable to the function of pride wear among some in the gay community. Clothing also serves a major role in gang affiliation, and clothing also brings unity and encourages excitement and spirit during election campaigns and sporting events.

This study provides a unique perspective to understand the role of Christian products in the lives of those who use them. Managerially, it is important to understand the motivations behind the use of the products. Academically, it is a unique context to examine the role of branding and the relationship of traditionally dueling social institutions, marketing, and Christianity. Study in this area may also broaden our understanding of the role of brands in other social and political movements.

# References

Aaker, D.A. (1996). *Building Strong Brands.* New York: The Free Press.

Baran, S.J. and Davis, D.K. (1995). *Mass Communication Theory.* Belmont, CA: Wadsworth Publishing Co.

Biel, A.L. (1993). Converting Image into Equity, in *Brand Equity and Advertising,* D.A. Aaker and A.A. Biel, eds. Hillsdale, NJ: Lawrence Erlbaum Associates, 67–82.

Carey, J.W. (1960). Advertising: An Institutional Approach, in *The Role of Advertising,* C.H. Sandage and V. Fryburger, eds. Homewood, IL: Richard D. Irwin.

Christian jewelry "Like sweet"—bracelets ask, "What would Jesus do?" (1997). *The Seattle Times* (June 21).

Christian retailing. Made in heaven. (1998). *The Economist* (May 23), 63.

Cobin, J. and Strauss, A.L. (1990). Grounded Theory Research: Procedures, Canons, and Evaluative Criteria. *Qualitative Sociology* 13 (1), 3–19.

Cordwell. J.M. and Schwarz, R.A. (1979). *The Fabrics of Culture: The Anthropology of Clothing and Adornment.* The Hague: Mouton.

Cunningham, P.A. and Lab, S.V. Eds. (1991). *Dress and Popular Culture.* Bowling Green, OH: Bowling Green State University Popular Press.

Dressler, C. (1996). Holy socks! This line sends Christian message. *Marketing News* (Feb. 12), 5.

Farquhar, P. (1989). Managing brand equity. *Marketing Research,* 1 (1), 24–33.

George, R. (1998). Would Jesus sue? *The Houston Chronicle* (July 5), 4.

Goffman, E. (1959). *The Presentation of Self in Everyday Life.* Garden City, NY: Anchor Books.

Guba, E.G. Ed. (1990). *The Paradigm Dialog.* Newbury Park, CA: Sage Publications.

Hamilton, W. (1932). Institution, in *The Encyclopedia of the Social Sciences, v. 8,* E.R.A. Seligman, ed. New York: MacMillan, 84–89.

Holbrook, M.B. (1994). The Nature of Consumer Value: An Axiology of Services in the Consumption Experience, in *Service Quality: New Directions in Theory and Practice,* R. Rust and R. Oliver, eds. Newbury Park, CA: Sage Publications, 21–71.

Hood, T.C. (1981). The uses of self in the conversion ritual. Unpublished manuscript.

Hood, T.C. (1984). Character is the fundamental illusion. *Quarterly Journal of Ideology* 8 (3), 4–12.

Hood, T.C. (1986). The marks of the Christian convert. Unpublished manuscript.

Hulsether, M. (1995). Interpreting the "popular" in popular religion, *American Studies* 36(2), 127–138.

Lee, L. (1997). Bringing the good book to the outlet mall. *Wall Street Journal* (Dec. 2), B1, B12.

Lincoln, Y. and Guba, E. (1985). *Naturalistic Inquiry.* Newbury Park, CA: Sage Publications.

Littrell, M.A. and Evers, S.J. (1985). Liturgical vestments and the priest role. *Home Economics Research Journal* 14, 152–162.

Mayo, J. (1984). *The History of Ecclesiastical Dress.* New York: Holmes and Meier.

McCracken, G. (1988a). *Culture and Consumption,* Bloomington: Indiana University Press.

McCracken, G. (1988b). *The Long Interview.* Newbury Park, CA: Sage Publications.

Moore, R.L. (1994). *Selling God: American Religion in the Marketplace of Culture.* New York: Oxford University Press.

Park, C.W., Jaworski, B.J., and MacInnis, D.J. (1986). Strategic brand concept–image management. *Journal of Marketing,* 50 (3), 135–145.

Rubinstein, R.P. (1995). *Dress Codes, Meanings and Messages in American Culture.* Boulder, CO: Westview Press.

Taylor, R.E. and Haley, E. (1994) The interview as an advertising research tool, *Proceedings of the American Academy of Advertising,* 221–232.

Wicklund, R.A. and Gollwitzer, P.M. (1982). *Symbolic Self-Completion.* Hillsdale, NJ: Lawrence Erlbaum Associates.

CHAPTER 17

# Media Literacy as a Support for the Development of a Responsible Imagination in Religious Community

*MARY E. HESS*

R ecent media studies scholarship suggests that our familiar
way of talking about the media—as instruments of transmission, vehicles for transporting messages—is less descriptive than understanding mass media as elements of a
culture from and within which we draw materials for forming and in-
forming our identities, relationships, and communities. Rather than being reliably produced and predictably consumed, media "rituals" provide space for the creation of, negotiation with, and even resistance to
meaning-making—including religious meaning-making.[1] This new
way of understanding a media culture landscape poses interesting
questions to religious educators. If mass media provide raw materials
and an environment for meaning-making, how are we (as representatives of historically grounded communities of faith) present in that environment? How does that environment shape our students before they
ever enter a single religious education context? To what extent do we

need to engage those raw materials and to what extent can and should we simply ignore them? Since communities of faith are clearly marginalized from the centers of power in the United States, and under- and misrepresented within mass media contexts, what ought to be our pedagogical stance?[2] At the same time, many members of communities of faith stand at the central nexus of various institutional systems of privilege and power: what ought our role as religious educators be to these members and within these systems?

These questions are large and vitally important. It is far beyond the scope of this chapter to adequately address even one of these questions, let alone the entire range. But it is necessary to begin to think through what is possible and effective for religious educators in this landscape. In this chapter I will try to do so from a very situated place. I am myself a white, middle class, highly educated (I hold a PhD from Boston College, a Jesuit university in the United States) parent of two small children. I grew up in the 1970s and 1980s in the middle west of the United States, and I currently teach in a graduate program in religious education and pastoral ministry in a Catholic context. I live in an urban, multiracial, multiethnic neighborhood in the city of Boston. I am naming these markers of my identity from the outset because I believe—and my argument in this chapter assumes—that context matters.

My focus in this chapter will be the contribution that media education tools bring to the task of religious education as we look toward the next millennium. To summarize that argument: religious educators need to recognize that the most powerful source of our strength and relevance within a media culture can come from our ability to give people access to the symbolic, narrative, and sacramental meaning-making resources of a faith community. Such a role necessitates standing as a witness to the prophetic voices emerging both from within and without faith communities. Media education tools are an essential element of that process because they support the development of a responsible imagination that can in turn nurture reinvestment in, and reconstruction of, religious community.

What do I mean by a "responsible imagination"? Laurent Daloz, Cheryl Keen, James Keen, and Sharon Parks completed a study a few years ago that sought to identify what if anything people who had lived long lives of commitment to the public good might share in common. Among other things, these scholars identified what they termed a "responsible imagination." Because their study is so important, and their eloquence so rare in academic analysis, I will quote them at length:

The people we studied appear to compose reality in a manner that can take into account calls to help, catalyze, dream, work hard, think hard, and love well. They practice an imagination that resists prejudice and its distancing tendencies on the one hand, and avoids messianic aspirations and their engulfing tendencies on the other. Their imaginations are active and open, continually seeking more adequate understandings of the whole self and the whole commons and the language with which to express them.

Their practice of imagination is responsible in two particular ways. First, they try to respect the *process* of imagination in themselves and others. They pay attention to dissonance and contradiction, particularly those that reveal injustice and unrealized potential. They learn to pause, reflect, wonder, ask why, consider, wait. . . . They also learn to work over their insights and those of others so that they "connect up" in truthful and useful ways. They seek out trustworthy communities of confirmation and contradiction.

Second, they seek out sources of worthy images. Most have discovered that finding and being found by fitting images is not only a matter of having access to them but requires discretion and responsible hospitality—not only to what is attractive but also to what may be unfamiliar and initially unsettling. . . .

Living with these images, the people in our study appear to know that two truths must be held together—that we have the power to destroy the Earth and the power to see it whole. But unlike many who seek escape from the potent tension this act of holding requires, these people live in a manner that conveys a third and essential power: the courage to turn and make promises, the power of a responsible imagination. (Daloz et al., 1996, p. 151–152)

It is this kind of responsible imagination that media education tools can help to nurture within religious education, and it is this kind of imaginative task that I will attempt in the rest of this essay.

## The Journey to Emmaus

I want to begin by moving into more explicitly theological language than I usually use and picking up a pericope from the book of *Luke* as a conversation partner. In using this story I am not performing detailed exegesis, nor am I seeking to work out a sophisticated liturgical theology, both tasks that might engage this text. Rather, I am simply imag-

ining ways in which this story might evoke a path toward more authentic and effective religious education amidst media culture.

The story I want to use is found in the last chapter of the book of
*Luke* and tells of two of Jesus' disciples who were walking to Emmaus
shortly after his crucifixion. During their journey they encounter a
stranger who is all the more strange to them because he seems at first
to be unaware of the world-altering events of the past days. As they
continue their walk, they discover that not only is he aware of their an-
guish but chides them for their foolishness in not believing in the
words of the prophets. This stranger, who unbeknownst to them is the
resurrected Christ, reinterprets their context to them, and then they respond by inviting him to dinner at the end of the day. He joins them,
and the author of *Luke* uses starkly ritualistic language to describe the
way in which this stranger blesses and breaks bread with them. At that
moment the disciples recognize Jesus, and he vanishes. They remark
on the way in which their "hearts burned within them" as he talked
with them and explained scripture to them. The story ends with the two
disciples immediately returning to Jerusalem and telling of their remarkable encounter.

There are, as with any scripture passage, multiple ways of hearing
and interpreting this pericope, some of which are central to the Christian community's Eucharistic traditions. But for the purposes of this article, I'd like to reflect upon the ways in which this story has come to
function as a mnemonic for me of the ways in which media education
tools can be integrated into religious education.

This particular story, found in this detail only in *Luke,* has been, like
the story of the "Father and Two Sons," one of the biblical narratives
that contemporary Christians find very resonant. There is something
profoundly familiar about the dilemma the disciples found themselves
in, something that resonates with great depth as a new millennium begins. We, too, as Christians struggling to be faithful after the *Shoah,* after Hiroshima and Nagasaki, witnessing to the devastation and despair
in Rwanda, Bosnia, and Kosovo, not to mention just around the corner
in our inner cities and rural farm fields, wonder where Jesus is for us,
what if at all his presence means. Our world is dying around us from
our own greed and wastefulness, our children often hold guns in their
hands, drugs (both legal and illegal) are flowing through our streets,
and church communities often seem like little more than fragile havens
in the midst of postmodern culture.

The story of the disciples on the road to Emmaus seeks to call us back into a primary relationship with God and suggests some ways in which we can learn to "open our eyes" once again. It has been for me a very apt mnemonic of a process for utilizing popular culture within religious education. First, the story tells about the mundane way in which the disciples met Jesus—as they were walking along the road, in the midst of their daily practices. Second, the disciples engaged in conversation with this stranger on the road, a conversation that included their retelling of the events of the past few days, and the stranger's interpretation of their embeddedness in a community that stretched back over several centuries. Third, and finally, they quite literally "broke bread together" in the midst of community.

Openness to encountering God in daily life, engagement in interpretive dialogue amidst difference (that is, "with strangers"), and sharing hospitality in a practice that has deeply symbolic resonance—these three actions produced a context in which the disciples could recognize the "burning in their hearts" and in which their "eyes could be opened." Neither one of these practices was enough in and of itself, but all together created a transformative framework.

My research into how religious educators can and should integrate popular culture materials into religious education has identified a similar process.[3] It is imperative that religious educators recognize, first, that it is more than possible, it is inevitable that people will encounter God in the midst of popular culture. Popular culture "rituals" are the "amniotic fluid" (to use Beaudoin's phrase) in which we swim (1998, p. xiv). I have argued in other contexts (Hess, 1998, and Hess, 1996), as have Hoover, Clark, and others (Hoover, 1998, Clark, 1998, and Hoover and Lundby, 1997), that, more and more, people use the elements of the cultural databases with which they are most familiar to name and claim transcendence. In many cases those elements are found within mass-mediated popular culture texts.

The second part of the "Emmaus process," and really the primary way in which media education tools are useful within religious education, has to do with exploring the ways in which various pedagogical interventions might open up such fledgling encounters with transcendence and create viable connections from them to elements of historically grounded religious practice. Within the Emmaus story, for example, Jesus spent an entire day in scriptural interpretation: "starting with Moses and going through all the prophets, he explained to them the passages throughout the scriptures that were about himself" (Luke, 24:27). What might religious educators do with scriptural interpretation amidst media culture? More than anything, we need to help people reencounter, reinterpret, or in some cases (perhaps many cases, given the increasing number of young people who have never been involved in any kind of church context) encounter for the first time, the scriptural "database," if you will, of our shared Christian heritage. I have found, over and over again, that working from popular culture texts into scripture and then back again can be enormously liberating and energizing. Such a process demands openness to critical engagement with difference. I will have more to say about this in a moment.

The third part of this kind of approach involves finding ways to reclaim and reconstruct elements of religious ritual practice so as to promote insight and resonant recognition of belonging in faith community. It is not enough to have the emotional, bodily "burning within," nor simply the cognitive, rational exercise of interpretative skills upon scriptural or doctrinal texts. Both of these can be practiced in individualist isolation—although that is not the story of the Emmaus journey, it is often a message of our contemporary culture. Instead, these elements—the affective, the physical, the intellectual—all must be integrated into practice within community. It is this latter part of the process that is so often lacking within contemporary communities of faith. We live immersed in a media culture that is rich in music, image, bodily posture, and other systems of communication. As Boomershine (1999) notes, we reason in this electronic culture more by "sympathetic identification" than by philosophical reasoning, and this form of identification is fostered by ways of knowing that are more than simply cognitive.

I have argued in other contexts for the ways in which the first step of this journey—the emotional or affective encounter with transcendence—can occur in mediated contexts.[4] For the rest of this chapter I'd like to focus on the second and third elements of this journey: (1) encounters with "strangeness" and embodiment in ritual practices and (2) the ways in which media education tools can help religious educators to engage these elements of the journey into communities of faith.

## Moving through Estrangement

The first element of the pericope that I would like to return to is the way in which it was crucial that the disciples on the road did not recognize Jesus until his point of departure. Throughout their long journey that day they were continually being confronted by his strangeness and his reinterpretation of the stories they had lived with and through. In what ways can religious educators participate in this kind of process? How are we inviting strangers into our midst, and how are we being open to reinterpreting our communal—and explicitly prophetic—histories/herstories/stories?

First: media culture stories often appear very strange to people who for whatever reason believe that they do not live their lives immersed in that frame of reference. That is one vital way in which popular culture texts have an important role to play within religious education: by making "strange" experiences accessible. I have something very specific in mind, here, however, not simply playing on the *X-files* trope or asking why it is that stories of the supernatural and the alien are so popular right now (although that is an interesting and useful question itself). Rather, consider how many ways popular culture has actually functioned to bring people into the orbit of experiences that previously were forbidden or even unmentionable. There is much to be concerned about with the ways in which popular culture texts may appear to glorify violence, or to applaud sexist harassment, and so on. But there are also many examples of ways in which popular culture texts have actually opened up conversations that people of faith ought to be having, judging only by dictates of justice and peace.

What does it mean to be gay, for instance? In what ways could women provide leadership to communities? How is it possible that a pregnant teenager might be responding to a will to live, rather than succumbing to suicide, by choosing to become a parent? How might people of various races and ethnicities live together in a common culture? Certainly these questions are neither completely answered nor even adequately asked within popular culture texts; but they are at least initiated. Part of the power of electronic media is their ability to promote, to use Boomershine again, "sympathetic identification." Ways of being in the world that institutional religious authorities prefer to ignore, or to condemn out of hand, are openly represented and at least in part explored, in popular culture contexts. Indeed, this kind of representation has been identified by religious institutions as the central problem they seek to solve.

In general such concern has centered around the sense that mass media communicate messages that are dangerous, and that if we could organize sufficient numbers of people to boycott the messages, we would go a long way toward easing the danger. But this strategy is only effective if you believe that it is possible for messages to travel in linear directions, from creator to receiver. If indeed media organizations create evil messages that vulnerable people receive, then boycotting the organizations as a way to stop the promulgation of the messages might work. But as I mentioned earlier, the process is far more complex that that. To pluck an example from recent history: there are numerous kinds of hate messages available to be "received" from the Internet.

To make the step, however, of going from the sheer availability of the material to its causal role in actual killings is a big step. We need to consider, instead, how people who act on such information, who actively seek it out and use it, are generally identified as people who are in some ways already isolated and alienated from more common cultural spaces. What are the cultural factors influencing their actions? As Katz and Jhally argue in relation to the shootings at Columbine High school in Littleton, Colorado:

> What this [event] reinforces is our crying need for a national conversation about what it means to be a man . . . Such a discussion must examine the mass media in which boys (and girls) are immersed, including violent, interactive video games, but also mass media as part of a larger cultural environment that helps to shape the masculine identities of young boys in ways that equate strength with power and the ability to instill fear—fear in other males as well as females. . . .
>
> There may indeed be no simple explanation as to why certain boys in particular circumstances act out in violent, sometimes lethal, ways. But leaving aside the specifics of this latest case, the fact that the overwhelming majority of such violence is perpetrated by males suggests that part of the answer lies in how we define such intertwined concepts as "respect," "power," and "manhood." When you add on the easy accessibility of guns and other weapons, you have all the ingredients for the next deadly attack (Katz and Jhally, 1999).

Rather than seeing this kind of material as causal, we need instead to recognize that it exists as raw material for people's imaginations, imaginations that have been socialized and developed within specific cultures. Rather than being so frightened by such material that we close our eyes and ears, and refuse to engage it, we need to confront it directly and inquire into its origins and consequences for our communities. It is not something to ignore. I would argue, instead, that one of the gifts of popular culture is its ability to bring disparate voices and representations into contexts in which people can begin to encounter them in settings and with resources that can actively engage them. Far from being a dangerous dilemma, popular culture and its very strangeness provides a very real opportunity, if only we, as religious educators can begin to embrace it. As Miles notes in writing about popular Hollywood films: "the representation and examination of values and moral commitments does not presently occur most pointedly in churches, synagogues, or mosques, but before the eyes of 'congregations' in movie theaters. North Americans—even those with religious affiliations—now gather about cinema and television screens rather than in churches to ponder the moral quandaries of American life" (1996, p. 25).

By utilizing this opportunity I do not mean that we ought to give unqualified acceptance to any and all ways of being that flash across our electronic screens. To return to my earlier example, we need to probe beneath the rhetoric of hate groups to help people discern the underlying problems of poverty and structural oppression that exist in those contexts. But the point is that the conversation can begin, it can be opened up, through engaging the meaning-making systems in our midst. We, as religious educators, ought to be reading, watching, listening, and acting within as many different kinds of mass-mediated popular culture contexts as we can so that we can discover what the cultural databases are that our students are drawing upon. Only in this way can we be relevant to and eloquent within their contexts.

## Engaging Media in Order to Make the Familiar Strange

How else might pop media function as "strange" in our midst? Tied into the previous examples was my notion that we ought to engage popular media as initiators of conversations. An important finding of recent educational research is the utility of dialogue across difference, of engaging difference as an essential element of helping students to embrace and construct more complex frames of reference within which to engage their worlds.[5] Part of the power of representational media, of evocative media (here I'm thinking of both image and sound), comes from their ability to provide multiple experiences to multiple people. In other words, three people could see the same film and arrive at three or more very different descriptions of what the film was "about."

Media can be "strange" if we seek to engage them in settings where our own differences can emerge. In many ways popular media provide an excellent opportunity to allow those differences to emerge in ways that allow them to be explored positively. As George Lipsitz, writing about teaching social history using popular culture materials, says: "as my students and I used popular culture texts from the past to gain insight into the complex stories defining our present identities, we found terrains of conflict and struggle in the most unexpected places and allies in the most improbable individuals. Not because these films, songs, and shows reflected our lives directly but, rather, because they reflected the core contradictions of our lives indirectly enough to make discussion of them bearable" (1990, p. xiii–xiv). It is in the process of reflecting our lives indirectly, particularly their core contradictions, that popular media texts and the media education tools developed in media literacy contexts can be so useful to religious educators.

How can we do this kind of critical engagement? In part by heeding one lesson from Emmaus—that we must be open to the strangers we encounter in our daily lives. Here I mean to suggest not only that we ought to pay serious and sustained attention to media texts but also, and perhaps more importantly, that we need to give ourselves over fully to questioning who and what is "strange" in our lives and "estranged" from us. For people like myself, who most often inhabit the higher end of the pyramidal structures of power, finding out from whom we are estranged often means that we must consciously and intentionally ensure that we are seeking voices from those who are oppressed by these same structures.

Media education tools are a crucial element of this kind of careful attention. In a world where billions of dollars are spent on "capturing" our attention for just a few seconds, "attention" is indeed a very precious resource. Just as historical critical textual tools have helped to focus attention on scriptural texts, and various kinds of spiritual formation practices have helped focus attention on interiority in the midst of community, media education tools help to focus our attention on a specific set of issues in relation to mass-mediated popular culture texts.

These issues include the following characteristics of mediated messages: "messages are constructions," "messages are representations of social reality," "individuals negotiate meaning by interacting with messages," "messages have economic, political, social and aesthetic purposes," and "each form of communication has unique characteristics" (Hobbs, 1997, p. 9). Each of these characteristics, which form in large part what media literacy activists refer to as the core group of "media literacy principles," helps us to focus our attention not only on the ostensible "meanings" of a particular message but also all those other ways in which media messages participate in our meaning-making. In particular, they give us some handy tools for keeping our attention clearly focused on the ways in which systemic structures of oppression help to reinforce and reproduce themselves.

Using these tools to consider how broadcast and daily news is presented, for example, leads to the inescapable conclusion that far from being an "objective" representation of shared reality, these newscasts are simply a construction of a very limited range of events, a construction that is heavily dependent on the resources involved in "gathering" and "choosing" what is newsworthy, and then in turn on the underlying decision of what is profitable, what will "sell" a newscast and capture people's attention. How do media education tools do this? In part by helping to bring into the conversation other voices that are not present, to stay with this example, in broadcast news.

A standard media education exercise might be to ask a group of students to trace the coverage of a local event through several kinds of news sources, including alternative sources such as neighborhood "'zines," and online sources. Once initial coverage is gathered, these same students are then asked to seek out people who were involved in the event in question, particularly those who were not represented in the gathered coverage. If the event is one that the students themselves were involved with, so much the better.

That reality is deliberately constructed, and that the construction involves multiple decision-making points influenced by multiple sources of power and location, is a recognition that is generally both alarming and potentially liberating to people. When media education tools are engaged primarily within contexts in which alternative forms of meaning-making are disallowed, this process can often fall more on the alarming side of the spectrum as people start to despair over how to ground and challenge their notions of reality. But when the same tools are engaged within a community that is conscious and intentional about its subversion of dominant structures of power—such as a vibrant community of faith—these tools are quite liberating. They can often lead directly to imaginative, creative, and empowering reinvestment in that community as a source for and compelling nurturer of these alternatives. Here again, paying attention to those things we have become estranged from, and seeking to make the familiar strange in order to focus a different kind of attention on it, are at the heart of this kind of discernment.

There is yet another way in which it is important to think about how we encounter alternative interpretations brought into our discussions through an openness to strangers, and it is highlighted by the most often raised objection I encounter to this use of media elements within religious education. That objection is that bringing all of these other ways of viewing the world into our midst will inevitably relativize and thus make useless a religious perspective.

## Multiple Ways of Knowing and Constructing Meaning in Our Midst

This objection is powerful only if it is possible to believe that systems of viewing the world exist as so many options, complete in themselves, and in clear opposition to each other, so that in recognizing that other options exist one has to affirm that no system can hold preeminence in one's life. That perspective has a lot in common with the kinds of perspectives often held by adolescents, who are just beginning to think in systemic terms,[6] and certainly there are more than enough examples that I could draw from within popular discourse claiming this to be the case. But part of the strength of religious communities, part of their ability to remain vibrant and strong incarnations of religious vision century after century, rises out of their commitment to understanding beliefs as embedded in traditions, in ways of knowing, that stretch out globally and through time and in the process are in a perpetual state of transformation. Religious educators know that we must teach not only about elements of traditions as practiced but also about traditions and the process of traditioning itself.

Mary Boys writes that "claiming identity as a Catholic school entails constructing a curriculum that teaches the tradition with all of its painful shortcomings and sinfulness as well as with its distinctive insights and grace notes" (1992, p. 19). Thomas Groome notes that "to come to religious identity requires that we wrestle, like Jacob of old, with ourselves, with our past, with our present, with our future, and even with our God" (1980, p. xv). I would extend their arguments by noting that, in our contemporary context, where a "hermeneutics of suspicion" should attend every powerful "master narrative," this kind of critical giving of access to a tradition, but also the very real ways in which that tradition is always in a process of transformation, is a highly effective way in which to practice religious education.[7] It also, by definition, assumes that not only are there various systems for knowing but that one can begin to perceive how those systems could be in conflict with each other and yet also be a part of a larger process that tends ever toward the heart of faith.

Thus, yet another form of "strangeness" that we must attend to is the strangeness within our own traditions. We must do so not only in terms of who is estranged from the community but also who has the power to construct that estrangement and in what ways the whole process transforms over time. These are not easy questions, and they raise difficult issues within communities of faith. They are vital questions, however, and if we do not face them, our communities will not survive. Media education tools are, again, very useful here because uncovering how the structures and grammars (including the visual grammar) of various media may assist us in constructing narrow or oppressive instantiations of religious community is ultimately quite liberating and leads to learning how to construct such locations differently.

## The Emmaus Journey and Ritual

What about the last element of the pericope, this story that I have chosen to use as a conversation partner? The disciples finally recognize Jesus in the "breaking of the bread," a phrase with acutely important resonance in far more complex theologies than I can discuss here. On a purely pragmatic level, it is an illustration of the ways in which we "perform" our beliefs in concrete and embedded ways. Breaking bread together at the end of a journey was an essential part of the process by which the disciples recognized Jesus, just as it was an essential element of their humanness. Who is not hungry and thirsty after a long day's journey? In this pericope we are alerted to a practice that has both normative liturgical elements and yet is at the same time a daily, quite ordinary element of being human. Both of these kinds of ritual practice need to be renewed if religious educators are to be effective in a media culture context.

What kinds of rituals can and do we participate in that shape our recognition of our "constitutive relationality," to use Goizueta's term (1995)? Contrary to what many institutional church officials might believe, the standard performance of the traditional liturgical rituals of our community (and here I will speak very clearly and specifically from my own location with the Roman Catholic community) is neither compelling enough nor accessible enough to vast numbers of people in the United States to be very useful as a means of religious formation. Yet at the same time, it is also our liturgical rituals that hold the most promise for providing access to the imaginative resources of our community, the symbolic, narrative, and sacramental resources.

What does this conundrum reflect? To answer this question, I need to consider the role of ritual in a broader frame than simply the specific practices of liturgical ritual before being able to elucidate some of the problematics involved therein. First, consider the point I made early in this essay: how we understand media has shifted from a "message transmission" model to one of cultural ritual. As I noted then, rather than being reliably produced and predictably consumed, media "rituals" provide space for the creation of, negotiation with, and even resistance to meaning-making. The same point can be made of liturgical ritual.

Indeed, how one engages a media "ritual" may have the same external appearance but a radically different internal appropriation. Recent experience suggests, for example, that how one appropriates the information the media has provided about President Clinton and the Starr investigations has as much to do with one's immediate contexts and concerns as it does with whatever the information was "on the face of it." This point is important enough that I should state it again: meaning-making practice may "look" the same externally—we may all watch the same newscasts, for instance—but the conclusions we derive, the actions in which we engage as a consequence of our news consumption, may differ radically. This same point can be made in relation to liturgical practice. Certainly the reasons I would offer, as a feminist Catholic, for my continued presence in our local parish liturgy have little in common with the reasons my elderly Dominican neighbor would offer; yet the practice, attending liturgy weekly, is the same. The ability to provide a common activity that serves widely divergent needs is part of the appeal of mass-mediated communications. It can also be the appeal of liturgy, but at the moment it quite often is not, at least in the ways in which liturgy is commonly celebrated in many local parishes across the United States.

At the same time as local parishes are struggling even to provide basic music and elementary interpretations of scripture, new media contexts are providing immersive experiences in which sound, color, physical sensation, bodily gesture, and so on are exquisitely tuned to create richly evocative and sensorily complex story experiences. Even those forms of media that have been around for that much longer, film and television for example, have begun to utilize the emerging digital tools, making it possible to enhance more traditional production with vibrant and extraordinarily evocative representations.

The cultural databases, or the "symbolic inventories" to use Stewart Hoover's term (1998), upon which we draw to construct our life worlds (our frames of perception, the descriptions of reality we claim as normative) are rapidly expanding into these new digital universes, while at the same time the symbolic inventories of communities of faith are fading away or being drawn into mass-mediated contexts in which their root meanings are transformed. Communities of faith that are seeking to enlarge their repertoire, and in doing so draw upon mass-mediated popular culture inventories, are finding themselves more capable of creating experiences that energize and challenge their participants. Communities of faith that fear these "databases," however, are becoming more and more marginalized.

Let me give you a very concrete and practical example. When I seek to explain something to my seven-year-old son, the examples I use are just as often drawn from videotapes that we watch as they are from books that we've read together, let alone liturgical celebrations we've participated in. My partner and I have worked hard to ensure that our son is just as familiar with "going to church" as he is with the ritual of "watching a video." It has been, however, much more difficult to find ways to interest him in "going to church" because the experience is in many ways alien from that in which he lives most of the week. In church he is primarily asked to sit and be still or to sing prescribed words at prescribed times. He rarely, if ever, sees other children lead any element of the worship, and God is most often spoken of in abstract or authoritarian terms. Even my son's school, which is a basic urban public school, is more innovative and creative in its educational processes. (Of course, this brief description will tell you a lot about the state of our neighborhood parish and should not in any way be taken as definitive of good liturgical practice.) Still, in order to draw on theological themes to talk with him about his daily life, we have to consciously and intentionally work to ensure that such themes emerge throughout the rest of the week.

For this reason, video series like the *VeggieTales,* an animated show geared toward young children, are an important resource for us. It places theological themes in the midst of his daily practices, it embeds them in a reality that is broader than our own family's stories, and in doing so it gives us a way to talk about God that grows naturally out of an activity that he enjoys. We do this in nonelectronic contexts too, of course, when we are enjoying a garden, or riding on a train, and so on, but electronic media has an aura of representing reality beyond simply our own neighborhood that is in some ways more authoritative than a local walk. Part of what is so attractive about *VeggieTales* is that it regularly quotes other popular media texts (such as *Monty Python,* the *Simpsons, Star Trek,* and so on) from nonbiblical contexts, thus in some ways pulling those stories into a religious context. Historians of religious community will recognize this strategy as a very ancient one, used over the centuries to form festivals and enhance celebrations.

This example not only points out issues around the cultural database or symbolic inventory in use but also our repertoire of practices. Singing together in public is a practice that is rapidly disappearing from many hegemonic contexts in the United States. People may sing "Happy Birthday," they may mouth the words to the national anthem, but people generally do not sing together in public. Similarly, there are very few occasions in which we gather together in large public groups to listen to speakers address us solely with words (as happens within sermons). The only context that comes readily to mind in terms of a place to which I regularly go, along with large numbers of people I may or may not know, and sit and stand together at preordained moments is the local movie theater. Such practices, assumed as ordinary but also essential components of liturgical ritual, are growing ever more strange and unusual in the daily progress of our lives.

By pointing out this shift I by no means intend to suggest that communities of faith should modify or drop their liturgical rituals. Instead, we need to think ever more carefully and intentionally about how to give people better access to them. How can we welcome people into worship spaces in ways that help to provide the necessary clues to what might seem, on first glance, to be inexplicable behaviors? One way to do that is to take cognizance of the ways in which we are currently socialized in nonchurch settings and think through ways to bring the best of those practices into church settings. We know when to become quiet in a movie theater, for instance, because the lights begin to dim. Hearing the same opening credits music alerts us to the beginning of a television show, just as a commercial break gives us permission to get up and move around.

Good liturgists know how to use light and sound to pass along these clues. Indeed, good liturgy is structured in such a way as to give people access to the experience with such ease that they can relax into it and "know" it in ways that stretch far beyond the cognitive. In our current cultural context, we need to help liturgists become more adept at translating and transitioning people from media culture contexts into church community contexts. Web pages that give immediate information and access to a community, for instance, are one way to help people "clue into" the often unstated and unspoken pathways of a community. Yet how often do such pages do more than list the time of worship and the worship leaders? Why not use those pages as a chance to chart out what an entire liturgy consists of? It is a great "teachable moment" and could provide far more information with deeper theological insight than would otherwise be easily accessible to people.

Another way to give people access to our traditional rituals is to take elements that are particularly evocative in nonchurch settings and bring them into liturgical ritual. Just as slide technology made it possible to project the lyrics to hymns on a screen up and in front of the worshipping community—thus ensuring that voices were raised up and outward, rather than down and into one's lap—emerging technologies have unique gifts to bring to worship.

Media education tools are useful in this context, as well, because in addition to "deconstructing" exercises (such as the one I noted earlier in relation to news) there are "producing/creating" exercises. Indeed, this is an element of media education that provides an important reciprocal benefit. By struggling to create their own media messages, students learn how media are put together. One of my favorite ways to teach people about scriptural exegesis is to utilize the ABS CD-ROMs, which provide multiple musical, textual, visual, and video representations of a specific short biblical text. In addition, they provide the space and tools so that you can think through how to go about producing your own video representation of a text. Asking students to do this not only teaches them about video production (which is an essential part of learning about video) but also gives them the experience of close work with a specific biblical text.

Religious educators can learn from media educators' experience here: we ought to teach about liturgy not only by "telling about it" and even by immersing students in it (both of which are important elements of the teaching process) but also by helping them to create liturgies that reflect their own concerns and that draw upon their own cultural databases.[8] Symbols are far more evocative when people are allowed to experience them and use them for meaning-making rather than when people are told what a particular symbol must mean. Music is an especially important resource in this context; both because it brings meanings, quite literally, "into" people (it is an internally located sense that accepts stimuli from external sources) but also because music evokes images rather than supplying images. Religious educators ought to be doing more to help our students identify and use music that moves them, particularly by bringing that music, and its embedded themes, into liturgical contexts.

## Daily Practices

In addition to transforming our liturgical celebrations, we need to think carefully and intentionally about our daily practices, about the ways in which we can perform our beliefs in settings and ways that make us consciously aware of them, even if the settings in which we are acting are not themselves explicitly religious. To return to the work of Daloz et al., with which I began this article:

> It is said that faith is "meant to be religious." Faith seeks language, a *shared* system of symbols with which to interpret the whole of life. If imagination is the process of "shaping into one," religion may be understood, in part, as the distillation of shared images, powerful enough to shape into one the chaos of our experience. In other words, stories, habits, and the rituals of everyday are the content of the imagination by which people know who they are and what they are to do in the world. It is the work of religion, in concert with the whole life of the commons, to do that well (Daloz et. al., 1996, p. 142).

One of the more useful resources available for thinking through practices of faith in a daily context is the "Education and Formation of People in Faith" project based at Valparaiso University in the United States. Out of that project comes a description of "practice" that is both specific enough to identify a set of historically grounded practices that are constitutive of Christian identity and also broad enough to be suggestive across creedal and liturgical boundaries. The practices identified are also those that can be practiced on a daily basis, not simply within liturgical celebration.

The Lilly project definition suggests that practices: "address fundamental human needs and conditions through concrete human acts," "are done together and over time," "possess standards of excellence," and help us to perceive how entangled our lives are "with the things God is doing in the world" (Bass, 1997, pp. 6–8). The practices they name in the book that lays out this project, *Practicing our Faith, A Way of Life for a Searching People,* include honoring the body, hospitality, household economics, saying yes and saying no, keeping Sabbath, testimony, discernment, shaping communities, forgiveness, healing, dying well, and singing our lives. Each of these practices has various representations within the mass media, and each can itself apply to how someone engages the mass media. What counts as "saying yes and no," for instance, particularly in terms of prayer and examination of conscience, within the world of the television drama is fairly narrowly described. This is an example of how a specific practice is "re-presented" to us by the mass media.[9]

What might we learn, however, by asking in what ways our practice of "saying yes and saying no" is permeated by the agenda-setting effect of the mass media? What might we learn by discerning in what ways it might be appropriate to "say yes and say no" to how we consume media representations, to how we engage various kinds of mass media? In what ways might our practices in relation to media—escaping into the dream creating space of entertainment, for example—support and/or interfere with finding the internal silence necessary for clear examination of conscience? In asking these kinds of questions, the resources of the media education movement can very easily be brought to bear within religious education.

Here my emphasis is not so much on bringing religious meaning-making into popular practices, as it is bringing popular practices into religious meaning-making. There might not appear to be any distinction between the two, but the difference I am trying to highlight has to do with the perspective from which one approaches popular practices. Rather than having religious communities make films with explicitly religious imagery, for instance, I would rather have them work on engaging the religious yearnings present in popular culture. Rather than condemning media culture and providing alternative texts, we ought to be discerning transcendence in that context and helping people connect their fledgling, fragile moves toward accepting God into rich and deep embeddedness in religious community. Given the ubiquity of mass-mediated popular culture, versus the distribution and creative difficulties present in the "religious media" realm, we might have a far greater impact on people if we could help them to enlarge their daily attention to encompass a transcendent dimension to all that they engage.

If indeed mass-mediated materials are raw elements in the repertoire from which we construct our sense of our selves and our relationality, then we can and should approach the making of communication ritual from a variety of vantage points. If what we are trying to do is influence the shape of religious action, not simply cognitive belief, and if that action is lived out on a daily basis, then we ought to be seeking to engage the materials that are present on a daily basis and shaping the attention and focus that people of faith bring to those materials.

This kind of religious education will have to be far more improvisational than previous conceptions. Meeting people where they are, helping them to articulate their vision, and then challenging it and ultimately helping them connect it to religious community is not something that can be done in predetermined or formulaic ways, at least not in our present chaotic and rapidly changing media culture context. Preparing to educate in this framework will require that religious educators themselves have a deep and expansive fluency in religious beliefs, practices, and locations. The institutions responsible for preparing catechists have struggled toward this recognition slowly and primarily by searching for ways to "certify" appropriate training programs that have appropriate curricula. Most of these curricula have emphasized relevant coursework in ecclesiology, moral theology, Christology, and so on. But while it is crucial that people be knowledgeable about doctrine, it is far more crucial that they be given the requisite formation to engage their own and their students' faith in vibrant and embodied ways. Few if any of these programs invite catechists into creative production, let alone with new media tools.

To return to the Emmaus story: we need to walk along the road, conscious all the time of encountering God, remaining open, even embracing strangers and present to our own embodiedness in practice. Media education tools are a wonderful way in which to engage that journey, particularly as the road meanders through the jumble of music, images, and sensations that pour in ever-increasing floods throughout media culture.

# Notes

1. For more on these assertions, along with background citations, please see my article "From Trucks Carrying Messages to Ritualized Identities: Implications of the Postmodern Paradigm Shift in Media Studies for Religious Educators," forthcoming in *Religious Education.*

2. Please note: since I'm trying to be as situated as possible in this argument, I will speak from and to a U.S. context. I do not assume that what I have to say applies across the United States, and I do not want to imply that anything I say has to be evident or applicable beyond that setting. It may be evocative, and I certainly hope it is useful, but it is in no way intended to be definitive.

3. For more on this topic, see M. Hess, 1998. See also the findings from the "Religious Education and Challenge of Media Culture Project," available on the web at http://www.bc.edu/bc_org/avp/acavp/irepm/challenge/mrcsource. html.

4. See note 2 above.

5. There is a growing literature addressing "teaching across difference." See, for instance, the Bergin and Garvey series of books, *Critical Studies in Education and Culture,* edited by Henry Giroux and Paulo Freire, especially the volume edited by Kanpol and McLaren (Kanpol and McLaren, 1995) from that series. The *Harvard Education Review* has published a set of articles that address these issues from the standpoint of "whiteness"; see in particular Fine, Weis, and Powell, 1997; Maher and Tetreault, 1997; and Giroux, 1997.

6. See in particular, Kegan, 1994.

7. For more on religious education that moves in this way, see Boys, 1989.

8. Every year I have graduate students who take my course in "media literacy and religious education" who put together liturgical season reflections (Advent reflections, for instance) and other kinds of educational experiences that utilize popular culture texts. Popular music has been a very important part of these projects. Some of these projects are accessible online at http://www.bc.edu/bc_org/avp/acavp/irepm/media/resources.html.

9. It is tempting at this point to explore the ways in which the practice of "forgiveness" has been argued about in recent months in relation to President Clinton. I simply note that this is one example of a "teachable moment" in which a profoundly theological question is being asked within contexts mediated by news formats.

# References

Bass, D.C. (Ed.). (1997). *Practicing our faith: A way of life for a searching people.* San Francisco: Jossey-Bass Publishers.

Beaudoin, T. (1998). *Virtual faith: The irreverent spiritual quest of Generation X.* San Francisco: Jossey-Bass Publishers.

Boomershine, T. (May 30, 1999). How to be a faith witness in the communications media? Conditions requisite for the public communications value of faith witnesses. Paper presented at the *Witnessing to the faith, an activity of the media* conference, St. Paul University, Ottawa, Ontario.

Boys, M.C. (1989). *Educating in faith: Maps and visions.* San Francisco: Harper and Row.

Boys, M.C. (1992). Life on the margins: Feminism and religious education. In *Initiatives: The National Women's Studies Journal* (Summer 1992), 17–23.

Clark, L.S. (1998). Identity, discourse, and media audiences: A critical ethnography of the role of visual media in religious identity-construction among U.S. adolescents. Unpublished dissertation, University of Colorado at Boulder.

Daloz, L.A., Keen, C., Keen, J., and Park, S. (1996). *Common fire: Lives of commitment in a complex world.* Boston: Beacon Press.

Fine, M., Weis, L., and Powell, L. (1997). Communities of difference: A critical look at desegregated spaces created for and by youth. *Harvard Educational Review, 67*(2, Summer), 247–284.

Giroux, H.A. (1997). Rewriting the discourse of racial identity: Towards a pedagogy and politics of whiteness. *Harvard Educational Review, 67*(2, Summer), 285–320.

Goizueta, R.S. (1995). *Caminemos con Jesús: Toward a Hispanic/Latino theology of accompaniment.* Maryknoll: Orbis Books.

Groome, T.H. (1980). *Christian religious education.* San Francisco: Harper-San Francisco.

Hess, M. (1996). What if God were one of us? Using popular culture transformatively in adult religious education. Paper presented at the Association of Professors and Researchers in Religious Education annual meeting, New Orleans, Louisiana.

Hess, M. (1998). *Media literacy in religious education: Engaging popular culture to enhance religious experience.* Unpublished dissertation, Boston College, Massachusetts.

Hobbs, R. (1997). Literacy for the information age. In J. Flood, S.B. Heath, and D. Lapp (Eds.), *Handbook of research on teaching literacy through the communicative and visual arts.* New York: Simon and Schuster Macmillan.

Hoover, S. (1998). Religion, media and the cultural center of gravity. Paper presented at the Trustees Meeting of the Foundation for United Methodist Communications, May 7, 1998, Nashville, TN.

Hoover, S.M., and Lundby, K. (Eds.). (1997). *Rethinking media, religion and culture.* Thousand Oaks: Sage Publications.

Kanpol, B., and McLaren, P. (Eds.). (1995). *Critical multiculturalism: Uncommon voices in a common struggle.* Westport: Bergin and Garvey.

Katz, J., and Jhally, S. (1999). The national conversation in the wake of Littleton is missing the mark. In *The Boston Globe,* May 2, 1999, Society section.

Kegan, R. (1994). *In over our heads: The mental demands of modern life.* Cambridge, MA: Harvard University Press.

Lipsitz, G. (1990). *Time passages: Collective memory and American popular culture.* Minneapolis: University of Minnesota Press.

Maher, F.A., and Tetreault, M.K.T. (1997). Learning in the dark: How assumptions of whiteness shape classroom knowledge. *Harvard Educational Review, 67*(2, Summer), 321–349.

Miles, M.R. (1996). Seeing and believing: Religion and values in the movies. Boston: Beacon Press.

# Contributors

**Jeffrey Brody** is an assistant professor in the Department of Communications and a member of the instructional faculty of the Asian American Studies program at California State University, Fullerton. A former journalist who specialized in covering the Vietnamese American community, Brody's research activities involve writing about minorities and media, the acculturation of Vietnamese, and the Vietnamese-language press. He is also coauthor of *The Newspaper Publishing Industry* and has written the chapter "The Structure of the Internet Industry" in *The Media and Entertainment Industries: Readings in Mass Communications.* Brody advises the student newspaper and teaches the course "The Vietnamese American Experience."

**Judith M. Buddenbaum** is a professor in the Department of Journalism and Technical Communication at Colorado State University. She is the author of *Reporting News about Religion: An Introduction for Journalists* and coeditor of *Religion and Mass Media: Audiences and Adaptations* with Daniel A. Stout and of *Readings on Religion as News* with Debra L. Mason. Her research on religion and the media has also been published in *Journalism Quarterly, Newspaper Research Journal,* and *Journalism History* and as book chapters.

**Yoel Cohen** is the head of the Department of Communication, The Lipshitz Teacher Training College, Jerusalem, Israel, and lectures in mass communication at the Holon Technological Academic Institute. He is a research fellow at the Center for Communication and International Policy, Bar-Ilan University, Ramat Gan. He holds a doctorate in mass communications from The City University, London, and a diploma in Jewish studies from the Jews College, London. Among his publications are *Media Diplomacy: The Foreign Office in the Mass*

*Communications Age* and *The Whistleblower from Dimona: Vanunu, Israel, and the Bomb.*

**Anne Cunningham** is an assistant professor of advertising at Louisiana State University. She earned her PhD at the University of Tennessee.

**Abdullahi A. Gallab,** PhD, a former journalist and officer in the information ministry in Sudan, teaches in the Communication Department at Hirum College in Hirum, Ohio.

**Eric Haley,** who has a PhD from the University of Georgia, is an associate professor of advertising at the University of Tennessee, Knoxville. He also serves as Associate Dean of the UT College of Communications.

**Mary E. Hess** has a BA in American Studies from Yale, an MTS in Theological Studies from Harvard, and a PhD in Religion and Education from Boston College. She is currently an assistant professor of educational leadership at Luther Seminary in St. Paul, Minnesota. Previously she was the director of the Religious Education and Challenge of Media Culture Project at Boston College and taught in its graduate program. Her research interests center on the pragmatic implications of emerging research in media and religion for communities of faith.

**Stewart M. Hoover** is a professor in the School of Journalism and Mass Communication at the University of Colorado at Boulder as well as a professor adjunct of Religious Studies and American Studies. He chairs the International Study Commission on Media, Religion, and Culture and directed the first international conference in 1996. He has authored *The Electronic Giant* (1979), *Mass Media Religion: The Social Sources of the Electronic Church* (1988), and *Religion in the News: Faith and Journalism in American Public Discourse* (1998).

**John Douglas Lepter** is an associate professor of communication studies at Trevecca Nazarene University in Nashville, Tennessee. He earned his PhD in communication from the University of Kentucky in 1996. Research interests include media audiences, media effects, and language and social interaction.

**Thomas R. Lindlof** is a professor in the College of Communications and Information Studies at the University of Kentucky, where he conducts research on media and culture. He is the author of *Qualitative Communication Research Methods* and the editor of *Constructing the Self in a Mediated World.*

**Rashmi Luthra** is an associate professor of communication at the University of Michigan-Dearborn. She received her PhD in communication from the University of Wisconsin-Madison. Her research on women and development communication has been published in the *Gazette,* in *Journalism and Mass Communication Educator,* and as a book chapter in *Feminism, Multiculturalism and the Media: Global Diversities.* Her research on women's movements and media has been published in *Knowledge, Women's Studies in Communication,* and *Feminist Issues,* and her research on gender and immigrant media has been published as a book chapter in *Making Waves: An Anthology of Writings by and about Asian American Women.*

**Gayle Newbold** is an associate editor of *Utah Business Magazine.* Her writing has appeared in numerous magazines and newspapers during a 20-year career as a freelance writer. She has done research on gender issues, including a study of readers of romance novels.

**Allen W. Palmer** is an associate professor in the Department of Communications at Brigham Young University in Provo, Utah. His work focuses on international communication problems. His research has appeared in *Journal of International Communication, Gazette, Public Understanding of Science,* and *Science Communication.*

**Stephen D. Perry** is an assistant professor of communication at Illinois State University in Normal. Perry has published articles on religious broadcasting and religious music formats in the *Journal of Mediated Communication* and the *Journal of Radio Studies,* respectively. His other research interests include media effects on culture and electronic media programming. His work has been published in the *Journal of Communication, Journal of Broadcasting and Electronic Media,* and *Journalism Quarterly,* among others. Perry also has six years of experience working in the broadcasting field.

**Tony Rimmer** is a professor in the Department of Communications, California State University, Fullerton. He was formerly a television producer in New Zealand. He has authored or coauthored several book chapters and journal articles on topics such as media and religion, media economics, media and politics, new media technologies, and methodological issues around the conceptualizing and measurement of media use. His research has been published in scholarly journals such as *Communication Reports, Communication Research, Journal of Media Economics, Journal of Public Relations Research, Journalism and Mass Communication Quarterly, Mass Comm Review, Public Relations Review,* and *Gazette.*

**Quentin J. Schultze** is a professor of communication at Calvin College, Grand Rapids, Michigan, and author of eight books, including *Dancing in the Dark: Youth, Popular Culture and the Electronic Media* (Eerdmans) and *American Evangelicals and the Mass Media* (Academie). His book *Televangelism and American Culture* (Baker Book House) won two national awards. He has also published several dozen scholarly articles and over a hundred essays in popular publications. He is finishing a book on the interaction of Christianity and the media in twentieth-century America.

**Daniel A. Stout** is an associate professor and associate chair of the Department of Communications at Brigham Young University. His coedited book *Religion and Mass Media: Audiences and Adaptations* with Judith M. Buddenbaum was praised as "a useful contribution to the literature" by the *Journal of Communication* and a "fresh approach toward research" by the *American Journal of Sociology*. Articles by Stout have appeared in the *Journal of Mass Media Ethics, Information and Behavior, Newspaper Research Journal, Public Relations Review,* and *Southern Speech Communication Journal.*

**Joseph D. Straubhaar**'s primary research interests are in (1) international communication and cultural theory and (2) comparative analysis of new technologies. He has published a book on international communications, *Videocassette Recorders in the Third World;* edited a book on international telecommunications, *Telecommunications Politics: Ownership and Control of the Information Superhighway in Developing Countries;* and written a textbook, *Communications Media in the Information Society,* along with numerous articles and essays.

**Hillary Warren** is an assistant professor of communication at the University of Wisconsin in Stevens Point. Her areas of research and publication include the economy of religious media, specialized audiences, and the application of chaos and complexity theory to the study of mass communication. She is currently collaborating on a political economic analysis of the production and consumption cycles of a religious media product.

**Candace White,** who has a PhD from the University of Georgia, is an assistant professor of public relations at the University of Tennessee, Knoxville.

**Arnold S. Wolfe,** who received his PhD in 1988 from Northwestern University, is an associate professor of communication at Illinois State University in Normal. Wolfe's research interests embrace mass media theory and criticism with an emphasis on semiotic and economic approaches. He has published articles on theories of the mass media audience in *Popular Music and Society* and on the enduring quality of popular music of the 1960s in the *Journal of the Northwest Communication Association* and the *Journal of Communication Inquiry.* His other research explores film and television semiotics, the world of the television critic, and the effects of foreign takeovers on freedom of expression in the film industry. This work has been published in *Critical Studies in Mass Communication, Mass Communication Review,* and the *Journal of Media Economics.*

# Index